About the Author

Dr R. Brasch is a well-known author with thirty-four books to his credit. A scholar in the fields of theology, philosophy and history, he has contributed to numerous international magazines and journals and has lectured at universities around the world. He is also a popular and respected telecaster, broadcaster and scriptwriter.

Among his many honours are the Coronation Medal (1952), the Order of the British Empire (1967), the Silver Jubilee Medal (1977), the Order of Australia (1979), and the Media Peace Prize (1979).

His books include *How Did It Begin?*, *How Did Sports Begin?*, *There's a Reason for Everything!*, *That Takes the Cake* and *Permanent Addresses*.

Dr Brasch has worked in London, Dublin, South Africa and the United States. He came to Australia in 1949 and now resides in Sydney. He travels extensively to research his books, and when not writing continues his busy schedule of public speaking and lecturing.

By the Same Author

That Takes the Cake

How Did It Begin?

How Did Sports Begin?

How Did Sex Begin?

Strange Customs

Thank God I'm an Atheist

There's a Reason for Everything!

A Book of Comfort

A Book of Friendship

A Book of Good Advice

The Book of the Year

Permanent Addresses

Circles of Love

Mistakes, Misnomers and Misconceptions

the Cat's Pyjamas

R. BRASCH

Angus&Robertson
An imprint of HarperCollins*Publishers*

Angus&Robertson
An imprint of HarperCollins*Publishers*, Australia

First published in Australia in 1997

HarperCollins*Publishers*
25 Ryde Road, Pymble, Sydney NSW 2073, Australia
31 View Road, Glenfield, Auckland 10, New Zealand
77–85 Fulham Palace Road, London W6 8JB, United Kingdom
Hazelton Lanes, 55 Avenue Road, Suite 2900, Toronto, Ontario, M5R 3L2
and 1995 Markham Road, Scarborough, Ontario M1B 5M8, Canada
10 East 53rd Street, New York NY 10032, USA

The National Library of Australia Cataloguing-in-Publication data:

Brasch, R. (Rudolph), 1912–.
  The cat's pyjamas.

  Includes index.
  ISBN 0 207 18970 6.

  1. English language – Terms and phrases. 2. Figures of
  speech. 3. English language – Etymology. I. Title.

422

Cover illustration by Evert Ploeg
Printed in Australia by Griffin Paperbacks, Adelaide

9 8 7 6 5 4 3 2 1
99 98 97

For
Gary and Lisa
Alan and Candice
as a token of our common bond

CONTENTS

PREFACE

James M. Barrie, the famous Scottish novelist and playwright, once spoke of an undertaker as a person who saw a potential coffin in every tree. A rather funereal choice of quotation with which to introduce a book, it is a fitting simile to my passion for 'finding out', getting information, seeing a question in almost everything. However, the difference is that my quest does not concern death but, on the contrary, birth. It's about *how it all started*: origins.

This book is another record of some of the results of my addiction. It contains over 400 more origins of the phrases, customs, symbols and concepts I have puzzled about and explored, seeking answers to them, as always, in cooperation with my wife Li, my constant companion and indefatigable help.

Discovering the answers was a most exciting, satisfying and enriching experience. It is one that I want to share with you. Words, sayings and customs all belong to our heritage and, even if only relating to a vogue word or a vague word, they reflect something of the realities of our present age, as well as those of past periods.

The Cat's Pyjamas contains many of the questions readers, listeners and viewers have asked me since my last publication on this topic, *That Takes the Cake*. They have drawn my attention to many a subject of which I myself would never have thought, and thus I owe a great debt of gratitude to their contribution to this book.

Why do some individuals walk around as if they were the cat's pyjamas, blowing their own trumpets, while others suffer fates worse than death? And speaking of fate, who first spoke, and in what circumstances, of the unlucky girl who was always a bridesmaid but never a bride? Fascinating indeed is the background of all these sayings, and no one needs to feel frustrated who cannot make head or tail of them.

To discover the origin of phrases, traditions or institutions, and to verify the stories told of them and the claims made, was a real adventure. It was necessary to go to their very roots, to visit the sites of their births, travelling often thousands of kilometres – always with Li. Thus we climbed the numerous steps of the spiral staircase of the tower in Blarney Castle in Ireland, there to view (and kiss) its famous Blarney Stone. Puzzled by the great variety of dishes served as Caesar Salad, we sought out the very place where it was first concocted and named – Tijuana, in Mexico. Whilst in that country we also took the opportunity to solve the mystery of the Mexican jumping bean – whether it was fact or all fiction.

Few people realise the circumstances and location of the creation of the shopping trolley, now adopted worldwide and taken for granted. In Oklahoma City, its birthplace, we uncovered its exciting story, an early experiment in trade promotion. Chilling and horrendous was the background of a murder we investigated in the county of Hampshire, England. It happened more than a century ago and, abstrusely, created the apparently endearing phrase 'sweet Fanny Adams'. Who was she, and what happened to her to become perpetuated in a sailor's ration?

On one of our exploration trips, when crossing the frontier from Mexico into the United States, we had to pass customs at Tucson, Arizona. At the time, drug smuggling was prevalent there, and the inspection very strict. When our turn came and the custom's officer asked me whether I had anything to declare, I gave him the firm answer of 'No'. In spite of it, he asked me to open our cases. Just when he was sliding his hand down the side of one of the bags, somewhat irritated I remarked, 'Officer, if you tell me what you are looking for, I'll tell you where you can find it.' His immediate reply was most unexpected. 'Sir,' he said with a smile on his face, 'I never know what I'm looking for till I've found it.'

This was the very experience I had encountered on not a few occasions in my research. In Germany we were following the footsteps of the Brothers Grimm (of fairy-tale fame) and had just reached Hamelin in Lower Saxony to explore the legend of the Pied Piper when, totally unexpectedly, we came across a war memorial with the inscription 'Hip, Hip, Hurray' – as a war cry! It led to the discovery of the disturbing history of these now totally misapplied words.

So many things happen to us in everyday life, coming quite out of the blue but proving of lasting effect. Such 'finds' are recalled in some of the pages that follow.

The vast realm of eating has never ceased to nourish our store of terms and phrases and, with it, has given food for thought as to their origins and their naming. We take the buttering of bread for granted, but who first introduced it and for what reason? Is there any foundation to the claim that 'an apple a day keeps the doctor away', or is it merely an old wives' tale? Crêpe Suzette makes a delicious sweet. Who invented it, on what occasion, and why was it so called? It is equally intriguing to know how the first 'fish and chips', that typical English combination, and the Scandinavian smorgasbord, came about. The ice-cream cone contains quite a story in itself – as an emergency measure that became a permanent fixture. It might be sensible not 'to teach your grandmother to suck eggs', but how did eggs find a place in the assertion that something is 'as sure as eggs is eggs'?

Eating leads straight to drinking and, if excessively done, to the drunk, with their own fund of puzzling expressions. People who 'wet their whistle' overmuch, having drunk 'one over the eight', will walk about like 'three sheets to the wind'. There is even a practical reason for the foil around bottle corks!

Throughout the ages, sex has given birth to offsprings of the most diverse kind. Its contribution to life is manifold, and therefore a topic which cannot be ignored in the exploration of the begetting of words, phrases and concepts. Once tabooed, 'screwing' presents a well worthwhile study, as does the 'hustler', 'hanky panky', being 'kinky', in 'drag' and 'bonking'. These are all topics, figures or figures of speech that might cause some films to be 'X-rated'.

A subject always of great concern, both in investigation and in everyday life, is the practice of peculiar customs and superstitions. To throw light on them tells much of the psyche of humans. What is behind the spraying of champagne in celebration of a win, the tying of a knot in one's handkerchief to remind one of something, and the tradition thrice to repeat the word 'rabbit', particularly so at the beginning of a new month?

Noteworthy are some features we encounter almost daily in life – so often, indeed, that they are mostly taken for granted. Have you ever thought why the ring in a water tap (the American 'faucet') is called a washer, and why an underground service access cover (the de-gendered former 'manhole' cover) is always round in shape? Odd is the reason why February is distinguished by being the only month of the year restricted to twenty-eight days. Those playing bingo (or 'housey-housey', its alternate name) well know that when the number 'one' is called out it is referred to as 'Kelly's eye', but why? People have been equally puzzled by models of ships enclosed in a bottle. How could they have ever been placed inside it with so narrow a neck, and what was their real purpose?

Our language and our life are truly colourful, in every sense of the word. Examples examined in this book tell of the origin of such sayings as 'true blue', being 'as brown as a berry' or 'tickled pink'. It also speaks of the blue-collar worker and why we 'nail our colours to the mast'. There is an explanation for the sailor's uniform being universally blue and the choice of the identical colour for the lights marking the stations and cars of the police force. Some people are 'green with envy', and green is also a prominent colour in the Islamic faith. And what is the meaning and history of 'a horse (being) of a different colour'? You can read all about it, written here 'in black and white'.

The modern world has created its own vocabulary of terms and expressions. Some are of recent coinage, whilst others are obsolete concepts which have been resurrected and completely updated. 'Ms' has replaced the Miss and Mrs. When and where did it first happen, and which way should it be pronounced? Other phrases and phenomena are of equal fascination. They include 'gazumping', 'laundering money', 'Giro banking' and the 'whistle blower'. Fans of Liberace might well be interested to learn of their idol's association with 'laughing all the way to the bank'. It is revealing to observe that the majority of the examples at hand reflect present-day society's preoccupation with material things, in 'making money hand over fist'.

As an Australian writer, it would be remiss of me if I omitted the discussion of some typical Australianisms that often bewilder the mind. Prominent among them are such sayings as 'up to dolly's wax', 'to cop the crow', 'further back than Walla Walla' and, last but not least, 'a wigwam for a goose's bridle'.

All these disparate questions, covering so many spheres and with startling insights and bizarre observations, are dealt with in alphabetical order. Where no definitive answer can be given, several suggestions are quoted – at times, indeed, a fascinating variety. Providing lots to talk about, no doubt they will beget further questions which, to receive from you, would be greatly appreciated.

R. Brasch

ACKNOWLEDGMENTS

My grateful thanks go out to the many people and libraries, organisations and institutions, consulates and firms who have been of great assistance to me in my research.

I am indebted to the librarians and staff of: ABC Reference Library, Ultimo (Judy Blood); Library of Australasian Dairy Corporation, Glen Iris, Vic. (Janet Werkmeister); Library of the Australian Film, Television and Radio School (Jillian Kelso), North Ryde; Catholic Inquiry Centre, Maroubra; Department of Defence (Army Office), Canberra (Lt. Col. A.A. Sillcock); History of Medicine Library of the Royal Australasian College of Physicians (Brenda Heagney); Library of the Museum of the Applied Arts and Sciences, Sydney (Margaret Rafferty); National Army Museum, London; NSW Branch Library, Police Headquarters, Sydney (Peter Wagner); St Patrick's College, Strathfield; State Library of NSW; Woollahra Library; University of Sydney Library, Information Service (Mary Rothe); *The Sydney Morning Herald*; Department of Germanic Studies, Sydney University; Library of the University of Tasmania; Library of the War Memorial, Canberra; Wine Society of Australia (Paul Soster).

Appreciation is due as well to the representatives of Belgium, Japan, Mexico, Sweden (the Trade Council, Carin Skold) and the United States (Information Service, Peter Gilbert).

I am equally grateful to the Commerzbank, Sydney (Werner Menges); Doyles Seafoods, Watsons Bay; Henselite (Australia) Pty Ltd; Norco Co-op Ltd, Sydney (Barry Shewan); Parke Davis Wellcome, Consumer Healthcare Pty Ltd (Sue Bell and Philip Johnston).

Last, but not least, I would like to acknowledge the help given to me by Stephen Baer, Gabriel Keil, Maureen Kremer, Dr A. David Packman of Oklahoma City (USA), George Richards, Bishop Donald Robinson, Phil Scott and Sir Alfred Shepperd (London). Many others, too, both at home and abroad, have given ready help with their information and by providing access to archives and documents. To all of them – thank you!

a

ALWAYS A BRIDESMAID BUT NEVER A BRIDE

Who would imagine that this expression of dismal frustration was inspired – in the 1920s – by an advertisement for a mouthwash.

To promote their product, the manufacturers of Listerine cleverly employed the personal experience of girls at the time who desperately wanted to settle down but seemed always to be left on the shelf. In text and image, the advertisement portrays such a situation and offers a possible explanation for such girls' lack of success.

Poor Edna was getting on for thirty, and most of her girlfriends were either already married or about to tie the knot. How she wished that, instead of being their bridesmaid, she could be the bride! However, any romance of hers invariably ended quickly. There was a reason. Unbeknown to her she suffered from bad breath, and no one would tell her so, not even her closest friends.

The advertisement sold millions of bottles of the mouthwash and, with it, gave the English language the saying which in the original advertisement spoke of 'Often a bridesmaid but never a bride'. Soon it was applied not solely to the unfulfilled longing for marital bliss but to any situation in which a party never was given the chance to play a major role.

AMPERSAND

The character '&' is known as the ampersand. A most useful contraction, it acquired its ponderous name by the slurring of speech. In fact, it could be described as a miscarriage.

To record speeches more easily and to shorten texts, people from ancient days onward made use of abbreviations. They did so long before the introduction of modern systems of shorthand.

It was logical that they chose special symbols for the words recurring most frequently. Not least, this applied to the conjunction 'and', which in Latin is *et*. By contracting its two letters into one, they created the now well-known character '&'. With a little imagination, in fact, it is still possible to recognise the 'e' and 't' intertwined in the symbol, particularly if the ampersand is reproduced in italics.

The new character proved so useful that it was commonly adopted as an abbreviation, eventually to be regarded as part of the alphabet and as such to be taught to pupils at school. Early textbooks and elementary primers (known as 'hornbooks') included it as the ending of the 'crisscross row'. The latter was a corruption of 'Christ Cross row', so named because a cross invariably preceded the alphabet.

Added to the alphabet, the character, like a twenty-seventh letter, followed the 'z'. Accordingly, when pupils recited the alphabet, they learnt to do so in its expanded version, saying immediately after the 'z', 'and by itself, "and"'. The 'and', of course, meant the '&' symbol. However, still using Latin terms, they expressed 'by itself' as *per se*. They would thus say '... x, y, zed and *per se* and.'

Mechanically reiterating the augmented alphabet numerous times, it was only natural for the students' speech to become slovenly and, when reaching the end of the alphabet, to run the final four words together, transforming 'and per se "and"' into 'ampersand'!

Eventually, people forgot its origin and mistook the corruption as a proper word, and as such it has been used ever since.

Nevertheless, the ampersand continued to intrigue the curious, who wondered how it all started. Some soon suggested that it really stood for 'Emperor's "and"', asserting that it was first created by a monarch, though they failed to identify which one.

ANAESTHESIA

Those undergoing an operation fortunately do so insensitive to pain. This they owe to the anaesthetist or, in the more stretched version of his or her impressive title, the anesthesiologist. These medicos are so called because they administer to the patient *anaesthesia*. This so-learned-sounding word, derived from the Greek and first used by the philosopher Plato, simply means 'no feeling'.

ANKH

Fascinating is the story of the Ankh, that looped cross so ubiquitous in ancient Egypt and known as 'the key to life'. In fact, in hieroglyphic script it stood for 'life' itself, in all its dimensions, but most prominently as the vital force of all existence – of the here and the beyond. Like the sun, it fructified the earth, ensuring deathlessness and, with it, revival. It was 'the key' to open up the gates to eternal life.

The shape of the Ankh has been open to a variety of interpretations. It has been seen as the stylised tree of life and as a magic knot. Others have recognised in it the Pharaoh's headdress or his sandal straps – an appropriate choice indeed, since he was, after all, regarded as the master of life and death.

The Ankh has also been explained as a simplified depiction of the female genitals and the womb, the very source of life.

Most convincing, however, is the suggestion that the Ankh is a replica of the key once used to open and close the dykes of the Nile. Its one-time function was to control the irrigation of the soil, so essential for the survival of all crops and, with them, the entire nation.

So laden with mystery and the arcane, it is no wonder that the Ankh was adopted as a popular amulet and regarded as the key to opening up the mind to the mysteries of hidden knowledge.

ANTIPASTO

Whenever the prefix *anti* is used, it immediately suggests some type of aversion or opposition. Antipathy is described as dislike, just as the antipodes are on the 'opposite' end of the earth's surface. Nevertheless, we can be misled in some cases when 'anti' represents the originally Latin *ante*, meaning 'before' or 'preceding'. Thus we 'anticipate' a situation, foreseeing it.

This applies to the Italian course referred to on a menu as 'antipasto', which is meant to be eaten 'before' (anti) the actual meal (pasto). It represents the Italian version of the French-derived *hors d'oeuvre*. The 'anti' in antipasto does not reflect any culinary aversion to pasta; 'pasto' literally speaks of 'food', from the Latin-derived *pastus*, a word still recalled in the English 'repast'.

Pasta itself was not introduced into Italy by Marco Polo from China, as is often claimed. It was already a much-favoured dish in the Mediterranean area in classical times, enjoyed by Etruscans, Greeks and Romans.

APOLOGY

An apology nowadays expresses regret for some offence given. As used originally, however, the term had a much more weighty connotation and, differing from its present-day sense, signified a formal plea – in fact, an explanation, a speech in defence. Not surprisingly, therefore, the term, from the Greek, literally refers to a 'speaking away'.

A classical example is the Greek philosopher Socrates' *Apology*, a version of which has been preserved in his pupil Plato's writings. The *Apology* was the unconciliatory speech he made at his trial in 399 BC, defending himself against the capital charges of impiety and of corrupting the Athenian youth by encouraging them to criticise the existing order.

APOTHECARY

Apothecary is the one-time name of the present-day pharmacist or, in American usage, the druggist. Though once it was exclusively applied to those dispensing and dealing in medications, originally the name had no medicinal connection at all.

The Greek *apotheke* generally referred to a 'storehouse' and was used in this sense in Britain till the seventeenth century. Accordingly, the apothecary was the keeper of a shop offering many types of products, which included medicines. Only in 1617, under the reign of James I, did the control of drugs come to be regarded of such importance that it was thought to merit a separate profession. Henceforth, by royal decree, grocers were asked to abandon the sale of any medical goods – an order they obeyed, though only under vehement protest. Ever since, and ignoring the title's literal meaning, the apothecary has specialised in the dispensing of medications, with grocers restricting their trade to the selling of food and other household goods.

As happens so often in life, the apothecary's concern – whether under the name of chemist, pharmacist or druggist – has come full circle. Once again, these shopkeepers sell a vast variety of goods, with medications occupying an ever-smaller section and, partially, even taken over by supermarkets.

APPLE A DAY KEEPS THE DOCTOR AWAY

The apple has played a significant role in the life of many races and nations, impacting upon their beliefs, traditions and daily diet.

For millennia it was thought that Adam and Eve were expelled from Paradise because of the apple they ate. It should be realised that Scriptures never mention an apple. They merely speak of 'the forbidden fruit' without specifying of what kind it was. In fact, it is now assumed that it was either a peach or an apricot.

In ancient times the apple was credited with the ability to improve the quality of life and even to prolong it. Legend tells that Alexander the Great, in a quest to find the water of life, discovered apples. These, it was claimed, had vastly extended the years of life of priests who ate nothing but the fruit.

An Irish legend attributes the apple with the capacity to endow humans with immortality. The Song of Songs, on the other hand, intimates the apple's potency as an aphrodisiac.

With such traditions in place, it was no wonder that apples were highly regarded, not least so for their curative powers. It explains the widely-held opinion that 'an apple a day keeps the doctor away', as humorously expressed in a rhyme by an anonymous author:

> Eat an apple when going to bed
> And you'll keep the doctor from earning his bread.

For some time, the claim of the apple's medicinal value was denied and decried as a myth and a fallacy. It was mere folklore, said the apple's detractors, perpetuated and further spread by orchardists to foster the sale of their produce.

Modern knowledge, however, and chemical analysis of the fruit have substantiated the beneficial effect of eating apples – and, with it, the fundamental veracity of the adage.

Though certainly unable to cure disease, apples may contribute to the preservation of good health. The potassium they contain is an essential mineral for the body. Equally beneficial is their pectin, which is said to be able to lower blood cholesterol. Everyone now realises the importance of fibre in one's daily diet for regulating bowel movements and possibly preventing some malignancies. Here, too, the apple is rich in this substance.

Though less significant, the role the eating of apples may play in cleaning the teeth, and thereby lessening the formation of plaque, is nevertheless well worth remembering. It accounts for the jocular description of an apple as nature's toothbrush.

Altogether it can be seen that 'an apple a day keeps the doctor away' is not a mere old wives' tale but a sound piece of folk wisdom gained as the result of experience. Though all statistics have to be taken with a grain of salt, a survey conducted by one of the English universities interestingly revealed that people who regularly ate apples had to consult their doctor much less frequently than those who didn't eat apples.

APRON

An apron, of whatever kind, contains a fault: it is so called by error. Its proper description should be a napron. However, the initial 'n' was mistakenly detached from the word to be joined to the indefinite article ('a') preceding it, thereby changing the napron into an apron, which it has remained ever since.

Derived from the Old French *naperson*, meaning 'cloth', the word is still part of all napery and every nappy (the American diaper).

Through the years, the apron has fulfilled a variety of functions. As an outer garment, it served both as protective clothing and adornment. Its individual features indicated the wearer's native region, social standing or occupation. A butcher's apron, for instance, was distinguished by its pattern of blue and white stripes. That of masons and blacksmiths was green and, to safeguard them in their work, was made of leather.

Special symbolic value belongs to the Masonic apron. Made of white lambskin, it represents the ideals of purity of heart and innocence of conduct. No doubt linked with the early mason, who was a master in his craft, Freemasons adopted it. It is still the first gift presented to a newly initiated member, one which he will always treasure and which, at his death, his brethren will place with him into the grave.

`ARMS' IN INN NAMES

Everyone has come across a hotel or a public house containing the word 'Arms'. Typical examples are 'The King's Arms' and 'The Cricketers Arms'. Their designation is linked with heraldic signs and goes back to the days when only a small minority of the population were literate. For this reason, buildings, instead of being numbered, were identified by some picture or illustration painted on their facades. This made it easy to locate a residence, business establishment or public house.

At a time when any association with royalty or nobility gave special status, among the most popular signs chosen were those showing a monarch's portrait or that of a close member of his or her family. Alternately, it might display a figure or symbol linked with the monarch. This explains the frequent use of names and signs such as 'The Crown', 'The Sceptre' and, not least, 'The King's / Queen's [coat of] Arms'. This, too, accounts for the ubiquity of public houses called 'The Lion'. As the 'king of beasts', the lion appears on numerous royal crests.

Other public houses adopted the 'arms' of the personage on whose property they were located or in whose proximity they were situated. More fortunate still were those which could boast of a nobleman's patronage, even if they had enjoyed it only once. Any such notable name gave special status to the inn, particularly when trade became highly competitive, and so a royal connection helped to attract customers. No wonder that every care was taken to display the arms conspicuously.

The practice had proved its value so much that even when literacy was widespread and pictorial identification no longer necessary, the tradition was retained. To those unaware of their background, it created the enigma of the 'Arms'.

ARMY BILLETS

Prior to the introduction of army barracks, soldiers were housed in civilian lodgings. For this purpose their commanding officer issued them with 'vouchers' which they had to present – for later compensation – to the owner of the residence to which they had been directed. The word 'billet' derives from the French phrase *billet de logement* – 'a ticket for lodging'. This original (French) 'ticket' – *billet* – completely detached from the private accommodation and application, has become the modern soldiers' quarters.

AVENUE

The French created the first avenue, that wide, tree-lined street, aesthetically so pleasing. They coined its name from the Latin *advenire*, for 'to come' and 'to arrive'. Initially intended to serve a very practical purpose by providing ample room for the population to walk about, the avenue was to assume an even more significant, political reason: the very spaciousness of the avenue permitted Napoleon's soldiers to move quickly, should ever the need arise, to put down an uprising.

AVOCADO

Digging for the linguistic root of the avocado uncovers a fascinating past and reveals a strange metamorphosis. The Aztecs enjoyed this tropical fruit, the shape of which reminded them of their testicles. It was for this reason that they called it after that part of their anatomy, *ahuacatl* in their language. Believing in sympathetic magic, that 'like creates like', they attributed to it aphrodisiac qualities.

On their conquest of Mexico, the Spaniards soon acquired a taste for the fruit, desiring it all the more because of its alleged sexual properties. Subsequently they imported it to Europe.

However, they found great difficulty in pronouncing its Aztec name. To make it roll more smoothly from their tongues, they substituted for it another word, eventually creating the present-day avocado.

They did not suppress or interfere with its sexual reputation, however. In fact, tradition tells of many desperate men, including a French king, partaking of the avocado to cure their impotence. No reliable record exists as to whether it had the desired effect.

AXMINSTER CARPETS

Axminster carpets recall the English country town of that name, located in the County of Devon. It was there that they were first made. Traditionally, credit is given to Thomas Whitty for creating the first Axminster. He had opened a carpet factory in Axminster in 1755, and fragments of some of his hand-knotted woollen carpets have since become treasured museum pieces.

Histories of the time tell of the high regard in which Whitty's carpets were held and how they not only graced many a mansion and country seat of the nobility, but even adorned the royal palaces at Brighton and Windsor.

Whitty employed almost one hundred people, most of whom were women. In teams of at least five they attended the individual looms. They excelled in their work, producing creations of unique beauty. In his recollections, the Reverend Thomas Moore tells how the thickness of the woollen fabric surpassed that of any other of its kind.

Sadly, the mechanisation of weaving, and the consequent appearance of much cheaper carpets, forced the factory to be closed in 1835. Yet the fame of 'the Axminster' persisted and, as late as 1937, a new carpet manufacturing plant was opened in that very town.

Tracing the Axminster to its earliest beginnings, however, takes us back further in time and reveals some fascinating data. The name of the township of its creation indicates that it was started as a minster on the river Axe. The word 'minster' refers to the 'monastery' that once was located there and, in fact, was the originator of the carpet.

Established in 1246 by Reginald de Mohun, the abbey was one of the first of the Cistercian Order in Britain. It is a historic fact that England owes the development of its wool resources to the White Monks of the Order, so called because of the white tunics they wore. This lends special weight to the possibility that the Cistercians were the real creators of the Axminster carpet, long before Whitty embarked on his venture. Not improbably, it may even be assumed that the White Monks' pioneering work in wool at that site led him to select it for his factory.

Frugal and industrious, the monks not only grew their own food but learnt to weave clothes. They became equally proficient in the making of carpets. Their type of rug became so renowned that it was called after the monastery – Axminster. It continued to be manufactured long after the monastery's dissolution in 1539. The Axminster carpet thus perpetuates the monks' art and can be counted among the many contributions religion has made to civilisation.

Today, the carpet continues to be favoured for its hard-wearing quality and, by those who love ornamentations, for its rich patterns.

BABY RATTLES

Among the first toys given to a baby is a rattle. Initially, this was not intended so much for the amusement of the infant as for its protection. The sound the rattle made was intended to drive away the evil spirits which were imagined to threaten the young child and were believed to be allergic to noise.

The earliest rattles go back to the dawn of civilisation. Beautiful specimens have been excavated at Tel-al-Amarna in Egypt, dating back to the fourteenth century BC, and others have been discovered in the famous ruins of Pompeii.

BACTERIA

People fight shy of bacteria. The less they have to do with them, the happier they are. Bacteria can wreak all kinds of havoc, something their name hardly suggests: 'little rods' is the plural of the Greek *bakterion*.

The name is an odd kind of memorial, commemorating the earliest identification of bacteria by the seventeenth-century Dutch naturalist Anton van Leeuwenhoek. When he first observed micro-organisms through a microscope, many of them looked like 'little sticks' or 'rods'. This suggested their name, which was subsequently also given to the science of bacteriology.

Indeed, bacteria were one of Leeuwenhoek's many remarkable discoveries, which included spermatozoa and 'animalcules' (protozoan). They were a find worthy of a man already so famous as to have been honoured by visits from the Queen of England, Frederick I of Prussia and Peter the Great, Tsar of Russia.

BAGEL

A ring-shaped bread roll, the bagel was popularised by American Jews who, having migrated to the United States from the European East, brought with them its recipe. Originally, this type of doughnut was crisp and dry, unsweetened but glazed. To make a bagel, humorists said, was easy: 'Just take a hole and put dough around it.'

Its Yiddish name, now part of the English vocabulary, was adopted from the medieval German *Beugel*, for a round loaf of bread. Nowadays, especially when eaten with cream cheese and smoked salmon, relished by many as a treat, its origin can be traced to totally different circumstances. The majority of eastern European Jews were poor. Their staple food, almost monotonously, consisted of black bread and herrings. However, once a week, in honour of the Sabbath, they substituted the coarse bread with white loaves. They could afford only a certain number of these *chalot*, as they were called in Hebrew, which was insufficient for their then still large families, so they supplemented them with round rolls with a hole in the centre. Indeed, they were almost a delicacy, and regulations issued in 1610 by the Jewish community of Cracow, Poland, recommended them as a most fitting gift for a woman who had just given birth to a child.

The circular shape of the roll had great symbolism to those early generations of bagel eaters. It called to mind the unending cycle of life. More so, it stood for the perfection to which all humans should aspire. The bagel thus offers a striking example of how even food can provide a spiritual message.

BALACLAVA

The balaclava, that woollen close-fitting head covering, worn also to protect part of the face, neck and even shoulders, by its very name recalls a famous site of the Crimean War. In 1854, the small harbour of Balaclava served the British forces as their base. The appalling conditions they had to endure at the time were further aggravated by the harshest of winters. It was for the protection of their heads against the biting cold that the men were issued with special hoods. Retained after the cessation of hostilities, they became useful items of clothing in wintry weather.

Ironically, in modern days the balaclava serves not only to give comfort and warmth. Criminals, not least bank robbers and intruders, have adopted it as a most useful disguise.

BAMBOOZLE

Though to bamboozle people generally means to mislead and confuse them, in nineteenth-century naval slang the term was specifically applied to 'deceiving an enemy by hoisting false colours'. The root out of which the term grew is obvious – the bamboo. A rapidly growing tropical plant, it is one of China's most important natural products. It has served countless and diverse functions, among them an instrument of punishment.

Once, people caught deceiving others were flogged with a bamboo stick. Eventually the description of their treatment was transferred to those meting it out. Anyone who 'bamboozles' others, therefore, linguistically speaking retains the (bamboo) stick once used to hit the hands and backs of offenders.

BATMAN

A batman nowadays is an army officer's personal servant. His designation, however, is not related to the baton carried by his superior.

In days gone by, the batman was not necessarily a member of the forces. He could be a civilian, attached to troops on foreign service. It was his duty to look after the men's cooking utensils, which were then carried in the saddlebag of a horse. The Old French word for a 'packsaddle' was *bat* (or *bast*), which made the soldiers refer to the animal carrying it as the bat-horse and the person attending to it as the bat-man.

Times changed and transportation was modernised. The packsaddle became obsolete and, with it, the man looking after it. Nevertheless, his services were retained both abroad and at home in civilian life. Instead of looking after the packhorse, he was now employed as the personal servant of those of superior rank. However, his change of duty did not alter or update his description, which continued to carry – verbally – the original (French) 'packsaddle'.

BATS IN THE BELFRY or BEING BATTY

Anyone who either has 'bats in the belfry' or is 'batty' is somewhat deranged.

The origin of the expression can be traced to one of two people. According to the first tradition, those who are 'batty' recall eighteenth-century author William Battie, who wrote a 'Treatise on Madness'. This work is said to have become so popular at the time of Battie's writing it that his name was soon adopted for the description of those suffering from the unfortunate condition he described.

Fitzherbert Batty is the other individual credited, unknowingly, with having given his name to the term. A lawyer in Spanish Town, Jamaica, he became insane. In 1839 it was found necessary for him to be confined to an asylum. When the news reached Britain, it made headlines in the London press. Becoming the talk of the town, Batty's name was soon applied to anyone thought to be mentally unbalanced.

In spite of these claims, it may be that no person is responsible for the word but rather bats, flying around in panic in a church tower when disturbed by the ringing of bells. After all, this would tally with the slang description of those living in a state of confusion as having 'bats in the belfry'. It is an apt simile, not least because of the added analogy between the bells being located in the highest part of a church and the head topping the body.

BEGINNER'S LUCK

It often happens that a complete novice at cards, or someone playing the poker machine for the first time, wins the kitty or hits the jackpot. The surprising success of this person is usually attributed not to pure chance but to 'beginner's luck', an ancient belief in the magic of anything new.

Traditionally, gamblers are superstitious. Thus they strongly believe in the luck of the beginner, which prompts some old hands at the game to make it their rule to follow the bids of newcomers.

BEST FOOT FORWARD

Everyday speech has made good use of many parts of the body, not least so the foot. People who assert themselves are said to put their foot down. Those making a blunder put their foot in it. People who are very conscientious in what they say or do cannot put a foot wrong. Those nearing death are said to already have one foot in the grave.

All these idioms are easily understood. Puzzling, however, is the origin of the saying that people 'put their best foot forward' when trying to make a good impression.

Both the occult world and the world of fashion have been quoted as the source of the phrase. Once it was believed that 'the left' was the realm of the devil, of evil and misfortune. This explains why *sinister*, the Latin word for 'left', assumed in English its ominous meaning. Hence it was advisable to keep the left foot behind and step forward with the best – which was the right – foot first. Advancing it would ensure good luck.

Much more recent and rational is a second interpretation. It traces the saying to male vanity, particularly apparent in the period of the dandy (the late eighteenth century). The dandy's desire to attract people's attention and admiration took strange and elaborate forms. In pursuit of his aim he made use of the entire length of his body, from the wig with which he burdened his head, down to the peculiar type of shoes he wore.

At the time, people imagined that their two legs differed in shape and that, 'normally', one was more becoming than the other. To draw attention to it they kept the worst one in the background, literally putting 'the best foot forward' and, with it, of course, the leg. (It must be realised that during the greater part of the eighteenth century people did not wear trousers, which hide the actual shape of the legs, but donned tight breeches and stockings which, hugging the legs, revealed the way these were formed.)

Yet a third explanation is based on the tradition, in speaking, of frequently using the singular 'foot' for both one's feet. In this sense, to put one's best foot forward would refer to walking as fast as one possibly could to reach one's destination soonest. This, no doubt, is the meaning of the words in Shakespeare's *King John*: 'Nay make haste; the better foot before.'

BEYOND THE PALE

Paling fences nowadays mark a property and keep out strangers. Obviously, their description derives from the wooden posts which make up the enclosure. The pale, however, for many centuries had a much more significant and, at times, ominous meaning. It was used to describe an entire restricted area.

Best known is its application in Ireland where, as first used in the fourteenth century, it referred to the district ruled by the English. In 1465 an English Parliament session defined 'the Pale' as consisting of four Irish counties. Thirty years later, another Act legislated that this 'British Pale' was to be enclosed by a vast ditch, an odd contradiction to the original meaning of the word.

People were said to live 'within [or beyond] the pale'. The significance of these terms changed according to which nation used them. For the English it described a region which, beyond British jurisdiction, abounded in savagery and lawlessness. To the Irish, on the other hand, it spelt out freedom.

These unfortunate historic circumstances now belong to the past. However, the terms then created survive, with 'beyond the pale' now being applied solely to those who live outside civilised conventions.

BIFOCALS

Bifocals were invented by Benjamin Franklin, the renowned American statesman who excelled equally as a scientist and innovator. His contributions to the improvement of the quality of life extend from the rocking chair and iron stove to the first lightning conductor.

How he came to create the first bifocals has been recounted variously. Though slightly different, all versions agree that it was personal experience that prompted him. One version tells that Franklin, travelling far and wide, had found it impossible to enjoy both the scenery in the distance and the company in the coach without constantly having to change glasses. Another suggests that at dinner parties, so much a part of his daily life, he wanted to see the food he was eating but at the same time clearly recognise the faces of his table companions. Once again, the task was impossible unless he switched glasses all the time.

He was well aware that this problem troubled numerous people. Not least, it handicapped artists, who frequently had to turn their eyes from the object or scenery they painted to the canvas, and back again.

Franklin's creative mind soon set to work. On 23 May 1785 he succeeded in making a lens that joined two segments of different strength – the bifocal. His invention dispensed with the necessity of carrying two sets of spectacles.

BISCUIT

What in the United States is a 'cookie' is in Britain a biscuit. Now served as a mere snack, its name points to much more substantial fare in days gone by.

From the French, biscuit (like *Zwieback*, its German equivalent) means 'twice baked'. Factually, it recalls the early method of its preparation. After a short time, particularly on voyages, bread easily went stale. Baking it twice, however, removed most of the moisture, and thereby helped in preserving its freshness.

BITUMEN

Bitumen, used for the surfacing of roads or for waterproofing roofs and boats, has traditionally been traced to the Vulgate, the Latin translation of the Hebrew Bible, in which it is used to render the Hebrew term now translated in English as 'pitch'.

The Douai Bible of 1609, which followed not the original Hebrew text but that of the Latin Vulgate, adopted the latter's version. Consequently, when speaking of Noah's building of the Ark (Genesis 6:14), it relates how in caulking it he followed the divine instruction to 'pitch it within and without with *bitume*'.

Scripture likewise tells that it was this substance which Moses' mother applied to the papyrus basket in which she placed her infant and set upon the waters of the Nile, in order to make it watertight and thereby to prevent it from sinking (Exodus 2:3).

BIZARRE

Bizarre indeed is the story of the word used nowadays to describe the odd, the unusual and the eccentric, for it is thought to be the only expression adopted from the Basque language.

The Basques, a people domiciled in a region of north-eastern Spain, for centuries were kept isolated from the rest of the country by a mountain barrier. This isolation led to the development of their own culture, traditions, dress and language. Even some of their proverbs are unique, such as 'a golden key will unlock any door', 'there is no tree without shadow' and 'a cheap mule is expensive'.

Basque men used to be distinguished by their beards, which they trimmed in a fashion different from any observed elsewhere. When visiting Spain, they immediately caught the attention of the locals, prompting them to identify the Basque by his conspicuous beard. They called him by the Basque word for beard, *bizar*, rendering it in Spanish as *bizarro*.

Equating hairiness with manliness, the Spaniards gave the term a new meaning, that of bravery and gallantry. It did not take long for the Italians to adopt (and adapt) the word. To them, however, the individuality of the Basques, those bold people who seemed insistent to see things done their way, made them associate their description with 'capriciousness'.

Still, it was not the end of the journey for the original *bizar*. Upon reaching the French the word was given a new slant. To them it came to signify the odd and the queer, an impression often created by anyone who talked differently or looked unusual.

That is how the originally Basque-grown 'beard' grew into a great variety of shapes – linguistically. Eventually it attained its present-day English connotation, pointing to the grotesque and fantastic, an interpretation it has retained ever since.

BLACK ARM BANDS FOR MOURNING

The wearing of black arm bands for mourning originated in England where, to start with, according to eighteenth century regulations they were restricted to military personnel. (A Gazette of 20 May 1775 specifically stated that 'His Majesty does not require that the Officers of the Army should wear any other mourning, on the present melancholy occasion, than a black crêpe round their left arm with their uniforms.') From England it found its way to the Continent, where it became prevalent.

Traditionally, those who had suffered a bereavement showed their sense of loss and honoured the departed by dressing entirely in black. They continued to wear this colour to the very end of the mourning period, which differed according to the degree of relationship, though Queen Victoria chose to wear black permanently after the death of her consort Prince Albert.

In English society it used to be the custom for the entire household, including the staff, to show their sorrow by donning black. However, to fit out servants in black clothes was too costly, so for them a black arm band had to suffice. The arm band therefore generally owes its existence to reasons of economy. To those acquainted with its history it recalls an age in which class distinctions were pronounced.

BLACK MARIA

For a long time, the American 'paddy wagon', which took those arrested to the police station or jail, was also popularly known as the Black Maria. The van was easily recognised, as it was painted black.

People like to personalise objects, and it can well be imagined that those unfortunate enough to be carried away in a police truck, in an attempt to soften the blow (temporarily at least), made it appear as if a woman was luring them away. They called the van Maria.

So says one tradition. Another links the first Black Maria with a Maria Lee who lived in the early 1800s in Boston, Massachusetts. A black woman, she was of powerful build and was said to have had a commanding presence. She ran a lodging house, on the waterfront of the city, which was frequented by sailors. They enjoyed not only her hospitality but her protection too. Staying with her, they knew, they were safe against any ruffians' attack. Maria was renowned for her courage, unafraid to tackle any 'resident' who was unruly, disorderly or drunk. On many occasions she helped the guardians of the law in subduing hooligans and, in one case, even to rescue a policeman from his assailants. To 'send for the black Maria' became a slogan whenever there was cause for alarm.

A celebrity in her own city, it was not unlikely that Maria's fame spread, her name even ultimately recommending itself to the English police, who called their early prison vans after her as well.

BLACKSMITH

The origins of the names of the goldsmith and silversmith are easily understood. But not so explicit is that of the blacksmith, whose best known job it is to shoe horses. Should he not, more appropriately, be known as a horsesmith?

There is a valid explanation. At one time the iron out of which the blacksmith fashioned shoes was known as 'black metal', and it was this that gave him his name. It also distinguished him from a smith working in tin, or other metal of a similar colour, who was referred to as a whitesmith.

BLOW ONE'S OWN TRUMPET

Anyone boasting overmuch of an achievement may be reprimanded by saying to them, 'your trumpeter is dead'. A mere metaphor now, its significance goes back to a former practice. Royalty and nobility at one time had their approach announced by a trumpet fanfare, which was sounded by a herald who preceded them. Equally, not so very long ago, a proclamation used to be introduced by trumpet blasts.

Those who wanted to be recognised for something they had done but found no one prepared to praise them lacked, as it were, a personal trumpeter. Obviously they had to 'blow their own trumpet'.

This figure of speech is used in the Gospel account (Matthew 6:2) in which those giving alms are reminded to do so inconspicuously and not to sound a trumpet before them 'as the hypocrites do'.

BLUE-COLLAR WORKERS

The colour of one's clothes often reflects the work one does. It can say something about a person's 'status' and even their mood. Colour has always attracted people's attention and influenced them, and not infrequently it has played a significant role in politics.

Those engaged in professional and secretarial duties were expected – first in the United States, in 1929 – to wear shirts with a white collar. Initially meant to distinguish them, it soon came to designate their very pursuit. Industrial and manual workers, on the other hand, became known in the 1950s as blue-collar workers. They were so called not because of any specific collar they wore, but because of their blue working shirt. Usually made of blue denim, the shirt was chosen for its durability.

BLUE LIGHTS ON POLICE VEHICLES

It is commonly believed, though wrongly so, that the police force adopted blue lights for their cars to differentiate them from the red lights of fire engines (obviously associated with flames), ambulances and other emergency vehicles. Though a very plausible explanation, it does not tally with the facts.

Initially, red identified the police as well. No doubt they had adopted it from the Bow Street Runners, a body of men previously employed to catch criminals. Going back to as early as 1749, the Bow Street Runners were renowned for their efficiency. They were nicknamed 'Robin Red Breasts', and for a very obvious reason. It was the colour of the red waistcoats they wore, chosen to make themselves specially conspicuous.

It was therefore almost a foregone conclusion that when in 1829 the modern police force was established, taking over the duty of those 'runners', it also appropriated their distinctive colour.

However, red was not to last. It reminded people of the Red Light District, and to be associated with prostitutes in any way was not in keeping with the dignity of the police force. Hence red was replaced by blue to identify a police station, a police vehicle and a policeman's uniform.

It is interesting to learn that for a short period in the 1880s, at Queen Victoria's request, the blue was abandoned. A frequent visitor to the opera at Covent Garden, Victoria had to pass the police station in its vicinity and, for reasons of her own, disliked the colour blue. Why she did so is not certain. It has been suggested that it is linked to an incident in which she stepped on a blue opal, crushing it underfoot. At her behest, the blue of the police was changed to white, at least locally. Soon after the Queen's death, however, it was changed back to the original blue, which colour it has remained ever since.

BLURB

The brief summary of the contents of a book and its author's qualifications, printed on its cover or dust jacket, is known as the blurb. It gives potential readers an opportunity to acquaint themselves with the subject matter discussed and the writer's background, then to decide whether or not to purchase the book.

In the beginning, however, 'blurb' was a very slanted term. It was coined by Boston-born Frank Gelett Burgess (1866–1915), a humorist, author and illustrator. Burgess was determined to voice his disgust at what he considered disreputable merchandising methods: namely, to give highly exaggerated accounts of a book and the status of its author.

To Burgess's mind such promotion – 'to flatter from interested motives' – was unethical. He felt that his chance to denigrate it had come when, in 1907, the United States Booksellers' Association invited him to be their guest of honour at their annual public dinner.

Traditionally, on this occasion the host presented each guest with a copy of a book most popular at the time. The choice for that year – and very appropriately so – was a book by Burgess himself. It was a satire on platitudes, which he had challengingly entitled *Are You a Bromide?* Each of the 500 people present found a copy of it placed next to their plate. To show his disapproval of the standard blurb, Burgess had, however, designed a special jacket. Instead of a rave write-up it displayed a picture of a 'sickly, sweet young woman' with conspicuously gleaming white teeth. (Most likely he had culled her from an advertisement for tooth powder!) Facetiously he called her Miss Belinda Blurb. In later years, Burgess confessed that he had intended to have her picture 'blurbing a blurb to end all blurbs'!

Whether or not he succeeded in putting an end to publishers' extravagant merchandising methods is a matter of opinion. Nevertheless, Burgess's 'blurb' became both a part of every book jacket and an accepted term of the literary vocabulary.

When, in the 1920s, the word blurb reached England, it did not immediately catch on. Though first listed in the Oxford English Dictionary in 1924, as late as 1942 Lord Dunedin, a Scottish peer, reprimanded the Edinburgh *Scotsman* for using it. He described the term as 'a monstrosity, imported, like so many others, from America'.

The very title of Burgess's book made yet another contribution to American speech. People came to refer to boring speakers, fond of using a multitude of meaningless clichés and platitudes, as 'bromides'. After all, their effect was identical to that of the well-known sedative.

BOBBY

English policemen have been nicknamed 'bobbies'. One explanation claims that they were so called from the very beginning of the establishment of their force. Their name was said to recall Sir Robert (Bob) Peel who, as the then British Home Secretary, in 1829 created the (London) Metropolitan Police Force. Those resenting its existence decried it as 'Peel's Bloody Gang'. Sir Robert's admirers, however, speaking of him as 'Bobby', transferred his nickname to the force he had established, calling it 'Bobby's men', eventually to be contracted into the now familiar 'Bobby'.

Previously, when as Chief Secretary for Ireland (1812–18) Sir Robert had instituted the Irish Constabulary, its members, too, were colloquially called after him, to become known in that country as the 'Peelers'.

BOMBAY DUCK

For a fish to be called a duck confounds the mind and potentially upsets the stomach. Those ordering Bombay Duck will be served dried salted fish, eaten in India as a savoury, often with curries.

Both sections of the name present a puzzle which, so far, has only partially been solved.

Bombay, no doubt, is the mistaken and misshapen rendering of *bombila*, the Marathi word for this type of fish, which is caught in great abundance in the area of the Indian Ocean coast where this language is spoken. Possibly the fact that the fish was exported in large quantities from Bombay contributed to the adoption of its misleading description.

This still leaves the 'duck' portion of the name unexplained. Some commentators have suggested that the word was chosen because of the habit of the fish to skim the water, reminding those watching them of the movement of ducks. Another explanation compares its origin with that claimed for Welsh rabbit. It is said that, just as the Welsh were so poor that they could not even afford the meat of a common rabbit, substituting for it toasted cheese (hence 'Welsh rabbit'), so impecunious Indians, unable to provide duck for their table, replaced it with dried fish.

Both tales of the Bombay duck seem a bit fishy. Perhaps the creation of this dish was due to the English presence in India. Serving on the sub-continent, the English soon became acquainted with the savoury. On their British tongue it deteriorated, as it were, beyond recognition, changing into the much more pronounceable – if not digestible – Bombay duck. Anglo-Indians then introduced it to Britain, where its earliest documentation goes back to 1860.

BONE CHINA

Bone china owes its name to the large quantity of bone ash it contains. This constitutes almost 40 per cent of the entire mix and is responsible for its special quality of translucency. Bone china was brought to perfection and popularised in the early 1790s by Josiah Spode II. The foremost English potter at the time, he was recognised as such by his appointment as Potter to the (then) Prince of Wales.

First known as British Cornish China, in 1810 it was very appropriately renamed Spode Porcelain. Bone china became its late Victorian trade name.

BONKING

Bonking has become part of the twentieth-century vocabulary as a colloquialism for 'having intercourse'. Its earliest literary mention has been traced to a 1975 magazine feature. Though everyone now knows what the term stands for, its origin is still uncertain.

According to one suggestion, it developed out of the early slang for 'hitting'. Others discovered in the word, as it were, an echo of 'banging'. In both cases, bonking would refer to violence, which, not rarely (and in many languages), has been associated with the sexual act, as in 'to knock up' and 'to screw'. Some, however, have seen 'bunk' as the cradle of bonking: a couple beds down to copulate.

Reversing direction, so to speak, there is also a hypothesis recognising in 'bonk' the 'knob', a well-known slang word for the penis, perhaps to camouflage it read from back to front. A variety of possibilities, they are as mysterious as sex itself.

BOOK COVERS

The modern type of book cover is thought to have religious origins. In its early days, the Church was an outlawed organisation, and the Roman authorities strictly banned the propagation of any of its ideas. Ignoring the prohibition, the Church published its teachings, doing so on leaves of papyrus joined together to form a volume. However, to conceal the contents of the codex, and thereby avoid its confiscation, they enclosed it in a wrapping. 'Covering up' the text, this wrapping came to be called a book cover.

Going to the other extreme, the cover now serves to publicise a book's contents – truly a contradiction in terms.

BOOKWORMS

An avid reader is called a bookworm. He or she is compared to those minute insects, mostly book lice, which have a predilection to live in, and feed on, old books. More correctly, it is their larvae that consume the books, with their preferential choice being the glue in the bindings of a volume. Only afterwards will they penetrate the pages as well. Humans who are bibliophiles also devour books, though fortunately only in a metaphorical sense.

BOTTOM DOLLAR

Being absolutely sure of something, people say that they would bet their bottom dollar on it, meaning the very last dollar they own.

It is easy to assume that the phrase was coined because people, with no other money left, found their last dollar right at the bottom of their purse or pocket and therefore very appropriately referred to it as their 'bottom dollar'.

At the best of times, money presents problems, and even if it 'talks', as the saying goes, it might easily be misleading. This certainly applies to the interpretation given to the bottom dollar. The dollar does not come from one's pocket at all, but rather from the gaming table, where the chips are stacked in front of the individual players. To make a bet the players take one or more from the top of the pile. Hence, betting their bottom dollar means to wager all they have, the entire lot – from the top to the bottom, including their very last dollar.

BOWING TO THE CHAIR

Common Parliamentary practice requires members of the House, on passing the Speaker's chair, to bow towards it. The gesture is assumed to express deference to the Speaker's high office and the impartiality of his or her position.

The custom in fact has a religious basis, going back to the mother Parliament at Westminster. Originally, this met in the fourteenth-century Chapel of St Stephen's. There the Speaker's chair occupied the former site of the altar, which, in turn, had replaced an image of the Virgin Mary.

Neither the altar nor the image exist any longer, but members continue to bow towards their former location. Unaware of the original reason, which has become redundant, the gesture has been reinterpreted and copied around the world, its meaning secularised. By bowing, members are said to show their respect to representative government.

BOWLING ALLEY

A bowling 'alley' is so called because the game was originally played in alleyways between houses.

BRAILLE

Until the advent of talking books and other modern electronic devices, for many years Braille writing was the most wonderful gift for those bereft of sight. By a simple system which used diverse combinations of six raised dots, it enabled blind people, merely by using their sense of touch, to read both literature and musical scores.

Its name honoured Louis Braille (1809–52), the man credited with its invention. He himself had been blinded as a child of three. Whilst cutting some leather in his father's workshop, the knife had slipped in his tiny hand.

At the age of ten, Louis won a scholarship for the National Institution for Blind Children in Paris. He soon excelled, his intelligence and gift for music leading him to be appointed as one of the teachers.

The head of the school, in search of some device to enable his charges to read, conceived the idea to provide them with texts in which the actual letters were embossed. This, however, presented an arduous task for youngsters, demanding much effort on their part to identify the individual characters by passing their fingers over them. It proved much too difficult to be applied by them for writing.

A visit by Captain Charles Barbier changed the entire situation, and the process. He displayed a gadget he had developed in the army. Whilst serving under King Louis XVIII he had invented 'night writing' to enable soldiers in the field and sentinels on patrol to inconspicuously, in the darkness of night, pass on or exchange short messages. To do this he employed a simple system of dots and dashes which could, without much difficulty, be embossed with a stylus on cardboard and 'read' by the recipient by the mere touch of the fingers.

Braille was immediately taken by the idea, but also realised its shortcomings. The officer's method could well serve in the conveyance of short army commands, such as to advance or retreat but, with its twelve-dot configuration, it was too cumbersome for any purpose beyond this. The symbols he had created occupied an area far too extensive to be covered by a finger tip.

So Louis set to work and, greatly improving on Barbier's idea, developed a very simplified system of raised point writing using six dots to represent each letter or symbol. He first had his system published in 1829. To start with, the authorities rejected it, but it did not take long for the blessing it represented to be recognised. The introduction of 'Braille', as it became known, would entirely change the quality of blind people's lives worldwide.

A heart-warming, though most probably apocryphal story, explains its sudden acceptance. As a lover of music, Braille had tutored a blind girl in playing the organ. She soon came to excel at the instrument. Invited by one of the then fashionable Paris salons to give a recital, she enthralled her audience, who gave her a well-merited ovation. When the applause had died down, the girl addressed the ladies. That she had pleased them so much, in spite of her handicap, she told them, was due only to one man. Louis Braille, totally ignored so far, had created a wondrous system to enable the blind to read musical scores and literature, she said. Almost abandoned, at the time Louis was dying from tuberculosis. Her words did not go unheeded and led to the final adoption of 'Braille'.

BROOCH

It has often happened that though once useful and practical objects have lost their function, they have not been discarded. Retained, they are given a decorative role. Eventually it is believed that this role was theirs exclusively from the very beginning.

This applies to the brooch. Initially, with buttons still unknown, it served as a necessary accessory to dressing, essential to fasten a garment. Having lost its purpose, the brooch has nevertheless been retained, mostly to be now worn as an ornament.

BROWN AS A BERRY

People might say of those with a deep suntan that they are as 'brown as a berry'. The comparison seems odd, as fruit berries are generally black, blue, red or green, but hardly ever brown, unless dried or in a state of decay.

Possibly, there is a simple explanation. A phrase might be adopted, whether it makes sense or not, merely because someone of prominence has used it. Its authorship alone makes it popular.

Geoffrey Chaucer, the renowned poet, in his *Prologue to the Canterbury Tales* (c. 1386) wrote of a horse (using for it the now archaic word 'palfrey') as being 'as brown as a berry'. If an authority as notable as Chaucer applied the comparison, it must be proper. Thus, even if for no other reason, it became part of everyday speech.

As for Chaucer himself, he might have chosen the simile thinking not at all of blackberries, blueberries, strawberries or gooseberries, but of certain brown berries grown on trees or shrubs, such as the hawthorn. Their existence was recalled again almost three centuries later when John Tatham, in his *Love Crowns the End* (1640), had one of his characters tell a person that 'Thy nose is as brown as a berry'. John Gay (1685–1732) made renewed use of the saying in his *New Song of New* [!] *Similes*.

However, other interpretations have been proffered as well. Some concern exists as to the real meaning of brown. Was it the colour we now associate with the word or, in Chaucer's time, might it not have related to some other shade? In parallel passages, in fact, it has been used for 'bay', a horse of a reddish-brown colour.

Perhaps the brown was not intended to be taken literally at all, but was meant to convey a quality. The sheen of a brown horse's coat was most striking and pleasing to the eye. This might have led people to apply the colour to anything pleasant-looking and attractive. Such a view would be reinforced by the fact that Chaucer attributed the colour specifically to a warhorse, which was admired for its powerful build.

Most acceptable could be a further and very simple suggestion: the saying might have been coined and become popular solely because of its alliteration. The words 'brown' and 'berry' have identical initials, making 'as brown as a berry' euphonious and memorable.

BUCK

The (monetary) 'buck' is pure American. Slang for a dollar, it derives from the terminology of deer hunters and trappers. When selling the skins of the animals they had caught, these men priced them not according to their quality but their size. Whilst charging for the smaller ones 50 cents, fittingly called a 'doe', they sold the larger ones for a dollar – a 'buck'.

A related derivation suggests that the buck is really a shortened form of 'buck-skin', which in the early trade with the Indians was used as a unit of barter.

BUDGERIGAR

By its colourful plumage and gift of speech, the budgerigar, this small Australian parrot, has become popular worldwide as a cagebird. Its description combines the Aborigines' words for 'good' (*budgeree*) and 'cockatoo' (*gar*).

Its indigenous name has misled authorities, who have, at times, made fantastic claims. Some have discovered in the 'budgie' (as the budgerigar is fondly referred to) the Old English for 'well-furred', though they give no explanation as to how that lovely creature had substituted a dense coat of hair for colourful feathers.

Even more far-fetched is yet another interpretation and rendering of the bird's name. First given in the early 1880s in an American dictionary, it has been repeated since. Establishing a French connection, it misrepresented the budgerigar as *beauregard*, no doubt influenced by its beauty – *beau* in French.

BUNGALOW

Bungalow is a Hindustani word. Meaning 'from Bengal', it recalls the region in the Indian sub-continent where this type of building was common.

During the British rule, Europeans living in the interior of India used to reside in such one-storey houses which, generally, were surrounded by a veranda. On their return to England they introduced the bungalow there, and by retaining its indigenous name acknowledged its original site.

An apocryphal story gives another reason as to why the bungalow was so called. A builder had been commissioned to construct a two-storey house, to be ready at a specified time. Unforeseen circumstances delayed its completion, however, with the result that on the stipulated date only one storey was finished. The client remonstrated with the builder, asking him what he proposed to do. Nonplussed, the latter suggested to *bung a low* roof on to the ground floor which was already finished. That is how, according to this tale, the word bungalow came into existence.

BUS

The bus is all that is left of the Latin word *omnibus*, meaning 'for all'. It is an apt description for this large vehicle designed to carry passengers.

Blaise Pascal, the famous seventeenth-century French philosopher and mathematician, was the first to have the idea of providing a carriage for public transport. With the financial support of a friend, he started such services in Paris in 1662. The carriage was an eight-seater. Whether full or empty, it kept to a schedule, running at regular intervals. Passengers paid a fixed fee for the trip, irrespective of whether they travelled all, or only part, of the distance covered. Known as a *carrosse* (for 'coach'), it soon caught people's imaginations, becoming quite a craze. Even the king made use of it. No doubt he must have been one of the few members of royalty ever to have travelled by bus!

Like all fads, however, it petered out – not least because, paradoxically, the service was restricted at the time to the aristocracy and the upper classes. It took more than one and a half centuries to be revived, once again in Paris, in 1819.

In the 1820s yet another Frenchman, Stanislas Baudry of Nantes, introduced a similar service to his city. It is to him that the world owes the vehicle's designation as a bus. Baudry had opened baths in a suburb of Nantes. To attract and oblige customers he inaugurated special transport services for them. Starting at the centre of the city, the vehicles took the clients straight to his establishment and, later, back again.

Soon other people availed themselves of the service, doing so for their own purposes to speedily reach their destination. Their abuse of something provided solely for the comfort of Baudry's patrons did not go unnoticed by the Frenchman. It gave him the idea of commercialising the venture. This he did, and by a combination of French and Latin words – *voiture* and *omnibus* – created 'a carriage for all'.

A strange coincidence suggested to him this name. It so happened that the city terminus of his service was located outside a store owned by a Monsieur M. Omnes. The firm was cleverly advertised by the punning slogan 'OMNES OMNIBUS', words which carried the message that the store of Omnes offered goods 'for all'. Instantly, Baudry recognised in the Latin term a most suitable name for his own conveyance. After all, it too was 'for all and everyone'.

Whilst working in France, George Shillibeer, an English coach maker, picked up the idea of the omnibus. He took it back with him to London, where on 4 July 1829, with two vehicles, he started the first 'bus service' in Britain. With a capacity to carry up to twenty-two passengers, it ran from Paddington to the Bank of England. The buses were drawn by three horses abreast. To start with, as an extra bonus, Shillibeer provided his passengers with literature so they could read on the way, but not for long. He stopped doing so when most of the books had disappeared!

It was merely a matter of time for the new type of service to catch on and to spread nationwide. Eventually adopted all over the world, the omnibus became popularly known by Shillibeer's abbreviation as 'the bus'.

Shillibeer's own enterprise, alas, was doomed to failure. Abandoning his buses, he became an undertaker. If the living could not help him to prosper, the dead would certainly do so.

BUTLER

Mostly redundant now, except in wealthy homes or at state functions, the butler has found a place in social history and 'Whodunnit' detective stories, movies and plays.

The butler, to start with, was the 'bottler' (in his French designation the *bouteillier*, from *bouteille*, the French 'bottle'). His was then a most responsible appointment, as it was his duty to look after the wine cellar and its much-treasured store. No wonder that, as chief steward of the household, he was held in high regard.

When in the eleventh century the Normans invaded Britain, they brought with them their tradesmen and servants, including their bottler. However, in his new home he had little or no work to do, as English soils produced far fewer grapes and therefore reduced the need to bottle wine. Nevertheless, the bottler was retained, and to keep him busy he was given odd jobs to do, thus taking on the duties of the modern butler.

BUTTERED BREAD

Copernicus is renowned for having revolutionised the world view of the universe, yet he may well have made yet another significant contribution, one which dramatically changed eating habits: it is claimed that he introduced the buttering of bread!

Generally, Copernicus is remembered only for his achievements as an astronomer. In actual fact, he was trained as a theologian and served as a Canon of the Cathedral of Frauenburg, situated on the Fisches Haff, a lagoon on the Baltic Sea in what was at one time East Prussia. He also studied medicine, and it is not surprising to learn that among many of his contemporaries he was better known as a physician than an astronomer. If patients lived too far away to be attended by him personally, Copernicus looked after them by correspondence. Sicknesses he treated included colic, gout and malaria. If puzzled by a case, he was not too proud to call upon the help of colleagues. It was said that the local poor, whom he treated with equal care to his wealthier patients, but without charge, worshipped him. To them he was a second Aesculapius.

When, during a siege, he was once put in charge of the local castle, he was greatly perturbed by the outbreak of some kind of 'plague' among the people. No known remedy proved effective. As a man of science, Copernicus applied a method of trial and error, anticipating modern experimentation. He suspected some link between people's diet and their state of health.

By daily changing the food, he eventually came to suspect that bread was the possible cause of the scourge. A staple food, he could not eliminate it from the people's diet altogether. He reasoned that by supplementing it with some other nourishing substance he would be able to counteract and neutralise its disease-causing effect. Thus he made everyone butter their bread. Whether because of this substance, or by mere coincidence, the 'plague' stopped.

Meanwhile the patients had taken a liking to the new combination. By buttering their bread, they enjoyed it all the more. What had been a temporary remedial measure became a daily habit, soon to spread far beyond the region, eventually to become the custom all over Europe.

This seems a most far-fetched story, but it has been advanced as a serious theory by a medical historian at Vermont University, USA. Subsequently, in 1970, it was reported in the *Journal of the American Medical Association* under the title 'Copernicus and the Inception of Bread-buttering'. Right or wrong, at the very least the theory is food for thought as to why and how people first started to butter their bread.

CABINET

In the British parliamentary system the inner circle of the government, and particularly so its executive and the leading members, are known as the cabinet.

Surprisingly, however, the original 'cabinet' did not refer to people at all. A French diminutive, *cabinet* meant 'a small room' (closely related to a ship's 'cabin').

The use of the word cabinet in its governmental sense goes back to the time when royalty not only reigned but ruled. To privately discuss affairs of state with one or several of his principal ministers, the king would ask them to join him in a small room. This would ensure confidentiality and secrecy. Using the French word, they spoke of the chamber in which they met as their *cabinet*.

The practice and room no longer exist, but the name of the cabinet survives in its now governmental sense.

CAESAR SALAD

Julius Caesar is famous for many things. However, Caesar Salad is not of his making, nor is it called after him. It is, in fact, of only comparatively recent origin, though as with other special dishes, opinions differ as to who should take the credit for having created it.

Generally, it is believed that the salad was improvised by the owner of an eating place in Tijuana, the Mexican city just across the American border on the other side of San Diego. One day in 1934, long after closing hours, a large contingent of tourists arrived at his restaurant. Not prepared to send them away and lose out on some good business, he happily welcomed them, then rushed into the kitchen to prepare a dish by mixing whatever ingredients were at hand in his larder.

Though made up in a hurry, the novel concoction he created proved a great success. Consisting of lettuce, bacon, anchovies, eggs, mayonnaise and garlic croutons, it soon became a regular feature on the menu, and was popular far and wide, though the recipe varied according to the chef.

The name of the ingenious owner of the restaurant was Caesar Gardini, and it was almost a foregone conclusion that he would call his fortuitous invention after himself – Caesar Salad.

An alternate claim changes the location to American soil and asserts that the salad was not the result of a crisis situation. On the contrary, it was deliberately created by a chef, anxious to contribute something special to the menu offered at the restaurant which employed him. Experimenting with a variety of mixtures, he finally produced a salad which seemed to be equal to none. Working at the famous Caesar's Palace in Las Vegas, his gamble paid off. It became known not by his personal name, now forgotten, but by that of the world-renowned establishment for which he worked.

CAHOOTS

Those who conspire together are said to be 'in cahoots' with one another. Now used for an unsavoury kind of partnership, the expression presents an example of how meanings can deteriorate.

The 'cahoot' of the phrase originally and simply referred to a 'small hut', as derived from the French *cahute*. Those who occupied the cabin – who were 'in [the] cahoot' – necessarily collaborated with each other. They did not always do so with good intentions, however. At one time, in fact, it is believed that the cahoot served as a retreat for gangsters. Those supporting them joined them in [their] cahoots.

A totally different derivation traces the phrase to ancient Rome and its military organisation. The *cohort* formed a tenth part of the Roman legion, being 600 men strong. It survived the Roman empire and, transformed into the English cahoot, eventually became the general description for a band of warriors, later to be applied to any gang. Those plotting with its members were 'in cahoots' with them.

CANDIDATE

People seeking office have almost always tried to convince those responsible for their election or appointment of the purity of their intentions and the spotlessness of their character. The Romans did so in classical times, and very conspicuously too. To draw the public's attention to their honesty and integrity they clothed themselves in white togas. The colour was symbolic of their untainted past and immaculate motives. As 'white' is *candidus* in Latin, these men became known as candidates.

Those having previously been wounded in battle introduced the further custom of wearing the toga loosely. By keeping their wrap partially open they displayed the scars on their body, thereby hoping to convince people all the more of their worthiness for election. After all, having served their country so valiantly in the past, they would not fail to serve it well in the future!

CAPITALISED 'I'

Appearances often deceive and, on occasion, even cause unfortunate misunderstandings. This has been the case with the practice of English-speaking nations to spell the personal pronoun 'I' with a capital letter. Misinterpreted, it has been seen by other cultures as symptomatic of an attitude of self-importance.

However, the use of the capital 'I' is due to totally different circumstances. It could be said that it was forced on the English; without it, they might have lost their identity.

To start with, the nominative of the personal pronoun was written not 'I' but *ic*, *ich* or even *ik*, and pronounced as in modern German, like the 'i' in 'little'.

Examples abound in early English literature, including Shakespeare's writings. Eventually, however, the pronoun was shortened so that all that remained of the *ich* was its initial, the small 'i'. On its own it was so minute a character that it could easily be overlooked or, whilst type-setting a text, even get lost.

It was for this reason that conscientious and concerned printers changed the small 'i' into the capital letter. Conspicuous now, it can hardly be missed or omitted.

CARDIGAN AND RAGLAN SLEEVES

For better or worse, warfare has had the most diverse effects. Perhaps one of its least harmful consequences has been the contribution it has made to fashion.

The Crimean War (1854–56) was not only responsible for the balaclava but for other innovations in dressing. These were not due to mere fancy but to dire necessity. Having not been properly equipped for a harsh winter campaign, soldiers needed some extra protection against the freezing cold conditions they had to endure.

One of them was the knitted jacket, now known as a cardigan. This garment perpetuates the memory of James Thomas Brudenell, the seventh Earl of Cardigan, who introduced it to keep himself warm.

Fitzroy James Henry Somerset, the first Baron of Raglan, was leading the British Expeditionary Force who, oddly, during that very campaign made yet another contribution to fashion. At the time, he had donned a woollen coat with loose-fitting sleeves, the seams of which extended up to the collar instead of the shoulders as was normal. Subsequently, this style of jacket was adopted at large, and has been called after him ever since.

There might have been an additional reason for Raglan's choice of this special kind of sleeve. Previously, at the Battle of Waterloo, his sword-wielding arm had been badly injured, necessitating its amputation. The sleeve helped to hide the loss of his arm.

CARRY THE CAN

Whoever is left to carry the can takes the responsibility or blame for an action or dangerous undertaking. Some would say that they are made the scapegoat.

The figure of speech may go back to the use of explosives in mining. To transport the tin (or can) containing the explosives to the site of operation was a hazardous job, shunned by many. Whenever possible, the man allotted with the task disappeared at the last moment, leaving it to one of his workmates to 'carry the can'.

Less dramatic is an alternate explanation which traces the idiom to a practice exercised among army personnel. When thirsty, the men of a company would make a raw recruit fetch for them tins of beer and then return the empty cans to their source of supply. Literally, he was made to 'carry the can(s)'.

CARTE BLANCHE

Anyone given carte blanche can do what they like, in any way they choose. They have complete discretion and full authority.

A French idiom, *carte blanche* literally means 'white sheet' (of paper). However, the white does not refer to its colour but to the fact of its being empty.

The English, who first used the expression in the early 1700s, confined its application to the military field. A defeated foe was given a blank sheet of paper which he had to sign. The victor would later record on it the terms of surrender. This practice was the forerunner of what is now termed 'unconditional surrender'. In a more positive sense, to give carte blanche could be compared to the modern phrase of giving a blank cheque.

CASH REGISTER

James J. Ritty of Dayton, Ohio, invented the cash register. In his case it could truly be said that necessity was the mother of invention.

Ritty ran a saloon in his home town. Although it was attracting an increasing number of patrons, its takings remained static. There was a reason, as James was soon to discover: a dishonest barman was pocketing the extra money.

To have a thief in his employ upset Ritty so much that he suffered a nervous breakdown. To restore him to health, his doctor, instead of prescribing a medication, suggested he go on a protracted sea voyage. Ritty followed his advice and returned from his trip fully recovered. However, the trip paid other dividends as well. During the voyage Ritty was invited to visit the engine room of the ship. Being a keen observer, he took notice of a device which registered the revolutions of the ship's propellers. This immediately gave him the idea of applying the same principle to a cash register.

The moment Ritty returned he set to work, helped by his brother John, who was a mechanic. Together thus they created the first automatic cash register. They patented their invention on 4 November 1879 and installed it in their saloon which, in no time, made the profit it so well deserved.

CAT'S PYJAMAS

To speak of anything superlative and remarkable as being 'the cat's pyjamas' is a somewhat strange expression to modern ears, as pyjamas no longer have the sensational effect on people that they did when they were first introduced in the United States in the early 1920s. At that time they struck people as something extraordinarily daring. This, in turn, made those who wore them (in defiance of traditional proprieties) feel specially proud. They showed their delight in their imagined superiority by wearing a grin reminiscent of that of the proverbial Cheshire cat.

Quite likely, the combination of the flamboyant attire with its wearer's demeanour was responsible for the odd metaphor.

CAVIAR TO THE GENERAL

Rarely heard nowadays is the phrase 'it's caviar to the general', used to describe something that is too good to appeal to popular taste. The saying seems to make little sense, and one might wonder why a general, of all people, is singled out to enjoy this delicacy.

Taken in context, however, the saying can be easily understood. The 'general' mentioned never had a place in the military forces; instead, the word appears in one of Shakespeare's plays, where it stands for people in 'general'. When Shakespeare wrote *Hamlet*, caviar had only just come on to the English market. It was so novel that it demanded an acquired taste. Common folk could neither afford nor appreciate the treat.

Shakespeare, in writing for the masses, made use of these facts by way of a metaphor. When in Act 2, Scene 2 the Prince discusses with a band of strolling actors the unsuitability of a certain play, he explains that it was too subtle for ordinary folk. In fact, he remembered how its performance had 'pleased not the million, [because] 'twas caviar to the general' – that is, to the masses.

CHAMPAGNE SPRAYING

It has become a custom at a party or when celebrating a sporting victory, particularly a motor racing one, to get hold of a bottle of champagne and, after vigorously shaking it, spray its contents over the participants. Such an action could be interpreted as an expression of exuberance – a liquid form of letting off steam, as it were.

However, akin to the practice of breaking a bottle of bubbly over the bow of a ship being launched, the jubilant spraying of champagne may have a deeply religious, now forgotten, background. This spraying of precious wine is like the libations once offered in worshipping the gods, presented in their honour and as a thanksgiving.

No doubt today's practice was greatly fostered by certain makers of the expensive liquid, who donated huge bottles of it for the occasion – not forgetting to have their names conspicuously displayed behind the dais on which the celebrations took place.

CHEESED OFF

Those disgruntled, bored or frustrated are said to be 'cheesed off'. They are fed up with prevailing circumstances.

The metaphor certainly gives food for thought, and its origin may be interpreted in a variety of ways.

Cheese, when having gone 'off', becomes not only discoloured but inedible, emitting a bad smell. These are all reasons for people to take a dislike to it, to regard it as something worthless, to be shunned.

To be 'cheesed off', on the other hand, might have no connection with this milk product which has served language in so many other ways, as when speaking of something being 'as different as chalk and cheese' or calling someone important 'a big cheese'. It may well have been created arbitrarily. Sounding a note of rejection, it could have been coined in conformity with already existing expressions, such as being 'browned off' or, in the vocabulary of vulgarisms, 'pissed off'.

CHEF

That the principal cook in a restaurant is called a chef merely refers to his being a 'chief' or a 'head'. The present-day title is due to a loss – not in status, but in words. His full description meaningfully spoke of him, in French (as was only appropriate, considering the Frenchman's traditional love of food), as *chef de cuisine* – 'the head of the kitchen'. He simply dropped the kitchen but kept his head.

CHEF'S TALL HAT

Considerations of hygiene led the chef to wear a hat. That his hat is tall is not, as may be imagined, to make him specially conspicuous. It has a very practical purpose: to let the air circulate inside and thereby, in the hot kitchen, keep his head (comparatively) cool.

CHEW THE RAG or CHEW THE FAT

To chew the rag is remindful of those people who nervously chew their handkerchief or lips, reverting to their days of infancy when they sucked on a dummy or suchlike.

A cow chews the cud, and whoever chews anything turns it over and over again – in their mouths, their minds, or in talking about it.

'Chewing the rag' has become a figure of speech for gossiping or discussing a matter complainingly, and for going on doing so ad nauseam.

It may be that the saying was initially used in a very literal sense, actually referring to a piece of cloth. At their sewing parties, women, gathered over their pieces of fabric (or 'rags'), started to gossip. Finding special delight in exchanging 'juicy' bits of information would account for the 'fat' in the alternate phrase.

It may be, however, that the rag did not relate to any piece of cloth at all but recalled instead the original meaning of rag. Used as a verb, in the sense of scolding and complaining, it was not just idle talk to which the saying alluded but grousing.

The phrase might also be linked to a completely different world, that of men at sea. Sailors, when bereft of their chewing tobacco, liked to keep their jaws moving, possibly to avoid seasickness. At times they actually chewed rags as a substitute. Whilst doing so they did not fail to give expression to their sense of deprivation.

It has also been suggested that when on long voyages sailors' rations of salted pork grew short or became stale, all that was left for them was the dried skin, specially stored for such an emergency. To make it digestible, if not palatable, they had to keep on chewing it. Whilst doing so, they no doubt voiced just how they felt.

With the passing of time, both phrases experienced a change. To chew the fat came to mean to keep on arguing endlessly, without ever reaching an agreement. The chewing of the rag became much more innocuous in its connotation, being applied merely to the drawn out telling of a yarn.

CLAPTRAP

Claptrap denotes nonsensical talk. In its original sense it also implied something contrived or lacking in genuineness.

The word claptrap certainly comes from the stage. Some playwrights would make use of any device to get applause – to *trap* the audience to make them *clap*! Now divorced from the stage, claptrap retains its meaning of worthlessness, of mere drivel. People speak of the claptrap of politicians. They, like those dramatists, would say anything to gain popularity and applause.

CLIFFHANGER

A cliffhanger nowadays mostly refers to an election in which the result is so close that neither party can claim victory. More generally, the term is applied to any dramatic situation in which the outcome is uncertain.

The expression dates back to the early period of American film-making, when movies were shown not in one session but in numerous instalments, anticipating modern TV serialisations.

Always melodramatic in content, each episode concluded with an exciting, 'up-in-the-air' ending. Typical situations saw the heroine about to lose her virtue or her life. Such closes represented a clever ruse to ensure the return of the audience for the next showing: movie goers could hardly wait for the next instalment.

The most popular star in this almost unending series of precarious 'endings' was Pearl White. Memorable was the scene in the 1915 Charles Pathé movie, *Perils of Pauline*, which showed her clinging to a cliff . . . 'to be continued' the following week. It was this specific 'finale' which created the cliffhanger.

CLIP JOINT

Crooks have employed every possible means to enrich themselves. When handmade gold and silver coins still served as currency, the cheats discovered an easy way. They clipped coins around their rims, and the gold and silver shavings they collected soon amounted to a considerable sum. Those who were paid with such clipped coins, unless they weighed each one individually, could hardly notice their reduction in size and value.

Eventually this malpractice grew to such proportions that governments felt it necessary to take stringent measures to stop it. They did so in a twofold way. The clipping of coins was made a serious crime, threatened with severe and gruesome penalties, such as the cutting off of a hand. Henry V of England declared the offence treason, punishable by death.

To make any future attempt at such fraud impossible, minters were instructed to produce coins with a milled rim. Any shaving of them would immediately be detected. Going even further, the authorities had the edges inscribed with a warning against any interference with the coin.

The clipping of coins was thus stopped, but not so dishonesty. In fact, the practice is recalled by so-called 'clip joints', those establishments which do not give value for money but which prefer to fleece their customers. No longer able to clip the coin, they 'clip' their patrons instead!

CLOCKWISE

Before the invention of clocks, the sundial served as one of the means by which people could tell (and measure) the passing of time. When clockmakers eventually replaced this primitive and natural timekeeper with their mechanical timepieces, they retained one of the sundial's features. Following the direction of the movement of the sun's shadows (as observed in the northern hemisphere), they applied it to the rotation of the hands of their novel gadgets.

Clocks and watches were universally adopted. Today, even with the invention and widespread use of digital systems, we continue to speak of a clockwise or anti-clockwise direction.

CLOUD WITH A SILVER LINING

The belief in happier days to come, despite current gloom, has been beautifully expressed by speaking of the now-proverbial 'silver lining' of a dark cloud.

A World War I song, intended to cheer up the folk at home whilst their menfolk were serving on the front, first popularised the words. They were part of the 1915 production of *Keep the Homefires Burning*, by Ivor Novello and Lena Guilbert Ford:

> There's a silver lining
> Through the dark cloud shining,
> Turn the dark cloud inside out,
> Till the boys come home.

The metaphor itself can be traced back many centuries to John Milton, one of England's greatest poets. In his *Comus* of 1634 he spoke of 'a sable cloud [that] turn[s] forth her silver lining on the night' (I. 221). The circumstances concerned a lady who, though lost in the woods, was determined not to give up hope.

COBBLER SHOULD STICK TO HIS LAST

On occasion, people well versed in their own sphere of work or learning try to impose their opinions in matters of which they have inadequate understanding. With their lack of qualification, such unjustified interference can have an embarrassing, if not unpleasant, effect. An age-old phenomenon, it is responsible for the advice that 'a cobbler should stick to his last'. Though now a figure of speech, the words are based on an actual incident which is said to have occurred as long ago as the fourth century BC.

Appeles, one of the great Greek artists of the time, was specially noted for his portraits. One day, a cobbler passing by stopped to admire his latest painting. Competent in the making of shoes, he called Appeles' attention to some inaccuracy in his representation of the sandals. Justified in his criticism, it was well received by the artist.

Possibly feeling flattered because his words did not go unheeded, he now began to find fault with other parts of the painting, arguing that something was wrong with the man's legs as well. Appeles, who apparently could not suffer fools gladly, cut him short by reprimanding him that 'the cobbler should not judge above the sandals' – the source of the modern saying.

COBWEB

A spider web is referred to also as a cobweb. An Old English word for spider was *cob*, a description thought to have been suggested by the shape of the spider's body. Thus its web became known as a cobweb.

COCA-COLA BOTTLES

Coca-Cola was first bottled in 1894, though its best-known bottle was designed only in 1913. Its inspiration and model, so it is told, was a mannequin in a department store who wore the then-fashionable hobble skirt. Few people nowadays realise that this has been perpetuated – in glass!

COLESLAW

Coleslaw, literally speaking, is Dutch-grown.

Unlike the names of some other dishes, it is not a fancy name. It means what it says. In Dutch, *kool* is the word for 'cabbage' and *sla* refers to a 'salad', specifically one made of lettuce.

People, not familiar with the Dutch tongue, wrongly assumed the *kool* to stand for 'cold'. It made them call this side dish 'cold slaw', a name which, though wrongly translated, would not be so incorrect. It might well be that slovenly speech produced the ultimate coleslaw.

COMING OF AGE

The day of 'coming of age' is a major event in people's lives. It is the attainment of the legal status of 'majority', with all the privileges and duties this implies. It is linked with the right (and, in Australia, the obligation) to cast a vote at elections, and, with it, the assumption of legal and social responsibilities.

The key, the symbol of 'coming of age', suggests the opening up of doors previously closed to its recipient. It has not always been merely symbolic, however. In former days, parents actually handed the house key to their son or daughter on their twenty-first birthday. Henceforth they were entitled to manage their own affairs and to come and go as they pleased.

Though modern legislation has brought forward the age of majority to eighteen, some of the magic attached to the age of majority still remains. Twenty-one, as the year of 'coming of age', was not determined haphazardly but was based on ancient occult belief in the significance of numbers. Twenty-one, as the multiple of three and seven – both of them numbers of supreme potency – was a number of great meaning.

Three was a magic number: life was divided into the past, present and future; body, mind and soul were believed to make up the wholeness of a person; Christians believe in the Holy Trinity. It is no mere coincidence that today one gives three cheers, permits three guesses and speaks of 'third time lucky'. According to the Greek philosopher Pythagoras, three was 'the perfect number'.

Seven, likewise, has been revered from the earliest days of civilisation. The Babylonians recognised seven planets in the sky and, deifying them, made their number sacred. Still today expressions like 'the seventh heaven of happiness', 'a seven-day wonder' and 'the seven seas' are common.

Multiplying the lucky three with the sacred seven resulted in a number so powerful that to attain it in the number of one's years was a most auspicious achievement.

Traditionally, the coming of age is an occasion for festive celebrations. The lowering of the legal age from twenty-one to eighteen has done little to diminish its significance.

COMMUTER

In Britain and Australia, commuting is a comparatively recent expression, adopted in the 1950s to describe the daily travelling from home to work and back. Americans have used the term for well over a hundred years, though initially it had a slightly different meaning and was used in a more specific sense. The word actually spoke of an 'exchange'.

Public transport at the time offered discounts to passengers who regularly covered a particular route, in the majority of cases to nearby beaches and seaside resorts. A voucher issued for the purpose was valid for a fixed period of time, just as the modern season ticket is. Those taking advantage of the cheaper fare acquired the voucher by an 'exchange' of money. Consequently, the voucher became known as a 'commutation ticket', ultimately responsible for the present-day commuter.

CONCERT and CONCERTO

Though speaking of a concert immediately suggests music, its description, like that of the concerto, does not strike a single chord. Both terms refer merely to a 'striving together', and to companionship. Hence, not music but melodiousness is the ultimate meaning of the terms.

In their original sense, and as actually first applied, a concert and concerto spoke of 'a *concert*ed effort' of a number of performers (often a family group) who, joining together, harmoniously presented a composition. For a single artist to give a concert as an unaccompanied soloist is, therefore, etymologically impossible. To the philologist's ear it would create the most atrocious dissonance.

CONSTABLE

Some words and titles have come a long way, during which time they have either gained or lost in status. A steward used to look after his master's pigs; literally, he was a stye-ward. A chamberlain's mission was to attend to the royal comfort in the king and queen's chamber.

Equally, a constable was not, in the beginning, a member of the police force. Rooted in the Latin tongue, as *comes stabuli*, he was the 'master of the stable', or chief groom. It was his job to look after the horses.

Nevertheless, the title can pride itself of some distinguished ancestry. In the Byzantine empire, to be the 'master of the horse' was a highly respected royal office. Adopted by the Frankish kingdom, it assumed an even higher standing. Eventually it designated the commander of the royal force, temporarily to become a hereditary appointment.

Still, it was not the end of the constable's career. After serving for so long in the realm of a nation's military forces, ultimately he became a member of the police force (the constabulary), with all his equine association forgotten.

CONTINENT

A huge mass of land is known as a continent. This explains why the British applied the term to the whole of Europe but excluded their own, separate, Isles. To them a 'Continental' was a member of any European nation except their own!

The name goes back to antiquity and was first coined by wayfarers. To them, the vast territory they traversed seemed to be never-ending, without any sign of the sea. Correctly they thus spoke of it as 'continuous land' which, in their Latin tongue, was *terra continens*. Finally dropping the 'land', it has remained the 'continent' ever since.

COP (or DRAW) THE CROW

To 'cop (or draw) the crow' is the Australian way of describing the sorry fate of coming off worse in a deal, being the loser or being allotted the hardest task in a joint endeavour.

Australian folklore traces the expression to a variety of incidents. One story from the days of colonisation is telling of the abuse meted out by the white man to Aborigines, who just could never win. One morning the foreman of a station asked his Aboriginal workman to come shooting with him. They were not lucky. At the end of the day, all they managed to show for their efforts was one rabbit and one crow. Magnanimously, as it seemed, the foreman suggested to Jacky (the name given to most Aboriginal men back then) that they should share the booty: 'I'll have the rabbit and you take the crow.'

When Jacky did not look happy with the proposal the foreman told him that he would change the offer. 'You take the crow and I'll have the rabbit,' he said.

Jacky was obviously still not satisfied and replied that he really wasn't sure about it, because whichever way the foreman said it, 'I seem to cop that ——— crow!'

Lacking all racial discrimination, yet equally revealing, is another tradition. This relates how a group of men, after a day's shooting, had bagged a number of birds, including a crow. Sharing out the spoils, however impartially, it was inevitable that one of the hunters was bound to 'cop the crow'.

Totally different is the scenario of yet a third version. It too dates back to the early days of the settlement. Hotels (the Australian public houses) then used to run raffles of a peculiar kind. Pieces of paper were put into a hat, one for each patron present. They were all blank, except for one. This had a crow sketched on it. Whoever drew this piece of paper had to pay for a round of drinks.

Newcomers, unaware of this lottery in reverse, were always given the first pick, apparently to show them how welcome they were. On such occasions, however, all the papers would be marked with a crow! Thus the guest was bound to 'cop the crow' and hence would have to shout drinks for all present.

CORNED BEEF

A mistaken notion claims that to speak of 'corned beef' is to reproduce the mispronunciation of *canned* beef. The true reason for its designation is in fact totally different. The granules of salt added to the beef to preserve it in the resultant brine were known, as far back as the seventeenth century, as 'corns'. No doubt this was because the grains of salt looked very much like the corn of the field, and this created the 'corned' beef.

CORNUCOPIA

A symbol of abundance, the cornucopia is the 'horn of plenty' in the literal translation of the Latin phrase *cornu copiae*. Figured in paintings, sculptures and even heraldry from ancient Greek and Roman times onwards, the cornucopia is always seen filled with fruit and flowers. Reputedly it had the magic quality of being able to replenish itself with whatever its owner desired.

The Greeks linked the cornucopia with the goat-nymph Amalthea. She nursed the infant Zeus who, in gratitude, presented the horn to her, endowing it with the miraculous power to be always abounding in the food or drink she desired at any moment.

The Romans made it the horn of Achelous. A river god, he had the power to assume three different identities. As a bull he confronted Hercules to wrestle with him for the hand of Deianira. When, in the struggle, Hercules hurled Achelous to the ground, he caused one of his horns to break off. Some nymphs picked it up and filled it with fruit and other gifts that – magically – would never grow less.

COUNTRY BUMPKIN

An unfortunate trait of human nature is to make fun of certain people's features, or of differences in build. Whilst those who are tall have been admired for their outstanding stature, the short and the plump have often been the target of ridicule. Such treatment has been meted out even more so to foreigners because of the regrettable dislike of the like for the unlike. It has also been shown to anyone having proved themselves superior in some respect.

This happened to the Dutch who, for centuries, were made the butt of English jokes. The Dutch had been strong and, at times, invincible rivals. To call anything Dutch, therefore, was prompted by the desire to degrade and cheapen it. This explains such expressions as the Dutch uncle, Dutch courage and Dutch treat. In the same vein, a Dutch auction is an auction at which the prices are not increased but lowered till a buyer is found.

Because some of the Dutch were thick-set and short, Englishmen compared all of them with a 'little tree' or, perhaps merely jocularly, with a 'little barrel'. Either way, the Dutch words for them sounded very similar: *boomken* and *buomekijn*. Assimilated into English, they became 'bumpkin'.

Going lower still, in more than just one sense, some heard in the bumpkin an echo of 'bum'. Bumpkins were such backward people that they merited being called 'little bums'.

Though former dislikes and antagonisms have long been forgotten, the word bumpkin has not disappeared. Still maintaining its derogatory meaning, it is no longer applied solely to people of a squat figure or of a particular nation. Prefixed with the word 'country', the country bumpkin has come to refer to a boorish person, a yokel – in short, a simpleton.

COWARD

Some apposite figures of speech have been derived from the coward's name. A composite of two words, the first part goes back to the Romans, to the Latin *cauda* for 'tail'. Always ready to turn tail, it can also be said of cowards that, like frightened canines, they slink away with their tails between their legs.

The suffix making up the word further shows up the coward's character and the way he is generally regarded. Derived from the Old High German *ard*, originally it used to add something 'hardy' or 'bold' to whatever word it was attached. However, when anglicised via the French language, it went to the other extreme. In English, the suffix acquired a note of disgust, depreciating to whomever or whatever it was joined. In this sense it is found in the weak-minded dot*ard*, the drunk*ard* and the cow*ard*. No one respects the latter.

COW BELLS

To put a bell on a cat serves an obvious purpose: its sound acts as a warning to birds, giving them a chance to fly away. However, why hang a bell around the neck of a cow? The original reason was a very practical one. In the European summer, cows stayed out all day and night, roaming around their pastures. This made it hard to find them at milking time, particularly in the Alpine meadows. The clanking of their bell helped the farmer to locate them.

CRÊPE SUZETTE

One of the world's great chefs, Henri Charpentier, created Crêpe Suzette. He did so in 1894, when still a young lad of fourteen, and he did it quite by accident!

At the time, he was employed at the Café de Paris in Monte Carlo. Among its regular patrons was the then Prince of Wales, the future King Edward VII. On one of the Prince's visits, his seven luncheon guests included Suzette, a beautiful young French girl. It so happened that Henri had the honour of serving the royal party. When the Prince chose crêpes for their dessert, Henri suggested a totally new kind, one of his own creation. (In fact, he had spent much time and effort on it, being guided and advised by the chef of the Grand Hotel, renowned as one of the most experienced members of his profession and, quite by chance, also a close relative of Charpentier.)

The Prince followed his advice and ordered the novel sweet. The excited young chef, preparing it in front of the royal guests, accidentally set the simmering sauce (his own special blend of liqueurs) on fire. Though deeply upset, he did not show it. On the contrary, he made it appear as if everything had gone according to his plan, and with an air of expertise poured the fiery sauce on to the crêpes.

The guests ate the pancakes with gusto. Indeed, they found the taste of them most delicious and, not least, that of the sauce, which the Prince scooped up to its last drop.

Young Henri, proud of his success and thrilled that a debacle had turned into a triumph, offered there and then to call his dessert after the Prince. Edward declined, explaining that ladies should always be given precedence. Henri therefore named his pancakes after the lovely girl in the party, Suzette.

Charpentier, who died at the age of eighty, in later years could not recall the girl's last name. It has remained a mystery to this day.

CUL DE SAC

A dead-end street leads no further. Those caught in it unawares will appreciate its description which, using the once-fashionable French *cul de sac*, literally means 'the bottom of the sack'. Having reached the cul de sac, it is impossible to go on. A colourful figure of speech, it depicts a situation from which it is hard to escape. So trapped, the only way out is to go back!

CURATE'S EGG

No one wishes to offend their host, least of all a man of the cloth and particularly not if the host is his superior. Of all people, a clergyman is expected to tell the truth. This makes it all the more awkward when his honest answer to a question is bound to embarrass and hurt the inquirer.

A young curate is once said to have faced such a dilemma. He did so, at least, in a cartoon, published in *Punch* magazine in 1895 and headed 'True Humility'. Invited for breakfast by his bishop, Mr Jones was served an egg that was off. When his venerable host inquired whether it was all right, the young clergyman did not dare tell the truth. Haltingly he replied, 'Oh no, my Lord, I assure you! Parts of it are excellent.' An accompanying drawing shows the breakfast table, shared by the two ecclesiastics and two ladies, with a uniformed maid and a butler serving them.

This 'curate's egg' has been preserved ever since – as a figure of speech. In a tactful way it describes a situation as only partially satisfactory. Critics, thus, when reviewing a performance they did not totally enjoy, might say that it was 'like the curate's egg' – good in parts. It is a positive way of giving a negative opinion.

CURE

To speak of a 'cure' literally implies that to restore a sick person to good health, much 'care' is needed. The term is derived from the Latin *cura* for 'concern' and 'attention'.

CURIOSITY KILLED THE CAT

Cats are notoriously nosy and in their eagerness to find things out can even endanger their lives. This would explain why we say that 'curiosity killed the cat'. The expression is used to warn people who want to know things that are none of their concern not to be so inquisitive.

However convincing, the saying is not authentic in its present wording but is the result of an early substitution. Originally, the expression did not relate to curiosity at all but to care, in the sense of worry. Worry can be a killer, to be avoided at all costs.

To emphasise the point, the cat was used as an example. Believed to be resistant to all types of dangers, the cat was said to have nine lives. Even so endowed, care (worry) could wear it out. The implications for humans were much more serious: for them, anxiety could prove lethal!

Quotations from early writers confirm this association of care and the cat. 'Let care kill a cat. We'll laugh and grow fat' boasted the *Shirburn Ballads* in 1585. In *Much Ado About Nothing* (1599), Shakespeare wrote: 'Though care kil'd a cat, thou hast mettle enough in thee to kill care'.

With the passing of time, people misunderstood the word. Well aware of a cat's nosiness, they corrupted the original 'care' into 'curiosity', and that was how 'curiosity killed the cat' was (mis)conceived.

CURRY

A highly seasoned dish, traditionally from India, curry consists of a great variety of ingredients. In actual fact, the real curry is the sauce added to these ingredients. It makes them 'hot', a description relating to the burning sensation it creates on the tongue. It is no wonder, therefore, that the word curry is derived from *kari*, the Tamil for 'sauce'. Members of the East India Company serving in India in the eighteenth century took a liking to it and on their return to England introduced it there, where curry soon gained wide popularity as an exotic dish.

Australians use curry to enrich their tongue. In their slang, 'to give someone curry' means to make it hot for them, to attack them verbally, if not physically.

Interesting in itself is the very origin of curry. Cereals of some kind were once (and still are) the staple food of the Indians: boiled rice or grain. Eaten on their own, these had little taste. To make them more appealing and palatable, Indians ingeniously added a savoury relish: curry. The earliest precise reference to it can be found in a record of AD 477. This tells how a certain Kassapo 'partook of rice dressed in butter, with its full accompaniment of curries'.

CURTAIN LECTURE

Wives have always had to bear many a burden. Unpaid and often unappreciated, they have been expected to look after the house. That their task could be described, even officially still today, as 'home *duties*', speaks for itself.

Adding insult to injury is the notion of the nagging wife. It was she who, fairly or unfairly, gave birth to the 'curtain lecture'. The wife would reputedly delay her criticism till she and her husband were on their own and then, when out of earshot of others, she would hold forth, telling her partner in no uncertain terms all he had said or done wrong . . .

For her discourse to be referred to as a 'curtain lecture' is not a mere figure of speech. It recalls early living and sleeping habits. Beds were once four-posted, canopied and enclosed by thick curtains. When drawn, these ensured complete privacy. No one could observe what was happening behind them nor hear what was being said. The thick drapes muffled the sound. It was the wife's opportunity to voice her reprimands – to give her 'curtain lecture'.

CUSTOM-MADE and THE CUSTOMER

'Custom-made', as a term, goes back to the United States, where it replaced the long-abandoned, archaic British 'bespoke'. The expression could be applied to a suit, shoes, a car – anything tailored or manufactured according to the specifications of the purchaser. As it was made for him personally, it was *customer*-made. In the process of speech, the word customer was merely cut short.

The word itself might be traced to the early days (first used in 1480), when most people had no permanent residence and therefore frequently moved about. In those circumstances, they obtained whatever they needed wherever they could find it. Those fortunate to have a fixed abode naturally gave their patronage to the local merchant. They became *accustomed* to making all their purchases in his store. It created the modern 'customer'.

CUT OFF ONE'S NOSE TO SPITE ONE'S FACE

Hatred can result in people acting most irrationally. Obsessed by this emotion, at times they will go to no end to hurt the subject of their animosity, even if they do so at their own expense. Trying to reek revenge, they injure themselves, and in the end find their own injuries far worse than those inflicted on their enemy. They 'cut off their nose to spite their face'.

Almost a cliché now, the saying was quoted as early as the first century BC. The Latin writer Publilius Syrus included it in his *Sententiae*, his collection of pithy aphorisms.

Its first actual use has been traced to the time of King Henry IV of France (1553–1610), whose reign was distinguished by the religious wars during which he had changed his religious adherence. Having become the head of the Protestant party, after the massacre of St Bartholomew he was promised that his life would be spared if he embraced the Catholic faith. He did so, but subsequently revoked his compulsory conversion.

No doubt, the mainly Catholic population came to loathe him. This applied not least to his Parisian subjects, who did not hide their feelings. In retaliation, the king intended to destroy Paris. However, realising that such a vengeful act would deprive his country of one of its most beautiful sites, he resolved to spare it. After all, it would be like 'cutting off one's nose to spite one's face'.

From France, the saying crossed the Channel to England, where Grose included it in his 1796 *Dictionary of the Vulgar Tongue*. Defining it, he wrote that it is 'said of one who, to be revenged of his neighbour, has materially injured himself'.

_d_

D-DAY

Various interpretations have been given for the choice of the name 'D-Day' for the significant date (6 June 1944) in World War II fixed for the invasion by the Allied forces of Nazi-occupied Europe.

The 'D' was said to stand for 'Deliverance'. Alternately, it has been suggested that it simply indicated 'the Date', the traditional description given to the date chosen for any important military action.

In actual fact, in the circumstances of World War II, the letter 'D' stood for 'Day'. As such it had been part of the military code on previous occasions. It is known, for instance, to have been employed in World War I for the date (12 September 1918) of the launching of the Allied offensive at Saint-Mihiel. One of the great battles at the close of that war, it was to drive the Germans from a salient they had held since 1914.

The reference to D-Day in 1944, therefore, is a tautology. Standing for 'Day-Day', it says the same thing twice.

DARN!

In modern times, coarse language no longer shocks people. Whilst Shaw was still able to bring down the house by the use of the word 'bloody' (which, in fact, greatly contributed to making *Pygmalion* an instant stage success), nowadays it would not ruffle a single person's brow. Centuries ago people minded their words. They carefully chose them to avoid any profanity, to give no offence to God or those to whom they were speaking. Whatever was regarded as a swearword was taboo.

In need of letting off steam, they cleverly substituted for the shunned oath a milder expression. They employed a euphemism which, as this term derived from the Greek says, was 'fair of speech'.

A typical example was 'damn(ed)'. Whoever uttered this word was thought to blaspheme. In search of some innocuous-sounding word that could replace the expletive, people originated 'darn'.

There has also been the suggestion that 'darn' was invented to camouflage the curse of 'eternal damnation'. Noah Webster held the view that it was derived from the Middle English for a 'secret'. Whichever way, 'darn', so meaningless now, was born to make people 'clean-spoken'.

DARTS

Darts is one of the most popular games in Britain, and has been for many centuries. Written evidence confirms that Anne Boleyn presented her husband Henry VIII with 'dartes ... richly ornamented', though the story that he had her beheaded because she beat him in the game is apocryphal.

From England, where darts came to be played in every public house, it spread to many other countries. The Pilgrim Fathers, who frowned upon all games, recognised the innocuous pleasure 'darts' presented and introduced it to America, where it caught the imagination and enthusiasm of the people there. There is also a tradition that credits American Indians with having played a similar game, prior to the Pilgrims' arrival, using arrows.

No one knows for certain who invented darts and where it was first played. Several theories have been advanced. The oldest one links it to the Vikings who, from Scandinavia, brought it to the British Isles.

It has never been resolved, either, what made people first take up the game. According to one school of thought, it was mere boredom. On cold winter nights, people threw darts to pass the time, and discovered in it a most absorbing pursuit. An alternate claim asserts that darts, like so many innovations, owes its existence to warfare. Throwing darts made from whittled-down arrows gave soldiers extra practice in archery, the principal form of warfare at the time.

Trees served as the earliest targets. Too cold to play outside in the depths of winter, people did the next best thing: they cut a cross-section from a tree trunk and used it as their indoor dart board. The board's natural concentric rings provided ready-made scoring divisions. With pubs becoming the most popular venue for the game of darts, players conceived yet a better idea for the board, making the bottom of an empty beer cask or barrel their target.

Darts no doubt grew out of the practice of archery or the throwing of javelins. Either of these could have been the source of the sharp small dart, merely a miniature version of the arrow or the long-pointed spear.

DEAD RINGER

Dead ringer is a colloquialism for a 'look-alike'. The metaphor has found its special place in the world of horse racing, where it was applied to describe a horse that tricksters substituted for another. Though very closely resembling the racing horse, the dead ringer was a far different performer – to the disadvantage of those laying bets.

This use of 'ringer' may well be traced to another sphere of deception. Counterfeiters replaced precious rings with worthless replicas, so similar in appearance that the exchange was difficult to recognise.

The 'dead' part of the ringer is easily explained. It denotes 'absolute' and 'complete', just as it is used in expressions like 'dead right' and a 'dead certainty'. A dead ringer was an exact double.

DEATHWATCH BEETLE

Beetles have crawled into the dark realm of superstition with both lucky and unfortunate consequences. The scarab beetle has done so on a happy note. Used as an amulet by the ancient Egyptians, it has long been regarded a luck-bringing insect.

Not so the deathwatch beetle, which is said to owe its name to its ominous reputation for inhabiting old wood, particularly, in former days, the timbers and roofs of churches. The chief cause of its ill fame was the eerie sound it made when tapping inside the wall of a home. Its inexplicable knocking, like all mysterious happenings, was given a sinister interpretation: it was death knocking at the door of one's home.

Another ancient belief added to the fear people felt in hearing the beetles' sound. They imagined that the ghost of a deceased person had come back with the intention either to cause trouble or, worse still, to summon some of the living survivors to join it in the beyond.

Oddly, it has been explained that the sound the beetle makes is not the result at all of its boring into the timber but – very pleasantly – of one beetle communicating with another.

DEBUNK

The practice of debunking has become a popular pursuit in modern times. It started shortly after World War I, at a time when several biographies appeared; it aimed at exposing the falsity of claims made by or about people.

The term itself might well be derived from the word 'bunkum', meaning empty talk and nonsense. There could well be a connection, too, with the Cockney slang 'bunk-up', used to describe the help given someone to enable them to surmount an obstacle. Those in need of a shove or lift would ask to be given a 'bunk-up'. Going the opposite direction, metaphorically speaking, suggested de-bunking.

DEPRIVED OF ONE'S RIGHTS

To be deprived of one's rights has a double meaning.

In a legal context, it refers to those who – for some specific reason – are denied the privileges of the ordinary citizen. They are excluded from certain entitlements and freedoms.

In a very intimate sense, the identical phrase can be applied to the practice of orchidectomy. This operation, performed on both testicles of a man, renders him infertile. It deprives him of his 'rights' to have offspring.

DEVILLED EGGS

Eggs have had strange associations. One African tribe, for instance, would not allow their children to eat them, fearing that they would make them thieves. This apparently odd practice was not the result of superstition but was based on practical reasoning. Potentially, each egg contained a chicken, and poultry comprised part of the community's diet. Eating eggs, children might take such a liking to them that they would go out of their way to obtain them, even resorting to theft, and in the process deprive people of essential meat.

Other cultures, however, have not been averse to the egg. Recipes using eggs have been found from as long ago as classical Greek times. Among the many dishes made up of them, one of the most peculiarly named is devilled eggs. Stuffed, these eggs were so called because of the early practice of smothering them with pepper. Figuratively speaking, they were as hot as the fires of hell. This made the devil (metaphorically, at least) their rightful companion, and thus they merited their description.

DIRTY WORK AT THE CROSSROADS

The phrase 'dirty work at the crossroads' leads back to a period of great violence. As well, it recalls times when people were haunted by supernatural fears. In order to counteract them they observed weird, occult practices.

To start with, the crossroads referred to were very real. They were the intersection of pathways; signposts did not exist. Unless guided and guarded, the few travellers on the road faced numerous dangers. They were exposed to the 'dirty work' not only of robbers lying in ambush at such road junctions, but to fiendish forces of the netherworld, for whom the crossroads were a choice position to do their nefarious work. They included malevolent ghosts, voracious vampires out for blood and, perhaps, the devil himself. For them it was a most promising site, as the mere fact of two or more roads meeting there ensured that they would encounter the largest number of travellers and, with it, possible victims. These wayfarers, having to halt at this spot to check which way to turn, made themselves all the more susceptible to attack.

Surrounded by those countless hazards, people applied every possible means to protect themselves and to frustrate the 'dirty work' threatening them. To chase away the evil forces, they placed sacred images at the junction, or set up a shrine or the potent phallic symbol. To placate the evil spirits they also offered gifts of food.

Added to the already existing perils of the crossroads was the danger of being pounced on by the ghost of a suicide. It was the gruesome custom to bury suicides at these intersections. Its purpose was to confuse their spirits, lest they find their way back and haunt the living. To 'nail' the suicide's spirit and prevent it from escaping, it became the practice to drive a stake through the corpse's heart.

Crossroads were frightening places indeed, even without the traffic hazards of today. Nothing illustrates the fear they evoked more than the expression 'dirty work at the crossroads'.

DISEASE

In days gone by, the term 'disease' covered a much larger area than that of medicine. It used to refer to any condition of life that caused discomfort. Those experiencing it were 'away from ease'. Literally understood thus, disease describes not the actual sickness but the state of mind it creates. Patients are dis-eased, or 'not at ease'.

DISHEVELLED

Anyone unkempt is dishevelled. Though now applied to people's general appearance, originally it specifically (and literally) concerned their 'hair'. Coming, not surprisingly, from the French (the language of those well-known for their elegance), it spoke of people's 'hair' (*cheveux*) being disarranged, the *dis* standing for the negative 'not' or 'un'. To speak of someone's hair as dishevelled is, therefore, a typical pleonasm, reiterating unnecessarily the 'hair'.

Through the centuries, 'dishevelled' experienced several changes of meaning. Originally it expressed the lack of a head covering, the baring of the hair. Still tied to the hair, it then came to refer to someone who was 'uncombed'. Only finally, letting down its hair, as it were, did it come to assume its modern sense.

DOCTOR

Medical practitioners were once known as 'sawbones' or 'leechers'. The title 'doctor' originally had no connection with medicine. It was purely academic. From the Latin, *doctor* referred to 'a teacher' – of any branch of learning.

On passing their examinations, students of the medical arts became Masters of Medicine. The degree qualified them to treat patients. If they so chose, it also entitled them to teach the subject, and it was in this case alone – and very correctly – that they could call themselves 'doctor'.

It was a reasonable distinction, but it did not last. Other non-teaching medical graduates presumptuously began to appropriate the title for themselves as well. Inevitably, this led to confusion. It made university lecturers in medicine realise that their designation as doctor had lost its significance. In fact, it had become misleading. To reassert their status, they called themselves professors.

The situation grew even more complex when graduates of other faculties, too, began to distinguish themselves by the title of doctor. Thus, apart from doctors of medicine, there were doctors of divinity and of law. The mere fact that the medical doctor had the most contact with the public soon led people to assume that anyone who was called doctor practised medicine. The misconception was generally adopted and became permanent.

DOG DAYS

Dog days are the hottest days of the year. Folklore derives their designation from the fallacious belief that the extreme heat prevailing during the summer season has the capacity to drive dogs mad, possibly even to cause them to contract rabies.

In reality, the name goes back to ancient Greek and Roman astronomers. They had observed that, during the period extending from 3 July to 11 August, Sirius, known as the 'dog star', rose at the same time as the sun. Mistakenly, they regarded Sirius as a 'hot' star, a misconception actually responsible for its very name – *seirios*, from the Greek for 'scorching'. By the conjunction, the star's heat was added to that of the sun, resulting in the specially hot and sultry weather.

That Sirius became known as the 'dog star' was due to its celestial position. Situated in the constellation of *Canis Major*, the 'larger dog', it is, in fact, its brightest star.

To suffer intense heat, no matter at what time of the year, renders people lethargic. It was this that led people to extend the use of 'dog days' and apply the phrase as a metaphor for any period of inactivity or general slowing down.

DOGWOOD

The most common explanation for why the dogwood was so called suggests that its odour reminded people of the smell of a wet dog. Certainly, it does not owe its name to any preference by canines for the tree.

The dogwood's gnarled growth has given rise to a legend. This tells that the Romans had chosen the dogwood (and not, as often assumed, the aspen) to supply the timber for the cross on which they were to crucify Jesus. At the time it had been a most sturdy tree, as tall and majestic as the oak.

Jesus had noted the tree's distress at being forced to fulfil such an ignominious role. Taking pity on the tree, and to prevent any future use of its wood for such purposes, he changed its entire nature. Henceforth it was to be a small tree with twisted branches, unsuitable for use as timber.

The dogwood was to serve future generations as a reminder of Jesus' sacrificial death. With two long and two short petals, its blossoms were reminiscent of the shape of a cross. A likeness of the crown of thorns could also be discerned at the centre of each bloom, whilst the petals on their outer rims carried what looked like nail prints stained with blood.

Thus the very appearance of the dogwood has a multiple message of agony and compassion. No one can overlook the tree which, when in full bloom at springtime, presents an unforgettable spectacle.

DOILY

By its very name, the doily pays tribute to the London draper who is said to have created and first supplied it. A Mr Doily (also spelled Dolley), he lived in the late seventeenth century and had his shop in the Strand.

An ornamental mat made of lace or some other cheaper substitute (paper or plastic), it is put on plates, inserted between a cup and saucer or placed under knick-knacks to protect furniture from being marked or soiled. There is the suggestion, however, that originally Mr Doily intended his invention to serve a different and more specific purpose. As a mini-napkin, it was meant to be placed under the then fashionable finger bowls, or other small basins.

In his time, Mr Doily was renowned for being an enterprising businessman, going out of his way to please his clientele. He frequently did so by offering them some novelty he had picked up. Indeed, he made a fortune by providing his customers, in the words of a later issue of *The Spectator*, with merchandise that was both 'cheap and genteel'.

DON'T COUNT YOUR CHICKENS BEFORE THEY'RE HATCHED

Though this advice is frequently quoted as having first been given in the sixteenth century, it has actually been linked with one of the many fables attributed to Aesop, the liberated Greek slave who lived in the sixth century BC.

The story tells of a farmer's daughter who was carrying on her head from the field to a farmhouse a full bucket of milk. She was going to exchange it for a basket of eggs. Daydreaming, she already saw the eggs being hatched. Even allowing for mishaps, eventually these would produce 250 chickens. If she sold them she would make enough money to enable her to buy a new dress. Wearing the dress at parties, she would attract many suitors. Proudly, however, she would toss her head at their offers of marriage, rejecting them all. Anticipating the action, unthinkingly she tossed her head, thereby spilling all the milk and, with it, destroying her hope.

It taught a lesson: not to count chickens before they are hatched. Ever since, the proverb has survived as a warning never to prematurely celebrate something that has not yet happened.

DOOR KNOCKERS

Originally, door knockers had a much more significant function than merely to make one's presence known.

People believed that evil spirits used to hover around the entrances to people's houses, anxious to 'possess' their home. The loud knock was intended to frighten them off and thus prevent them from getting into the house with the visitor.

Identical considerations (and fears) explain why, frequently, door knockers represent some figure, object or animal, such as a lion's head. Just as in the case of gargoyles, those grotesque carved creatures seen projecting from roof gutters, these fanciful knockers were meant to scare off demons.

`DRAG`

To be 'in drag' describes men wearing women's clothes. The practice goes back to the early days of the stage, when women's parts were taken by men. As the dresses they wore often 'dragged' along the ground, in the jargon of the theatre such roles became known as 'drag roles'. It was but a small step for people to refer to the actors taking the part as being 'in drag'. Eventually the term was applied to everyday life as a description of those who, in search of extra sexual stimulus, donned the clothing of the opposite sex.

DRINKING HORNS

Throughout the ages, people have loved their drink. It has cheered them up, contributed to the spirit of a gathering and made meals more enjoyable. At one time it also offered an opportunity to eliminate one's enemies. Fear of one's drink being poisoned, in fact, is the basis of some modern drinking habits, including the custom for a host to 'taste' the wine prior to having it served to his guests. The practice was intended to reassure them.

Identical qualms contributed to the introduction of the horn as a drinking vessel. As a naturally-grown 'cup', it was believed it could prove a life-saver. If the wine poured into it contained poison, the horn would start 'sweating' or, acting like an antidote, extract the lethal 'additive'.

e

EGG ON ONE'S FACE

American in origin, the saying 'to have egg on one's face' most likely goes back to the late nineteenth century.

It is not difficult to trace this figure of speech to an actual practice still followed. Individuals (not least politicians) who have roused the public's anger have rotten eggs pelted at them. Their treatment is very much like that of (bad) actors, who are booed off the stage. Those thus 'defaced' are deeply embarrassed.

EGG ROLLING

In some Christian countries the rolling of eggs is an Easter custom. Mostly on Easter Monday, hard-boiled eggs are rolled down a hill or a slope. The explanation given is that the rolling of the egg symbolises the rolling away of the stone from Jesus' tomb. This links the practice with the chief message of the festival, the resurrection of Christ.

The observance, which evolved through the years, assumed a variety of forms, often differing locally. Particularly enjoyed by children, they frequently came in their hundreds to find out whose egg was fastest or rolled the furthest. Whoever kept their egg unbroken for the longest time could claim the eggs of all rivals. On the other hand, those whose eggs got cracked were out of the race.

No Easter egg-rolling event surpasses that held on a lawn of the White House in Washington. It is attended by thousands of people each year. In fact, it is the only time when the public is permitted to use the lawn, and then it is only children who are admitted, with the exception of parents accompanying them.

The 'White House Roll' took place for the first time under James Madison, the fourth President of the United States (1809–17). It had been his wife Dolley's idea, and on that occasion the rolling was held on the grounds of the Capitol. It was to become an eagerly looked-forward-to tradition. When, however, years later (in 1878), some children in their exuberance badly damaged the turf, the practice was abandoned. The fervent pleading of children not to be deprived of this enjoyable Easter treat made the wife of the then President Rutherford Hayes resume the practice, though at a new site – on the White House lawn. There it has taken place (with only two interruptions during the two World Wars) ever since.

The origin of egg rolling, like that of so many customs, goes back far beyond its 'Christianisation', to pagan days.

The egg has always been symbolic of fertility and life after death. The practice of rolling it along the ground was once part of ancient solar worship. Rolled across fields, especially at the time of spring (which coincided with the later celebration of Easter), it was a magic rite which fructified the earth and thereby ensured a bountiful harvest.

Eggs were also rolled for the purpose of divination, to discover some future event or the time at which it would happen. In some districts of Britain, for instance, unmarried people divided into two groups, men and women. Individual members of each group took their turn in rolling an egg. The one whose egg proved the fastest would be the first to get married.

EIGHT-SIDED BAPTISMAL FONT

That some baptismal fonts are neither round nor square but octagonal is not accidental, nor is it merely decorative. The shape in fact has a theological message.

Eight has been regarded as the number of renewal and rebirth. According to Christian doctrine, the sacramental rite of baptism admits the recipient into the Church. The eight sides of the bowl reflect the seven days of creation, with the eighth day symbolic of a new beginning, the spiritual rebirth and regeneration of the baptised.

For the identical reason, some churches are built in an octagonal shape, and domes are often supported by eight pillars.

EQUESTRIAN STATUES

Famous warriors have been the frequent subject of statuary, not least so to honour their achievements after their deaths. In most instances they are shown conspicuously on horseback.

The equestrian statue, by the very stance of the horse, is a record in stone or bronze of a man's final fate. For those killed in battle, the horse is presented rearing up on its hind legs. If death was the result of injuries suffered in action, one of the horse's feet is shown raised. A horse standing firmly and relaxed on all four of its feet indicates that its rider died of natural causes.

ESCALATORS

Escalators are an American invention. They were first conceived in 1892 by Jesse W. Reno of New York, the son of an illustrious army officer. An engineer by profession and a true entrepreneur by nature, in 1894 he made a novel contraption, publicised as 'the Reno Inclined Elevator', and offered it as part of the entertainment on Coney Island. It provided a unique kind of joy ride.

Soon afterwards, Charles D. Seeberger, another American, was able to come up with an improved version of the 'elevator'. Realising the enormous potential of the invention, the Otis Elevator Company of New York City bought up both Reno's and Seeberger's designs, combining the best of their features. The resultant machine acquired the name 'escalator'. Making it their trademark, the company registered the name on 29 May 1900.

Forging ahead, the company exhibited a model at the Paris Exposition in the same year. On taking their sensational 'moving stairway' back to the United States, in 1901 they installed it – the first of its kind in America – at Gimbels' Department Store in Philadelphia, where it remained in continuous use for forty years.

Britain did not lag behind. In fact, as early as November 1898 the country's first escalator operated in Harrods, the world-famous London store. A novel contraption, it gave fright to many of the ladies and gentlemen who adventurously mounted it. This led the manager of the store to post one of his salesmen at the top of the stairs, ready to serve a tot of brandy or provide smelling salts to those overcome by the experience.

Though little realised, the choice of the name 'escalator' has an intriguing, if not very peaceful, past. Incorporating *scala*, the Latin for a 'ladder', the same word was part of the escalade. A military term of medieval times, it was then applied to a method of attack on fortifications: mounting the walls by 'scaling ladders', the forerunner of the escalator! Actually, the modern name 'escalator' is a contraction of its original description as an 'escalading elevator'.

ETC

'Etc' is the abbreviation of *et cetera*, the Latin for 'and the other [thing]', or 'and the rest'. It is meant to include further but unmentioned items of the same type as those referred to by name. Correctly, therefore, 'etc' should never be used for persons but solely for inanimate objects. These days, however, the restriction is no longer observed. Though rarely spelled out in writing or print, in speech 'etc' is always fully pronounced.

FATE WORSE THAN DEATH

Words date, just as attitudes change. The unutterable becomes the everyday and conditions or experiences once never talked about are able to be freely discussed. This makes it difficult, on occasions, to understand a saying which, though very apposite in its time, has become totally outdated.

According to the period, background and prevailing culture, what could be considered 'a fate worse than death' might refer not just to one specific situation but a great variety of circumstances. But the phrase, when first coined, had a very definite meaning and strongly reflected a contemporary attitude. Virginity was treasured then as one of the highest virtues. For a girl to lose it – prior to marriage – was the worst fate that could befall her. She would be ostracised by her family and her friends – in fact, by the entire community. Defiled, no decent man would ever marry her.

This applied even more so if she had been 'deflowered' against her will. Almost beyond imagination was the treatment meted out to such an innocent victim. People would not dare explicitly to refer to her rape, a tabooed word then. Instead they used a euphemism, immediately understood by everyone. They said that hers was 'a fate worse than death'.

Times have changed. The moral standards responsible for the observation no longer apply, and so the saying has lost its original meaning. Nevertheless, it has been retained. Totally divorced now from rape, it is used as a general metaphor in everyday speech.

FEBRUARY – THE SHORTEST MONTH

In the early Roman calendar, the lengths of the months alternated between thirty and thirty-one days. It was soon realised, however, that this method made the year too long, with the result that seasons fell at the wrong time. According to the calendar, for example, the date of a spring festival might be celebrated in winter. To rectify this situation they decided to shorten every year by one day.

That February was chosen to lose that day, making this month count twenty-nine instead of its rightful thirty days, had its special reason. In the traditional sequence, August had thirty days. This, however, was regarded a personal insult to Emperor Augustus. Why should the month named in his honour be shorter than the preceding July, named after Julius Caesar, his uncle? Would it not create the impression that Augustus was inferior to him? To please the Emperor (no doubt at his persuasion), the Roman Senate decided to add one more day to August, thereby giving it thirty-one days, exactly as many as July had.

There still remained the problem, however, of how to obtain this extra day. As February was already shorter than all the other months, it was thought that it would not really matter if it were further reduced by yet another day, which could then be added to August. This explains how February became the shortest month of all, counting a mere twenty-eight days in ordinary years.

FEET OF CLAY

A futuristic dream related in the Bible created the expression 'feet of clay', now used as a vivid metaphor to describe the vulnerability of a person in a position of power, and the instability of fame: a hidden flaw might ultimately cause a person's undoing.

The Book of Daniel, the source of the metaphor, gives a detailed account of the circumstances of its creation. They concerned Nebuchadnezzar, founder and lord of the Babylonian empire and conqueror of the Holy Land. At the time of this story his rule seemed to be firmly established, spreading ever more widely. One night, Nebuchadnezzar was greatly perturbed by a dream in which he had the vision of a giant. The figure had a head of gold and his breast and arms were of silver. With a thigh of brass and legs of iron, the entire body seemed to be of strong metal, except his feet, which were of a fragile mixture of iron and clay.

In the dream, Nebuchadnezzar watched as a stone struck the giant's feet, making the entire image collapse. Breaking into many pieces, these were scattered by the wind.

On waking, Nebuchadnezzar was terrified. He was convinced that the dream contained a message. He called upon his personal counsellors to interpret it. When they were unable to do so he consulted Daniel, one of the Jewish exiles, renowned for his wisdom.

Daniel explained that Nebuchadnezzar's had been a prophetic dream. It was meant to warn him that his mighty empire was not going to last. His were the 'feet of clay', and some power from outside (the stone in the vision) would cause his destruction.

History proved the veracity of the interpretation: Nebuchadnezzar's empire was conquered and divided. All that was to survive of his might and glory were the feet of clay. A metaphor now, the expression is used in reference to all those who imagine themselves invincible, or are regarded as such by others and who, ignoring their hidden defects, will one day find themselves destroyed by them.

FELT

No doubt apocryphal is the story of how felt, that matted fabric of wool, came into existence. The story attributes its creation to St Clement, who was later to become a pope (the third after Saint Peter).

It all happened by chance. Covering long distances in his pilgrimages, Clement's feet became sore, making walking ever more arduous. To ease the pain, he wisely placed some fleece from a sheep between the soles of his feet and his sandals. The pressure exerted by his weight, combined with the moisture from his feet, changed the wool into felt.

No wonder that hatters, grateful for his (alleged) contribution to their trade, made him their patron saint, remembered on 23 November of each year. Perhaps very appropriate in this connection is a message of his in which he observed that:

We all need each other: the great need the
small, the small need the great. In our body
the head is useless without the feet and the
feet without the head. The tiniest limbs of
our body are useful and necessary to the
whole.

FIRST-RATE

'First-rate', the description of the truly excellent, was once
upon a time not generally applied to anything or anyone of
outstanding quality. It was naval in origin and was part of a
system of classification, introduced into the British navy by
Admiral Lord Anson who served as the First Lord of the
Admiralty from 1751–56.

Warships were then graded into six different 'rates',
according to the number of guns they carried. To fall into the
category of 'first-rate' required a minimum of one hundred
guns. HMS *Victory*, the best-known of all the royal navy's
warships, was equipped with this number of guns.

FISH AND CHIPS

Fish and chips is so popular a combination that it seems to
have always existed, particularly as a British national
institution. Surprisingly, though, the pairing of the two fries
dates back only to the 1860s.

Who it was that first had the idea of this tasty combination,
and where exactly it was conceived, has been a matter of
controversy. The credit has been given to places ranging from
Oldham in Lancashire, the Scottish seaport of Dundee, and
London.

The most plausible story has it that it was all due to an
itinerant Cockney entrepreneur. Moving through the streets of
London, he prepared his 'novel treat' on a small stove on top of
a handcart.

FOIL AROUND BOTTLE CORKS

Contrary to what might be imagined, the silver or gold foil around the corks of wine bottles initially had no decorative purpose. It was not there to make the bottle look more expensive and attractive. Rather, it served a very practical and essential purpose.

Brown moths were known to feed on the cork and thereby destroy it as well as the contents of the bottle. To protect the cork from thus being chewed up, it was enveloped in the foil.

FOR SHOW BUT NOT FOR BLOW

Anything which is just for show but not for blow is not to be used but merely to be displayed.

The saying goes back to a period in men's fashion when, to appear elegantly groomed, the man would have the corner of a neatly folded handkerchief sticking out of his breast pocket.

As only part of the handkerchief was visible, some clever person conceived the idea of dispensing with the handkerchief altogether, replacing it with a small piece of triangular white linen stitched to cardboard. The latter part would be hidden inside the pocket.

Obviously, this type of 'handkerchief' was useless for blowing one's nose on. It was truly for show and not for blow. Most people have discarded the custom, but it survives nevertheless in the metaphor.

FORESTALL

Forestalling used to be a trade malpractice of medieval times. The term was very literally understood: it referred to goods which, illegally acquired, were disposed of before they reached the stall to which they had been assigned.

In the fourteenth century when the word was first used, forestall was a term for an ambush. It joined be*fore*, in the sense of 'in front' with *steall*, indicating a 'place'. It was the placing of oneself in front of another person.

FORLORN HOPE

Literally, there is no hope in 'forlorn hope'! The description of a desperate situation or an undertaking that is doomed to failure comes from Dutch *hoop*, which is related to a 'heap' denoting a squad or a small troop of soldiers. 'Forlorn', the Dutch *verloren*, referred to them as being 'lost'.

Just as is the custom of other armies to send out an advance guard to reconnoitre and prepare the ground before the battle, so it was part of Dutch strategy. A very hazardous mission, it was bound to suffer a high percentage of casualties. The majority of the squad, therefore, had little chance of returning alive. With this in mind, the military command, after having dispatched the assault force, counted it as 'lost'. Indeed, they were 'a lost troop', a forlorn hope.

FORTY WINKS

Insomniacs complain that they have not slept a wink all night. In fourteenth-century England, a 'wink' meant a quick dodge or a move from side to side. 'Forty winks' related to a short nap. The figure was not meant to be taken literally; though it now seems a rather large number, at the time it stood for just 'a few'.

Indirectly, religion might well have been responsible for the general use of the phrase (though not as the result of a dreary sermon). The 'forty winks' related to the reading of the 'Thirty-nine Articles of Faith'. In 1571, an Act of Parliament made it obligatory for the clergy of the Church of England to adopt them.

To peruse the set of doctrinal formulae became a tiresome task. Years later, in 1873, it was lampooned in *Punch*, the famous British comic periodical. In a feature entitled 'Refreshing Slumber' it stated that if a conscientious right-minded man, after steadily reading through the Thirty-nine Articles were to take 'Forty Winks', the Archdeacon himself would look upon it merely as a venial offence, easily excused and forgiven. The magazine, though not creating the metaphor, certainly gave forty winks its modern currency.

FREELANCE

A freelance (or freelancer) nowadays is a writer, artist or other skilled person who is not employed by any specific company. Their own masters, freelancers take on special commissions or assignments.

The original freelance was a volunteer fighter, a soldier of fortune. Unattached to a feudal lord, he gave his services to whomever he chose. His interest lay in the reward he received and not the cause. As a mercenary he was *free* for hire by any prince or government. And because a *lance* was his knightly weapon, he could aptly be called a 'free lance'.

The name was conferred, posthumously as it were, by Sir Walter Scott. He coined the name in 1819 in his novel *Ivanhoe*, spelling it in two words as 'Free Lance'.

In spite of the obvious meaning of the name, the circumstances of its creation were soon forgotten and, with it, all martial association. The two words were fused into one, to become the modern freelance. In the case of a writer or a journalist, the lance was transformed into a pen (or, these days, the keys of a word processor).

FRENCH FRIES

French fries, the modern, refined name for potato chips, well merits its designation, as France is the country of its origin. Fries owe their description to Thomas Jefferson, who was to become the third president of the United States. When Ambassador to France (1785–89) he first ate them there. He took a liking to them and, on his return home, served them to guests on his plantation at Monticello. Appropriately, he called them 'French fried potatoes'.

The novelty soon caught the public's attention. Making them part of their fare, people shortened the name to 'French frieds'. Possibly because it was so much easier on the tongue, in the early 1930s their name was changed to the present-day 'French fries', to be re-exported as such worldwide.

There was yet another significant reason for the choice of name. The French like to serve and eat their food delicately, and therefore cut up their meats and vegetables into thin slices before putting them into the frying pan or cooking pot. In the case of beans, they cut them into narrow strips. It was only natural that potatoes were treated in the same manner, to become known and served as 'French fries'.

FURTHER BACK THAN WALLA WALLA

'Further back than Walla Walla', an Australian idiom for being at a great disadvantage, recalls Walla Walla, a famous trotter of the 1930s who could never be beaten. To handicap the horse he was put back ever further, eventually – at a race at Harold Park, Sydney, in 1933 – to a distance of 180 yards (163.9 metres). Still, he came first, 12 feet (3.6 metres) ahead of his nearest rival.

To have to face almost insuperable difficulties was therefore said to be placed 'further back [even] than Walla Walla'.

Walla Walla died in 1952 (at Dalton, New South Wales) at the age of thirty, but his fame did not die with him. It survives in the Australianism.

GARGLE

GARLIC

GAVEL

GAZUMPING

GERRYMANDER

GET DOWN TO BRASS TACKS

GIFT COUPONS

GIFT OF THE GAB

GIRO BANKING

GIVE A DRESSING DOWN

GO BY THE BOARD

GO OFF HALF-COCKED

GOOD CHAP

GRAPEFRUIT

GRAVES FACING EAST

GREEN COLOUR IN ISLAM

GREEN WITH ENVY

GREETING CARDS

GRIM REAPER

GROTTY

GUIDED TOURS AND TRAVEL AGENCIES

GUTTERSNIPE

GYMNASTS AND THE GYMNASIUM

GARGLE

An onomatopoeic word, 'gargle' echoes the gurgling sound it makes. Not merely of imitative origin, the word also incorporates the French for 'throat', *gargouille*, thereby locating the action.

This very same (French) throat was responsible too for the naming of the gargoyle, that conspicuous face or creature seen protruding from the roof gutters of some medieval buildings. Grotesquely shaped, these 'throats' acted as drain-pipes for rainwater.

GARLIC

Garlic has played a significant role for thousands of years and has done so in many ways.

Its pungent odour was thought to act as a devil-repellent. As such, mothers placed garlic in the cradles of their children. To this very day, particularly in the Mediterranean area, people hang up strings of garlic in the doorways of their homes and restaurants. They do so in the belief that it serves as a safe-guard against malevolent forces.

Other qualities also attributed to this malodorous bulb led to a diversity of practices. Roman soldiers ate garlic before going into battle in the belief that this would give them extra courage. Bullfighters in Bolivia carried a piece of garlic on their person, convinced (or at least hoping) that its smell would turn away the bull. Housewives guarded their kitchen with it to keep out evil spirits which otherwise might ruin the food or interfere with the churning of butter.

Most lasting and universal has been the tradition that garlic possesses antiseptic properties, preventing those eating it from catching diseases. Jocularly, this has been regarded as a very reasonable practice, as its smell would keep people – and their germs – out of catching range. Modern science has, in fact, discovered that there might have been some unrealised truth in the superstition. Analysis has shown that garlic contains some antibiotic substances, though these are probably not present in sufficient quantities to be effective in the killing of germs.

Whilst the smell of garlic is offensive to some people, others cherish it as an aromatic plant which greatly improves the taste of food. Long ago, the ancient Israelites, after leaving Egypt, hankered after the garlic that grew there in abundance, its taste haunting them as they crossed the desert (Numbers 11: 5).

That garlic was popular with the early Anglo-Saxons is testified by its linguistic roots. Garlic is a combination of two Old English words: *gar*, for 'spear', and *leac*, for 'leek'. The choice was influenced by the spearhead-like shape of its cloves and the ancient classification of garlic as a leek, one of the onion family.

GAVEL

The gavel with which a chairperson calls a meeting to order was originally a small hammer. One of the working tools of a stonemason, its cutting edge was used to smooth rough stones.

The gavel owes its description to its shape which, viewed from the front, reminded people of the gable of a house. Gable, in turn, is derived from the German *Gipfel*, meaning a 'top' or 'summit'.

GAZUMPING

Gazumping is an unethical practice. Though not illegal, it is certainly frowned upon. When about to buy a house or property, both parties concerned agree on the purchase price. With nothing yet put down in writing, in the proverbial phrase, theirs is a 'gentleman's agreement'. In other words, it is not legally binding. It often happens, however, that the vendor makes use of the offer as a bargaining tool to get more money from another interested party, or to force the original buyer to raise his bid.

The word gazumping is of Yiddish origin, in which tongue it means to 'swindle'. The term is an even more appropriate choice if it is realised that gazumping is derived from the German *Sumpf*, for a 'bog' or 'swamp'. Is not the falling through of the deal like being 'bogged down'?

GERRYMANDER

The political malpractice of redrawing the boundaries of constituencies for the benefit of gaining more votes for a party is oddly described as a gerrymander. The term fuses the name of Elbridge *Gerry*, a once notable American politician, with the end part of a sala*mander*. A queer combination indeed, it was well deserved.

Gerry had played a significant role in American history. He was paramount among those who had stirred the people of Boston to rebel against the British. A member of the Continental Congress, he was one of the signatories to the Declaration of Independence. Twice – in 1810 and 1811 – he served as the Governor of Massachusetts. Nevertheless, he is best remembered by an act of deception, perpetuated in the vocabulary.

Supporting the Republican party, Gerry was determined to do his part to help it retain its majority at an election held during his term of office. With this in mind, in 1811 he connived in a scheme to reshape the electoral districts. The new boundaries would favour the Republican vote. His plan succeeded, creating strong resentment on the part of the opposition.

A map of the new electoral districts was displayed in the offices of the Boston *Centinel*. When a local artist by the name of Gilbert Stuart saw it, he was immediately struck by the fact that its outlines resembled the shape of some weird creature. He made the similarity even more apparent by adding, with a few strokes of his pencil, a head, claws and wings. The newly-created monster of political manipulation was a salamander, he remarked to Benjamin Russell, the editor of the paper. Russell, like a flash, retorted, 'Not a salamander, but a Gerrymander'!

Thus the gerrymander was born as a political term. A queer hybrid, it has survived to the present day and crept into the politics of many a country.

GET DOWN TO BRASS TACKS

To refer to one's going down to the essentials of a matter as to 'get down to brass tacks' seems an odd expression to modern ears. The very description of the tack is misleading. Brass tacks never existed; only their heads were of brass.

The metaphor goes back to a very simple, but now obsolete, method of measuring fabrics in stores. Brass-headed tacks, nailed to the edge of one of the counters and evenly spaced at intervals of a quarter of a yard, enabled drapers easily to measure goods sold. To 'get down to [the] brass tacks' therefore meant business!

GIFT COUPONS

Gift coupons are not a novel method of trade promotion. Benjamin Talbot Babbit (1809–89) of the State of New York, the inventor and owner of more than one hundred patents, is said to have been their pioneer.

After having designed a novel process for making soap, Babbit sold his new product – in 1865 – in the form of individually wrapped cakes. Lest would-be customers should wrongly assume that they had to pay extra for its wrapper (and therefore not buy the soap), the label carried the word *coupon*, with the promise that ten of them would entitle the customer to a special gift.

Coupons thereafter became popular with promoters of merchandise. Americans used them to further the sale of cigarettes. Many of their packs then carried not a health warning but the promise that a 'Valuable Coupon [is] Enclosed'. It could be used to obtain a free gift which the purchaser could select from a vast range of goods, extending from a photo album to a pair of stockings.

The English, on the other hand, first promised in a Peterborough advertisement of 1876 that anyone who purchased a minimum of quarter of a pound of tea would get discount 'Tea Tickets'. These could be exchanged for a variety of 'useful' items.

The term 'coupon' itself was adopted from early bonds. These had 'certificates of interest' printed on them which, for redemption, had to be 'cut out' – *couper* in French.

GIFT OF THE GAB

To have 'the gift of the gab' is regarded as lucky and is admired by many. Those so endowed have no difficulty conversing or holding forth on almost any topic and at any occasion, and do so fluently, extensively, and usually convincingly.

Words just seem to flow out of their mouths, and it is this very 'mouth' which the phrase highlights. The root of gab is the Gaelic *gob* for 'mouth'. As such it occurs in several tongues and combinations, as well as in colloquialisms.

In Old French, *gobe* stood for 'a mouthful' and *gober* for to 'swallow', like the English 'gobble'.

In slang, the gab and gob are used in a variety of expressions. Those trying to show off in conversation are said to 'flash their gab', whilst whoever is asked to stop talking is called upon to 'stop your gab'. In the jargon of boxing, a 'gob-full of claret' was used to describe a bloody mouth.

Although those having the gift of the gab talk so much, they might in fact say very little. Covering lots of ground, their words may lack depth. It is not surprising, therefore, that a connection has been suggested between the gab and gabble, idle talk. Some believe, in fact, that gab is a linguistic back-formation of gabble.

GIRO BANKING

Giro banking is intended to provide an inexpensive and easily accessible way of transferring money or settling debts. Both the use of the term and the institution originated in Italy centuries ago and were most probably pioneered by the Florentine Medicis.

The word 'giro' is derived from the Greek *gyros* for 'circle' or 'circuit'. The Italians applied it to a monetary exchange, specifically to the transfer of a letter of exchange. Theirs was a very appropriate choice of word – after all, the transaction made the money 'go round'.

Merchants and financiers migrating from northern Italy introduced the system to England, where their original settlement in London is still recalled by the name of Lombard Street. In fact, it was through the activities of these people that the entire district surrounding the street became a centre for the exchange of money and for banking.

Giro has been linked as well with *Agio*, another financial term. Its linguistic Italian root being *aggio*, meaning 'convenience', it might be seen as a very wisely chosen word. It emphasised that this type of money transfer served the comfort of the customers, making it easy for them to accomplish.

To widen its scope and make Giro banking even more easily available to the public, the British post office in 1968 included it in the services it offered. When, twenty-seven years later (in 1995), Australia adopted Giro, its postal authorities followed the English example.

Anglicised in its pronunciation, in English Giro is pronounced not with the original hard 'g' (like in guest), but with a soft 'g', as if spelled Jyro.

GIVE A DRESSING DOWN

Anyone given a 'dressing down' is one who has been scolded. The expression may originally have belonged to the phraseology of the butcher, its birthplace being the abattoir.

After an animal had been killed, its carcass was prepared for the market. De-hided and with its intestines removed, it was cut into quarters or halves. This process technically became known as 'dressing', as recalled in the 'dressed chicken'.

Whoever is the target of a 'dressing down' is equally thus cut into pieces, though fortunately merely metaphorically. They feel all cut about, sliced up – just as has happened literally to the slaughtered animal.

Others, less bloody-minded, trace the phrase back to mining. To 'dress down' ore was to break it up and to crush it; exactly as a person may feel – all broken up and crushed – who has been given a severe talking to.

GO BY THE BOARD

Anything that 'goes by the board' is neglected or lost. The expression was born at sea, at the time of wooden sailing vessels. Just as those embarking on a ship climbed '*aboard*', anything disposed of at sea, went 'over*board*'.

When, in a storm, a boat's mast snapped, the captain had to make an instant decision. He could either salvage it for repair or let it go 'by the board', slipping it into the sea and reckoning it as a total loss. The latter practice is recalled whenever present-day social critics complain that manners have 'gone by the board'.

GO OFF HALF-COCKED

People who embark on a venture inadequately prepared for it are said to 'go off half-cocked'.

The expression dates back to eighteenth-century gunnery. When, in loading muskets, the hammer – known as the 'cock' – was prematurely released (either through a mechanical fault or the shooter's haste), the discharged gun was said to have 'gone off half-cocked'.

GOOD CHAP

To call someone 'a good chap' has an intriguing background.

Originally, people were known by their first names alone. This soon created confusion. With so many Johns, Jacks and Harrys about, they needed some additional identification. Eventually, this led to the introduction of family names.

There were several methods by which these were chosen. The simplest way was to call a family after the occupation of its bread-winner. This created the Bakers, Coopers, Fletchers, Taylors and Chapmans, the last being the name for a tradesman who bought and sold a great variety of goods.

The original linguistic root of the chapman already pointed to his occupation as a tradesman. Derived from *kupa*, a Sanskrit word, this referred to a beam of scales. (This, incidentally, indicated that goods were once sold by weight.)

When the Normans invaded Britain they replaced many Anglo-Saxon words with those of their own. In doing so, they changed the chapman into a 'merchant'.

Nevertheless, the indigenous chapman of Old English root did not disappear immediately. His name was retained, though his status was devalued: the title was now applied to peddlers and itinerant traders. But not for long. The chapman did not even survive in his new, inferior function.

Although the chapman died out as a salesman of any description, he continued to exist as a family name. Once bestowed (and inherited), the name was not abandoned. Eventually, its 'man' part was dropped and all that remained was the present-day 'chap'. No longer used in its original sense to describe a person engaged in trade, it assumed a new role as a jovial term for a good sort of person, a fellow whom one liked.

Those early chapmen have left other marks in word and phrase. As they used to sell their wares at a lower price than did the established merchants, the 'chap' gave the English vocabulary all that was 'cheap'. 'Chopping and changing' recalls the chapman's practice of changing his type of merchandise and the prices he charged as he travelled from town to town. On top of this, in the traditional manner of bargaining, he usually reduced the amount initially quoted.

GRAPEFRUIT

A rather fanciful resemblance was responsible for the naming of the grapefruit which, in actual fact, has no relationship, either botanically or in flavour, to the grape.

The way the fruit looked when hanging down in large clusters from heavily laden trees reminded some imaginative people of bunches of grapes. This prompted them to call this type of fruit a grapefruit.

No one knows for sure in which part of the world the grapefruit first grew. Generally it has been assumed that it was the West Indies, whence it spread eastward and westward. J. Lunan, who first encountered it in the West Indies in 1814, gave it its name. It was commercialised as late as the 1880s in Florida.

GRAVES FACING EAST

Though nowadays, with the exception of some faiths, no special significance is given to which way a grave faces, this has not always been the case. Some races and religions were very concerned that their dead were placed in the ground in the right direction. In antiquity, migrant tribes were anxious that their departed headed towards their ancestors' home. Moslems still strictly adhere to the tradition of their graves facing towards Mecca, their holiest shrine. Jewish graves face Jerusalem where, according to orthodox belief, the resurrection of the dead will occur.

The positioning of Christian graves in an easterly direction goes back to early theological beliefs. According to the prophet Malachi (4:2), it was in the east that 'the sun of righteousness [would] arise with healing in his wings'. This was interpreted as the second coming of Christ, the time of resurrection. For the dead to be ready fastest to answer the call, they were laid in the ground with their heads to the west, enabling them to look eastward, awaiting the Final Judgment. The ecclesiastical east did not necessarily coincide with the topographical one, but the symbolism was always apparent.

GREEN COLOUR IN ISLAM

The verdure of an oasis, situated in the arid desert, gave special significance to its green colour. To the thirsty and hungry nomad it promised refreshment and the vigour of life. Tellingly, the word green is derived from the same root as to 'grow'.

No wonder, therefore, that green became one of the sacred colours of Islam. It was the colour of wisdom and prophecy. As green symbolised the blossoming of the wilderness, so it proclaimed the bringing of salvation to those living in a spiritual desert. Thus did Mohammed's followers go out under a green banner to spread his faith. This explains why green is present in most of the flags of Muslim nations.

GREEN WITH ENVY

Closely related to the green-eyed monster are those who are green with envy. It could almost be said of them that they are mentally sick.

To be 'green around the gills' is regarded as a symptom of sickness, just as a greenish pallor was once thought to indicate the presence of anaemia or some other unhealthy condition.

Envy is a terrible sickness. Sufferers are full of aches and pains, psychologically. Colourful indeed is their description thus as being 'green with envy'. On the other hand, the phrase might well go back to the ancient belief that a person's condition was influenced by four specific bodily fluids, termed 'humours'. These were blood, choler (or bile), phlegm and melancholy. If the proportions were not properly balanced they caused sickness, showing up in the patient's general appearance. Envy was a powerful poison, most likely resulting in discolouration, and was caused by an excess of bile.

GREETING CARDS

The modern greeting card goes back thousands of years to the time of the ancient Egyptians. There was only one type: good wishes cards for the New Year. Initially, these took the form of messages attached to gifts. Earliest examples unearthed from tombs date from the sixth century BC. The custom was adopted in the Roman empire in the second century, to lapse altogether until it was reintroduced in Germany as late as the fifteenth century. The giving of cards still remained confined to the one special date of the calendar. Mostly woodcut prints to begin with, these employed religious motifs. With time and some interruptions, the practice of sending New Year greeting cards expanded all over Europe. Late in the eighteenth century a new type of card came into being: the Valentine card.

Sir Henry Cole's introduction of Christmas cards (in London, 1843) added further to the range. His novel idea, once it caught on, was specially helped and popularised by the inauguration in Britain of the penny post.

Only slowly did other cards follow, with the birthday card coming next. After initial rejection, it eventually caught on. Finally, in the 1860s, business succeeded in entering the market. Greeting cards thereafter became a huge industry, proliferating in ideas, shapes and sizes, covering every occasion of the life cycle.

GRIM REAPER

Depicted as a man or a skeleton holding a scythe, the 'grim reaper' has been a traditional personification of death. Frighteningly, death is compared with the mowing down of a human life, just like stalks of wheat cut down with a scythe. The metaphor can be traced to a variety of sources: ancient mythology, New Testament writing, a superstition and the imagination of poets.

Greek mythology portrayed Kronos, the god of agriculture and harvesting, holding a sickle.

Mysterious and powerful is a vision related in the Book of Revelation (14:14–20). The figure of the 'son of man', seated on a white cloud, is described as holding a sharp sickle in his hand. The symbolism is clear: with the earth's crop 'over-ripe', the time has come for harvesting.

An early superstition may well have contributed to the spreading of the idea of death as a reaper. People, afraid of the dead, imagined that they could harm them even from their graves. During the night, the dead might rise to visit and haunt their former homes. To prevent them from doing so they were interred with a sharp implement, usually a scythe or a sickle. Should the deceased ever intend leaving their grave, they would see the sharp instrument and, afraid of injuring themselves by moving about, prefer to stay put.

When, in later times, some of these graves were excavated, the discovery of the scythe with the skeleton could easily have given rise, or at least reinforced, the image of death as a reaper.

The metaphor was finally popularised by Henry Longfellow, the American poet who wrote 'The Reaper and the Flower'.

> There is a Reaper whose name is Death,
> And with his sickle keen,
> He reaps the bearded grain at a breath,
> And the flowers that grow between.

The reaper described as 'grim' recalls the 'Grim Death' of Milton's *Paradise Lost*.

GROTTY

'Grotty', a word now applied to anything which is seedy, crummy or generally unattractive, is English slang. It is all that is left of the original 'grotesque'. Part of twentieth-century Liverpool jargon, it would probably have never gained wider currency had it not been used by the Beatles in their first film, the 1964 'A Hard Day's Night'. This immediately popularised the word, particularly among teenagers.

GUIDED TOURS AND TRAVEL AGENCIES

Guided tours were the result of early fifteenth-century religious fervour. Members of the Christian faith, anxious to visit sacred sites in the Holy Land or other shrines far away, at the time felt too insecure to do so on their own. There was safety in numbers, and they soon learnt to join other pilgrims making the same journey.

Even package tours, as they are now commercially known, had their genesis in religious zeal. They owe their existence to one man – Thomas Cook (1808–92).

By occupation a wood turner and printer, Cook became the first travel agent. A devout Baptist, he was a teetotaller and was anxious to see people abandon drink. He became involved in the Temperance Society of Market Harborough, his home town in the English Midlands, and acted as its secretary.

On 5 July 1841 a Temperance Convention was to take place in Leicester, a town some considerable distance away. Cook wanted to ensure a good turn-out of his local members. To encourage them to attend, he offered transportation in a special train at a greatly reduced fare – one shilling (ten cents) per person for a return trip.

His efforts proved an outstanding success, prompting him to organise other excursion tours to different parts of the country. To make these tours all the more attractive, their price included accommodation in Temperance Hotels. Motivated by the result, Cook gave up his work as a printer and wood turner to devote all his time to the new venture.

A man of imagination and business acumen, he soon realised how his idea could be applied profitably in fields far removed from religious endeavour. Thus he inaugurated a program of the most varied tourist excursions, wisely chosen and well organised. They were to grow into the versatile tourist industry of modern times.

In 1855, Cook personally conducted the first overseas trip and, with it, laid the foundation for what was to become known worldwide as 'Cook's Tours'. The firm's name became a slogan and a figure of speech for any sightseeing tour – wide-ranging but quickly done – that gave travellers a good view of diverse sights and places in the shortest possible time.

GUTTERSNIPE

Snipes are birds that live mainly in marshes and on river banks. With their distinctive bill, they 'snap' up their food from the scum and the mud. It seemed appropriate, therefore, that those living from scraps of food picked up out of the refuse lying in the gutter should be called guttersnipes. Expanding the application of their name, the description was given to foul-mouthed, bad-mannered people, not least to youngsters who, reared in squalor, behaved like street urchins.

GYMNASTS AND THE GYMNASIUM

The ancient Greeks realised the value of physical culture. As revealed in their marble statues, a finely-proportioned beauty was their ideal. To reach the utmost of physical strength and health they regularly exercised and, to obtain maximum freedom of movement, did so naked. For this reason they became known as gymnasts, the Greek word for 'the nude one'. Accordingly, the place of their exercise, because of their nakedness, was called a gymnasium.

Though the literal meaning of the terms has been lost, gymnasts and the gymnasium survive, though good care is taken to have the 'naked' ones properly covered.

HAIRBRAINED

HANGED, DRAWN AND
QUARTERED

HANGING FIRE

HANKY-PANKY

HARD UP

HAVE AN AXE TO GRIND

HAVE IT IN BLACK AND
WHITE

HAVE ONE IN STITCHES

HAVERSACK

HAWKS AND DOVES

HELL-BENT

HELL FOR LEATHER

HEYDAY

HIDE ONE'S LIGHT
UNDER A BUSHEL

HIP, HIP, HOORAY

HIS NIBS

HIT A SNAG

HOBO

HOISTED BY ONE'S
OWN PETARD

HOITY-TOITY

HOMO SAPIENS

HONKY

HOOLIGAN

HORSE OF A DIFFERENT
(ANOTHER) COLOUR

HOWLING SUCCESS

HUE AND CRY

HUMBUG

HUSTLER

HAIRBRAINED

Anyone hairbrained has little or no brains, just as a hair-brained scheme is a badly conceived one. In either case, the description makes no sense. Properly presented and spelled, however, it does. To be hare-brained or to act in such a fashion is more fitting to the brain of a hare than that of humans.

HANGED, DRAWN AND QUARTERED

A metaphor used for the fate merited by those guilty of heinous deeds is that they deserved to be 'hanged, drawn and quartered'. This expression relates to the actual treatment once meted out to criminals, particularly traitors. Each of the individual words indicated a part of the punishment, though they were not inflicted in the sequence stated.

The person to be hanged was first dragged – *drawn* – through the streets to the place of execution, either on a hurdle or tied to a horse's tail. On arrival at the scaffold, the condemned was *hanged*, after which the body was cut down and beheaded. The remaining torso was cut into *quarters*, which were displayed as a warning to others.

It was a ghastly procedure, enacted as a public spectacle. Samuel Pepys watched one such execution. Commenting upon it in his *Diary* on 13 October 1660, he wrote: 'I went out to Charing Cross to see Major-General Harrison hanged, drawn and quartered; which was done there, he looking as cheerful as any man could do in that condition.'

There were variations in the practice of this judicial perversion. A 'refinement' was the introduction of the additional custom of cutting down the hanged victim even before he had expired, then disembowelling (termed 'drawing') him while still conscious so that he himself should witness this part of his punishment. In such an instance, the execution of the sentence would follow in the order of the quotation.

In judgments still in existence, the final fate of the dismembered body was left to the king's discretion.

HANGING FIRE

A matter kept in the balance or left pending is said to be 'hanging fire'. The phrase has no connection with burning of any type, but refers to the suspense derived from the delay in the firing of a gun or its failure to go off.

HANKY-PANKY

Hanky-panky has been compared with hocus-pocus. Both were acts of showmanship, used for attracting spectators; and speechwise, both use the device of reduplication.

Anything hanky-panky is 'underhand' and not to be trusted. Dubious altogether, even the very origin of the expression can be so classified. Itinerant jugglers of seventeenth-century England announced their arrival by chanting these meaningless words. 'Hanky-panky' became, as it were, their signature tune.

According to another explanation, the term may recall a well-known popular trick performed by magicians. In full view of their audience they displayed what seemed to be an empty piece of cloth, such as a handkerchief (in its shortened colloquialism, a 'hanky'), and then magically drew from it objects or even animals. This made 'hanky-panky' a most appropriate word for their trickery. The word was eventually expanded to include all kinds of shady business, including illicit sex.

HARD UP

To call those who are in financial straits 'hard up' is to employ a nautical term from the days of sailing ships.

In severe weather, special measures had to be taken to keep a ship afloat. Most important among them was to turn the ship's head away from the wind. To do so, the tiller which controlled the rudder had to be put over as far as possible and be kept in this position, demanding much effort on the part of the crew. In fact, it necessitated the combined strength of a maximum number of men. In an emergency of such a kind the command was: 'Hard up the helm!'

Metaphorically speaking, the situation paralleled that of people who were in desperate need to weather the storms of economic adversity. With the original meaning of the words forgotten, 'hard up' was transferred from the sea to describe their condition.

HAVE AN AXE TO GRIND

Those who have an ulterior motive in what they do or say proverbially have 'an axe to grind'.

The figure of speech is generally attributed to Benjamin Franklin (1706–90) and is associated with an (alleged) early incident in his life, one which he was reported never to have forgotten.

One day, so the story goes, a neighbour visiting the Franklins' home started chatting with Ben. He showed special interest in the family's grindstone and asked the boy to explain to him how it operated. Quite by chance, it seemed, the man was carrying with him a blunt axe. Young Benjamin, probably highly flattered to be consulted, fell for the ruse. He not only explained the grindstone's workings in every detail but, to demonstrate its effectiveness, used the man's dull axe and in the process sharpened it!

This experience taught the boy a lesson and in future made him wonder, whenever people flattered him, whether it was not because they had 'an(other) axe to grind'.

Though Benjamin Franklin's fame no doubt encouraged people to credit him with being the author of the words, they might in fact be of much earlier origin. Charles Miner (1780–1865), in a story he published in 1810 in his *Essay from the Desk of Poor Robert the Scribe* entitled 'Who'll Turn the Grindstone?', claimed to have been the victim of such deception, though the circumstances he describes are slightly different.

A stranger carrying an axe had asked him whether his father owned a grindstone, as his tool needed sharpening. It so happened that they had one. Praising the boy for being so alert, observant, handsome and, most of all, for looking much stronger than his age, he flattered young Miner into taking up the blunt axe and, to prove that the impression the stranger had gained was not wrong, sharpen his axe.

The moment he had done so, the man's attitude changed. Hearing the school bell ring, he taunted that the boy was not to miss his class, though he probably would like to, being such an apparent lazybone. There was no tip, not even a word of thanks.

And yet, it was all worth the experience. The lesson he had learnt would serve others well, both in his time and for generations to come. Miner concludes the story by observing how, 'When I see a merchant over-polite to his customers . . . think I that man has an axe to grind.'

HAVE IT IN BLACK AND WHITE

The request for a written statement confirming the facts or terms of an agreement made demands 'to have it in black and white'. Clearly, what the phrase is really saying is that the statement must be written in black ink on white paper.

HAVE ONE IN STITCHES

To 'have one in stitches' has nothing to do with sewing or being sewn up.

Anyone having experienced a 'stitch' in their side knows what it feels like. If one laughs long and loud it may result in such a sharp pain – totally inappropriate for something which should cheer one up.

HAVERSACK

The haversack no longer lives up to its original meaning and usage. Now referring to the canvas bag carried on the back of hikers and soldiers to hold provisions and other gear, the haversack has been appropriated from the equine world. There it served the horses for their fodder and described the 'sack' (from the German *Sack*) out of which they ate their oats or 'haver' (also derived from the German *Hafer*).

HAWKS AND DOVES

Hawks are fiercely aggressive birds of prey. Built for a predatory life, their beaks and talons can be deadly. Doves, on the other hand, are known as gentle and peaceful creatures. From biblical times they have served as symbols of peace. A dove, so the Bible tells (Genesis 8:8–11), brought back to Noah's Ark the olive leaf, indicating that the Flood had subsided and that humanity had been saved from annihilation. It is not surprising, therefore, that the hawk and the dove have become metaphors for aggression and peace, respectively.

The modern use of 'hawks and doves' as a political simile can be traced to the United States. The term 'war hawk' was coined by Thomas Jefferson in 1798, first to be applied to the Federalists who agitated for war with France. 'Hawk', describing a staunch supporter of belligerent action, was to gain modern currency in 1962. It was then used in the United States–Soviet confrontation during the Cuban Missile Crisis. On that occasion the dove also acquired its new role in political parlance.

Hawks and doves were finally adopted into the modern universal vocabulary at the time of the Vietnam War. Picasso further enhanced the traditional symbolism of the dove by his use of the bird in one of his famous drawings, '*La Colombe*' (French for 'The Dove'), then to be appropriated in numerous peace posters.

HELL-BENT

Whoever is determined to attain a goal, no matter at what cost, is said to be 'hell-bent'. They are prepared to endure the worst merely to get the object of their desire. Indeed, for it they would even suffer the pangs of hell! Though nowadays many people no longer believe in the existence of an actual hell, people keep on using the expression. Its concept continues to convey to them a picture of tribulation and anguish.

The employment of the phrase in the arena of political battle in the United States last century was most likely the cause of its popularisation. During an election campaign for governorship in the state of Maine in 1840, those supporting the (successful) candidacy of Edward Kent were said to have been 'hell-bent for [his] election'. In fact, 'Hell-bent for Kent' had been their slogan.

Long forgotten is a former theological application of the saying. Proclaiming that all sinners were destined for damnation, they were said to be 'hell-bent'.

HELL FOR LEATHER

'Hell for leather', meaning 'at great speed', further expands all that is meant by hell-bent. In actual fact, to begin with the expression was 'hell-bent for leather'. Ignoring all danger, people gallop ahead (with the leather possibly referring to their saddle).

However, a totally different explanation claims the phrase to be a corruption of 'all of a lather'. The furious speed at which a person in a hurry moves will cause them to break out in a sweat. It might equally be applied to a horse which, ridden or driven at a fast pace over a long distance, will become coated in a lather.

HEYDAY

'Hey!' is an exclamation that, for one reason or another, sought to attract people's attention. The cry gave rise to the word 'heyday', which refers to the stage or period of highest vigour or fullest strength. A heyday thus is a 'high day' – a stage in one's life distinguished by vigour and success.

HIDE ONE'S LIGHT UNDER A BUSHEL

The well-known phrase 'to hide one's light under a bushel' comes from the Gospels (Matthew 5:15; Mark 4:21; Luke 11:33). It refers to the restraint demonstrated by some people in showing their talent. They fight shy to display their qualities and, unassuming in character, conceal their abilities.

The bushel was originally a container, made either of wood or earthenware. It was normally employed as a measure for grain, but the poor made other good use of it. Turning it upside down, they used it as a table, and it is this practice which explains the figure of speech. Jesus wanted to admonish his disciples not to conceal his message but to spread it – to light up the world. He compared his word to a lamp, something not to be hidden under a bed or under a bushel. Placed there, its light would be almost invisible. A light was meant to be placed on a lamp stand to be seen by all and to illuminate the room, he said. Likewise should the Apostles be seen.

HIP, HIP, HOORAY

'Hip, hip, hooray', the popular cheer repeated three times in honour of a person to be celebrated, presents a puzzle. Its origin is steeped in mystery and is a subject of confusion and controversy. Now part of happy celebrations, once it was used as a battle cry, still recalled as such on monuments, and on a great variety of occasions.

'Hip' on its own has intrigued people and created several theories. To begin with, so it was believed, the word was not hip at all but 'hep', a shout used by herdsmen and shepherds to drive on their cattle and goats. Jew baiters then adopted the cry to hunt and haunt their victims. To them, Jews were less than cattle, and their beards reminded them of those of goats. During German anti-Jewish riots in 1819 (spreading from the city of Wuerzburg over wide areas), 'hep, hep' became a rallying call of anti-Semites. It was particularly used in academic circles and in student associations which, at the time, vehemently opposed Jews being given equal rights.

Whilst the 1819 events are historically documented, nothing supports another claim of the exclamation's much earlier birth. This dates back to medieval times, to the Crusades. It tells that German Knights, before embarking on their mission to the Holy Land, headed Jew hunts in which they roused the mob with the shout. Not a real word, 'hep' was in fact a contraction, a combination of the initials of their slogan: in classic Latin, *hierosolyma est perdita* – 'Jerusalem is lost [to the enemy]'. It celebrated, in anticipation, the capture of Jerusalem from the Turks. Eventually, possibly through the slurring of speech, the acronym 'HEP' changed into 'hip' and was exclaimed thrice to rouse the masses.

It has also been suggested, much more simply, that 'hip' merely joined the first two letters of *hi*erosolyma to the initial of *p*erdita. Either way, the acrostic became a joyous cry proclaimed by those who vociferously celebrated the liberation of Jerusalem from the hands of the 'infidels'.

Equally doubtful and complex is the background of the second part of the cheer, the 'hooray' (or hoorah, as it is also rendered).

Those who believed the 'hep' to be the Crusaders' creation discerned in the 'hooray' a Slavonic root – *hu-raj*, meaning 'to Paradise'. Hence the call, taken in its entirety, was intended to express how, with 'Jerusalem lost' to the infidels, the victors were on their way 'to Paradise'.

Of much later date, but still linked with a hostile pursuit, is another derivation. This traces the modern hurrah to *ura*, an indigenous Russian cheer with which Cossacks launched their attacks. Yet a further theory sees in the exclamation a modified form of *huzza*. Once a sailor's cheer and salute, it was also a hauling cry. This then grew into a general shout for both a charge and a jubilation.

Going back to the ancient past, hurrah has also been explained as a survival from pagan days. It is all that is left of *thor-aie*, the Scandinavians' invocation to Thor, their god of war, asking for his help in battle. That modern, enlightened people on festive occasions would thus continue to call on a pagan deity would not be surprising. After all, once every week we still honour the identical god – on Thursdays, the day called after Thor.

Much more civil, simple and peaceful is a final interpretation. This finds in the 'hip' a call to attention, and in the 'hurrah' an encouragement to 'hurry along'.

Numerous and perplexing indeed are the paths along which the expression travelled and the changes in meaning and purpose it experienced on the way. A chilling reminder of horrendous deeds for the student of history, it has become a joyful toast to those happily unaware of the background of the cheer.

HIS NIBS

'His nibs' is closely related to former *nob*ility, though it cuts it short. Once reduced (in name, if not in status), a further change took place, this time to a vowel. From 'His Nobs' it became 'His Nabs' and ultimately changed to 'His Nibs'.

More respectable is another suggestion. This derived 'his nibs' from the Hindi language, in which a governor was known as a Nawab. His title was also responsible for the *Nabob*, a name applied to a delegate of the supreme head of state, a Viceroy or chief governor under the Great Mogul.

Of whichever root, 'his nibs', copying 'His Honour', was used as a mock title with which to address (or speak of) someone who, though in charge, was not taken very seriously.

HIT A SNAG

It is an experience of everyone's life that not everything always goes smoothly. Sooner or later, some unexpected difficulty impedes one's path – one 'hits a snag'. The 'snag' is of an Old Scandinavian root, related to the Norwegian word for a 'spike' or 'sharp point'. It was applied to anything obstructing one's passage, such as a tree trunk or a craggy boulder.

To 'hit a snag' was first used in American navigation when some sharp object sticking out of the river bed brought a boat to a standstill. The phrase was also common among Canadian lumberjacks. They applied it when, in floating logs down the river, they were stopped by some such obstruction – a 'snag'.

HOBO

Most people will associate the 'hobo' with someone who is 'down and out' – a vagrant and a vagabond. Doing so, they fall far short of the original meaning of the name, though it is still a matter of controversy as to how it first came into existence and what it initially represented.

Though it is certain that the hobo's original home was America, there are at least three major 'explanations' of the name.

Least degrading is the claim that it was first applied to veterans of the Civil War. Returning from the battlefield, at times they had a long distance to cover; they were '*ho*meward *bo*und'. Combining the first two letters of each word, they became known as hobos.

A second suggestion says that tramps, meeting on the way, exchanged jovial greetings and did so by using as their salutation 'Ho! Beau!'. Translated into present-day language, this could be rendered as, 'Hello! Handsome!' The *beau*, of course, was the French for 'beautiful'. This was the general term used at the time for a dandy, a man who was out to impress people by the way he dressed. The hobo who appropriated his name was his very antithesis!

There is also the theory that itinerant workers used to carry with them their own hoe. This made people soon refer to them as the hoe-boys – which, slurred in speech, deteriorated into the hobo.

Others have tried – rather far-fetchedly – to see in the hobo an Indian or Chinese root. Even Latin has been cited as the source of the name, with hobo explained as an abbreviated combination of *homus bonum*, 'a good fellow'.

HOISTED BY ONE'S OWN PETARD

To be hoisted by one's own petard means to become the victim of one's own evil design. People who experience this fate are caught in the trap they have set for others.

The original petard was a device employed in medieval warfare. Loaded with an explosive charge, it was attached to the gate or the wall of a fortified city and detonated. If successful, the explosion would create a breach large enough for the attacking force to enter and capture the town.

It was a hazardous undertaking. Whoever was commissioned with the task of fixing the petard was fully exposed to the enemy. Once spotted, he was an easy target. To detonate the charge was even more perilous. Not infrequently, the gunpowder exploded prematurely, with the result that the soldier lighting the fuse was lifted into the air by the blast. 'Hoisted by his own petard', he was killed.

Derived from the French for 'breaking wind', the petard was given its name because of the sound it made when it exploded.

Petards have long become obsolete in warfare, but they survive in the figure of speech and, not least so, because Shakespeare used the expression in Hamlet.

HOITY-TOITY

Stuck-up people are dubbed as being hoity-toity. The very sound of the characterisation seems to point to the haughtiness of such people. Just as conspicuous as they tend to be, the word, by its reduplication, reflects their air of self-importance.

The now double-barrelled expression goes back to 'hoyden', the name once given to a tomboy. Her description, in turn, had its root in 'to hoit', meaning 'to romp riotously'.

People who are hoity-toity are arrogantly standoffish. This gives credence to an alternate derivation of their description. It claims that those 'high and mighty', as it were, acted as if they were standing on a high roof – *haut toit* in French – from which they condescendingly looked down on the common folk. It was the fashionable French of the 'high roof' that – Anglicised – became their stigma.

HOMO SAPIENS

A member of the human race is referred to as homo sapiens. From the Latin, this speaks of man (which, of course, includes woman) as the 'wise man' – that is, a reasoning, thinking creature.

Carolus Linnaeus (1707–78), the renowned Swedish botanist, was the first to coin the term. In his methodical pursuit to divide all living things into categories, he felt that wisdom, being rational, distinguished humans from all other creatures. Hence his choice of their name! Centuries later (in 1935) it made Henri Bergson, the famous French philosopher, remark that '*Homo sapiens*, the only creature endowed with reason, [is] also the only creature to pin its existence to things unreasonable.'

As intriguing as Linnaeus's designation of wisdom as the specific quality of humans is his use of the Latin *homo* for 'man'. Though God is said to have formed man out of the dust of the ground, breathing into him the divine spirit, his '*earth*ly' feature has nevertheless remained the basis of his designation as 'human'. This is derived from the Latin *humus* for 'soil'. Its etymology merely adopts the original Hebrew tradition, in which it is said that Adam, the first man, was so called because he was fashioned out of the 'soil' of the earth, which is *adamah* in Hebrew.

It should be noted that *homo* used in the sense of 'man' has no connection with the *homo* of *homo*sexuality. Of a different, Greek, root, this means 'identical'.

HONKY

Beginning in the United States in the 1950s, then catching on in Britain as well, blacks came to refer to the white man as a 'honky', also rendered honkey or honkie. Though a comparatively recent practice, the origin of the word is uncertain and has been given a variety of explanations.

Most far-fetched is the idea that blacks chose it because the Caucasians reminded them of white geese and their *honk*ing. The name, it is said, was coined in imitation of the supposed nasal timbre of white people's voices.

Another unlikely suggestion links the name with a practice observed in some inter-racial relationships. White men who had black girlfriends would pick them up after work at their place of employment. They announced their arrival by *honk*ing the horn of their cars. Its sound was transferred as a nickname to all white males.

A further derivation traces the honky to earlier days when Europeans who had joined the American labour force were resented. Since many of them had come from Hungary, they were contemptuously referred to as 'hunkies'. This, corrupted into honky, was then applied to all white men.

HOOLIGAN

A hooligan is a lout, a vandal, a 'no-gooder'. His description as such has been claimed to be the corruption of Houlihan, the name of an Irish family who lived in the Southwark district of London. Patrick, one of its members, worked as a bouncer at a number of local establishments. An evil character, he became notorious for beating people up, sometimes even robbing them. Clarence Rook made Houlihan's lawless life the subject of a book which, published in 1899, he called *The Hooligan Nights*. With fact and fiction intermingled, soon the hooligan assumed its present-day meaning.

Police reports dealing with the prosecution of 'Hooligan Gangs' (sometimes referred to also as 'Hooley Gangs') further contributed to the adoption of the family name as a description of ruffians and hoodlums.

Another suggestion, which antedates this claim by many years, traces the hooligan to a farce shown in London in the early 1800s. Its main character was called Hooligan. A butler, he was a great bungler and was mostly in a state of intoxication, much to the amusement of the audience.

Simple but very convincing is yet another explanation. The Hooligans, an Irish family living in London, were so notorious for their rowdiness that their name became the byword it now is.

HORSE OF A DIFFERENT (ANOTHER) COLOUR

To convey the fact or opinion that something is a completely different matter, it is said that it is 'a horse of a different (or another) colour'.

The origin of the phrase has been traced to the English village of Uffington in Berkshire. On a hill just south of the village can be seen the outlines of a galloping white horse of gigantic dimensions. Covering an area of almost 0.8 hectares (2 acres), it is 112 metres (374 feet) long and, on a clear day, can be seen from as far away as 18 kilometres (12 miles). Thomas Hughes made it the scene of the opening chapter of his 1857 classic, *Tom Brown's Schooldays*. 'And what a hill is the White Horse Hill!' he wrote. 'There it stands right up above the rest . . . the boldest, bravest shape for a chalk hill you ever saw.'

The horse probably dates back to the Iron Age. For the ancient Celts it was a shrine in honour of a deity. It was inevitable, however, that with the passing of time fresh vegetation and weeds overgrew the figure, which thus became 'a horse of a different colour'. To retain it for years to come, it became the custom periodically to 'scour' the horse and thereby restore its original hue.

An alternate claim attributes the white horse to totally different circumstances: not to ancient mythology but to the history of the English people. Apparently Alfred the Great, the Saxon king, placed it there after his victory over the Danes at nearby Ashdown in AD 871. This led to the enemy's eventual complete withdrawal from English soil.

The horse was to serve as a perpetual monument of the Saxons' casting out the foreign invader. As the traditional emblem of the Saxon people, the white horse proclaimed from on high the message of Saxon supremacy. This would be threatened if ever it became 'a horse of a different colour'. To prevent this from happening, the population regularly went up the hill to restore the horse to its original white.

Different again is a third explanation. This links the saying with medieval tournaments, those jousting matches in which armoured knights competed against one another on horseback. Whilst it is the modern method to distinguish the various race horses by the colours their jockeys wear, at that time it was the colour of the horse which identified its rider. If a favourite knight was expected to win a race but did not succeed in doing so, his supporters, and particularly so his lady, would sadly remark that it was 'a horse of a different colour' that came first.

Shakespeare must have been familiar with the phrase when, in *Twelfth Night* (Act 2, Scene 3), he made Maria say to Sir Toby Belch, who shared her opinion on a certain matter, that 'My purpose is, indeed, a horse of that colour'.

HOWLING SUCCESS

Anything preceded by 'howling' is intensified. A howling error is thus an error which, though easily noticed, is hard to rectify. On the other hand, a howling success is a supreme achievement.

The earliest use of the phrase has been attributed to the stage. A comedy that was so amusing that it made the audience *howl* with laughter could rightly be called a 'howling success'.

All the world is a stage, as a well-known quotation tells us, and it is no wonder that, from the theatre, the expression was soon adopted to describe life situations which were the acme of accomplishment.

HUE AND CRY

To raise a 'hue and cry' is to create an uproar to attract public attention. The words go back to the world of hunting. A vocabulary of 'shouts' was developed within the sport to indicate whether, for instance, the quarry was a deer or a fox.

It did not take long for the practice and the words to be adopted in the pursuit of justice. Representatives of the law raised their own distinguishing hue and cry when chasing a criminal, often hunting him with their hounds. Easily recognised as a sound of alarm, it was meant as a call to others to join in the chase. It was people's duty, in fact, to do so 'with horn and voice'. Anyone refraining from doing so committed an offence, just as to raise a hue and a cry without reason was equally punishable.

Declared redundant in Britain in 1827, the old law no longer applies. However, the hue and cry has been retained in the vocabulary and now refers to any type of uproar or public outcry. At times, though, making a lot of noise may mean very little.

The two words making up the term merely reinforce one another and, in different ways, say the same thing.

'Hue', from the French *huer* for 'to shout', is merely another 'cry'.

HUMBUG

Humbug is nonsense and deceit. No one knows for certain how the term originated. This gave all the more scope for people to suggest various kinds of sources, some so odd and convoluted that they themselves could fall under the category of humbug. Though by and large incorrect, they have contributed, each in their way, to perpetuate and spread the use of humbug. They present a most fascinating miscellany of curiosities.

The Irish, Welsh, Scots and Germans have all taken credit for having created the word and concept. 'Bug' (like the bugbear and the bogey) has been traced to the Welsh root *bwg*, responsible for the naming of the ghost and other evil spirits haunting humans. The English then adopted the word and, rendering it as 'bug', made it the name of insects. They possibly did so because these bugs, like the imagined ghosts, flitted around alarmingly.

Of course, there were thousands of different species. Some of these were harmless, whilst others could be lethal. Did not the Bible, in one of its versions of a Psalm (91:5), call on the faithful not to be afraid of 'the bugs that fly by night'?

One type of bug made its presence known by a loud humming sound. This, as can easily be understood, caused people to be alarmed. However, once they realised that the humming bug was not at all dangerous but that its loud noise in fact meant very little, they used the *hum*ming *bug*, contracted in their speech to 'humbug', as a description of the bluffer, a person out to deceive the gullible.

The Scottish claim belongs to the realm of genealogy and the joining in marriage, very long ago, of a man called Hume to a girl whose family name was Bogue, pronounced Bug. They lived in the eastern county of Kincardineshire, then known as The Mearns. One of their descendants was referred to as Hum o' the Bug. He had the habit of telling whomever he met, and on every possible occasion, of all the great things he and his forebears had done. He did so not once but innumerable times. Everyone was aware of the spuriousness of his assertions, and it did not take long before Hum o' the Bug became synonymous with claptrap and absurd, empty talk. Shortened to humbug, the family's (abbreviated) name survives to this day.

Historically, humbug has also been traced to the German city of Hamburg which, at the time of the Napoleonic wars, assumed great importance in the blockade of Britain. Anticipating modern psychological warfare, it became a centre of disinformation, a place from which false rumours intended to undermine British morale and economy were spread. For the British, this made all that was falsehood synonymous with Hamburg. Forgetting the actual circumstances, the city's name survives, though slightly deformed on English tongues, in all that is 'humbug'.

The Irish money market has also been cited as a possible source of the term. During the reign of King James II, faked coinage then circulating was appropriately dubbed 'base copper'. In Gaelic, this was *uim bog*. Was not all humbug as spurious as those coins?

Much more simply, the humbug has been seen as a fusion of a 'hoax' (called in slang a 'hum') and a 'sham' or 'bogy' (the 'bug').

There is no doubt that, among the English, humbug was most popularised by Charles Dickens who, in his *Christmas Carol*, made Scrooge repeatedly exclaim, 'Bah, humbug'. In America, on the other hand, it was P.T. Barnum, the great showman, who was responsible for the word gaining currency. Proudly, he called himself 'The Prince of Humbugs' and even wrote a book on the *Humbugs of the World*. In his office he kept a locked chest, which in large black lettering carried the instruction that it was to be opened only after his death. The object of great anticipation, his entire staff imagined that it contained rewards for their loyal services. At his death the box was opened to reveal numerous copies of his autobiography, with the further instruction that the copies should be given to all those who had been longest in his employment! He thus acquired the reputation of being a fraud and charlatan.

HUSTLER

There is quite a story behind the hustler, now specifically used in American slang as a name for a prostitute.

In Dutch colonial days the name was applied to fast and energetic workers who, as it were, were hustling along in their jobs. The term then suffered a change of meaning, becoming tainted. Hustler came to describe a dishonest person who lived by their wits. Pool hustlers, for instance, created the impression that they were mere novices at the game, misleading the other players and by their ruse gaining high wins.

Whichever way, the individual concerned had to be fast. Perhaps, then, there is not so great a difference between such a person and some 'sex workers'.

i

ICE-CREAM CONE

An emergency created the ice-cream cone. During the 1904 World Fair in St Louis, USA, an ice-cream vendor ran out of his stock of small paper plates on which he served his frozen treat. Desperately he needed some replacement to continue his business. The owner of the neighbouring stall suggested that he could solve the problem by shaping waffles into small vase-like cups. The ice-cream seller took up the idea, which proved an instant success! In fact, it helped both men, as the neighbour, a baker by trade, was selling the necessary waffles.

In a slight variation of the story, more credit is given to the ice-cream vendor. The baker, indeed, had suggested the waffle, but merely as a sort of flat plate. Adopting the idea, the ice-cream seller went one step further by twisting the still hot and pliable waffles into cones.

It was a splendid invention that not only helped two astute businessmen in increasing their trade but added to people's gastronomic enjoyment of an already popular food. In the past, ice cream had been served on paper plates, saucers or similar small dishes. Henceforth these became redundant, making washing up of the used dishes unnecessary. So the novel cone, as well as being a culinary delight, proved a work-saving device.

INDIAN GIVER

Remnants of outdated prejudice and racial discrimination have tainted the vocabulary of everyday speech. Unfortunately, this applies to many languages.

Colonising nations occupying alien lands used to look down on the indigenous populations, frequently using their name derogatorily to express inferiority of anything, whether of an object, custom or season. A typical example concerns American Indians. Anything short of perfect was called Indian. An Indian summer, thus, was merely a temporary return of the real one.

Most notable of this type of disparagement and misconception is the 'Indian giver', an expression perpetuated in modern speech. An Indian giver refers to someone who, after having given a present, subsequently asks for its return.

It was an Indian tradition to exchange ceremonial gifts. As was only to be expected, these had to be of comparatively equal value. Europeans, however, when thus being honoured, either out of mere ignorance or a feeling of superiority often felt it sufficient for their gift to be of much less value. The Indians, deeply hurt, not only rejected such a present but asked for the return of theirs. It was incidents of this kind that, most probably, created the contemptuous designation of the 'Indian giver'.

INNINGS

Like so many other sports, cricket has given everyday language some memorable idioms. And one of these is 'innings'. Whoever has 'a good innings' is lucky, either by a long run of success or, particularly so, by being blessed with longevity. At the end of such a life, obituaries and eulogies frequently speak of the deceased as having had 'a long innings'.

But innings, although having a final 's', is not a plural. Referring to the batting time of a team or players, it is also used for the total number of runs scored by them during such a turn. When the Americans adopted the word for their baseball games, at first they retained the Englishmen's spelling (innings with an 's'). It appears in the earliest treatise written on the sport by Henry Chadwick in 1868. Subsequently, however, the delusive final 's' was dropped.

Originally, the term was used – and most plausibly so – in the shortest possible form. Clearly and simply, it referred to the part of the game during which the player or side was 'in'.

INNUENDO

To express anything by innuendo is to give a subtle indication of something, not voice it explicitly in so many words. The word innuendo recalls the language of gestures. It is derived from the Latin *nuere* for 'nod', the movement of the head with which people conveyed a message. Giving a nod, winking or merely raising an eyebrow could say a lot. Indeed, it could be sufficient to destroy a person's reputation. Verbalised, the nod (still retaining its Latin roots) became the innuendo.

A nod can be interpreted in many ways and it is essential to know that it means different things to different people. Whilst Englishmen, Americans and Australians, for instance, mean 'yes' by nodding their head up and down and 'no' by shaking it from side to side, elsewhere, such as in Bulgaria, Turkey, Iran, Bengal and parts of Greece, the same gestures may express the very opposite. There are so many types of nods indeed, that, not surprisingly, they have led to some confusion.

IRISH BULL

The Irish have often been the butt of jokes, some of which they have even fostered themselves. Perhaps, at times, the only way to survive has been to make fun of themselves. Typical is the reputation of being ludicrously illogical, best illustrated by what came to be known proverbially as the Irish bull. It referred to foolish, incongruous statements. In Middle English, 'bull' stood for 'falsehood' and at some time was used to signify a 'bubble'.

Regrettable historic circumstances might well be responsible for the expression 'Irish bull'. Early antagonism between the English and the Irish resulted in the English making Irish a byword of all that was inferior (just as the Americans had done with the Indians). Bricks were thus called 'Irish confetti', a wheelbarrow was described as an 'Irish buggy' and 'Irish apricots' were potatoes. 'Irish bull' could well be a testimony to the Irish people's desperate struggle for survival in the face of oppression. 'Bull' is the Anglicised form of the French word *boule*, meaning 'fraud' and 'deceit'. To save their lives and independence, Irishmen were forced to mislead their oppressors which, cunningly, they learnt to do by confusing them with senseless, contradictory talk. Eventually, this was designated by the English as being just 'Irish bull'.

Another possibility is that the 'Irish bull' might have been suggested by the 'cock and bull stories' Irishmen were fond of telling.

IRONING

Concepts and descriptions, once adopted, have a tendency to survive, even if they have become obsolete. A typical example is the household chore of ironing clothes. 'Ironing' being so called goes back to the days when the task was done by an instrument actually made of iron. The modern gadget contains not a single scrap of iron, yet the now inapplicable name for the practice is maintained.

IT DOESN'T MATTER

When we say of something that 'it doesn't matter' or 'it matters a lot', we use 'matter' in the sense of a vital substance, of real consequence.

From the Latin, 'matter' was used specifically to describe wood, a material out of which a diversity of objects could be shaped. Significantly, the words 'matter' and 'mother' are closely related, their linguistic root being *mater*. Anything that matters has great potentiality. Creative and fruitful, it should be taken due notice of.

ITALICS

Italics were introduced into printing by Teobaldo Mannuci, who is better known by his Latinised name, Aldus Manutius. A printer by trade, Manutius was an Italian scholar, renowned for his love of classical literature and aesthetics.

In 1490 he established in Venice his own ('Aldine') Printing Press, to produce beautiful editions of Greek, Latin and Italian works. He realised, however, that he could not do so with the traditional 'roman' (vertical) characters. In his opinion, these were unworthy of the books, which needed special lettering of graceful distinction. Thus he adopted for his printing types the handwriting of Petrarch, the great fourteenth-century Italian scholar and poet, whose calligraphy he admired. He made first use of it in 1501 when publishing an edition of Virgil.

It was an historic moment in the development of printing and, proud of his country, Manutius dedicated the first volume in the new type 'To Italy'. This led people to call the conspicuously slanting letters 'Italian'. Anglicised, it created the 'italics'.

Manutius's original intention in creating an italic typeface was to add to the aesthetic value of his books. Then a change occurred. Printers discovered another significant function for italics. The distinctiveness of the type made it specially suitable to give emphasis to important words and phrases within the text. Italics could thus do to print what a raised voice could achieve in speech.

The modern age found further ways to take advantage of the type. It italicised the names of newspapers, book titles and foreign words.

Italics came to assume a multiple purpose in printing, proving a useful means to beautify, to clarify and to emphasise. However, there was one instance in which the employment of italics led to confusion. The seventeenth-century translators preparing the Authorised King James version of the Bible came across passages which, if literally rendered into English, would make little sense or be subject to misinterpretation. By the mere addition of a single word or phrase, however, they could elucidate the text. Mindful of the sanctity of what they regarded a divine revelation, they did not want to create the impression of having improved on the text. So, to indicate that certain words appearing in their translation were not part of the authentic text but additions of their own, they put these in italics.

Later readers of the Authorised version, unaware of the reason for the italics, rashly and wrongly assumed that they indicated the special importance of the word or phrase so reproduced!

j

JACKET

JAW

'JOHN' FOR TOILET

JOINT

JUDGE'S BLACK CAP

JACKET

In the fourteenth century, a short, close-fitting coat was part of everyday dress for French peasants. Using the diminutive of Jacques, the most common name for men at the time, they called it 'Jacquette'. This, in turn, created the modern jacket which, in its English cut, still conspicuously preserved the original 'Jack'.

The jacket has also been seen as a civilian adoption of a once military coat, the *jacque*. This belonged to soldiers' uniforms between the fourteenth and seventeenth centuries. Sleeveless, made of leather and at times quilted, it was usually worn over their coats of mail.

Even the navy adopted the jacket, adapting it to their own uses and renaming it a pea-jacket. It became a short, heavy overcoat, worn for sailors' protection during severe weather. The coarse cloth out of which it was made was responsible for the 'pea', derived from the fifteenth-century Dutch *pij* describing such a thick and rough type of material.

A modern American appropriation of the pea-jacket changed it into the P-jacket, often (though mistakenly) seen as an abbreviation of a '*pilot's jacket*'.

With the passing of time, on the loom of language the jacket has come to cover so much more than the human body. As a 'dust jacket' it is wrapped around books, whilst at the dinner table, when potatoes are served unpeeled, they are presented 'in their jackets'.

JAW

Cartoonists have found in the jaw one of the most welcome features of the human face. This is because it lends itself so splendidly to caricature.

The jaw is truly Anglo-Saxon – in its etymology. The name has nothing to do with its appearance but is related to what seems part of its function. All that the 'jaw' says – not only in its body language but by its linguistic root – is 'I chew'.

When nature called, people once used the so aptly called 'necessary' or 'privy' to relieve themselves. Bathroom, toilet, comfort station and WC (short for 'water closet') then took their place. Another euphemism was the lavatory. Of French root, from *laver*, it described the smallest room in the house as the place where a person would 'wash [up]'.

In England and Australia, those who need to 'spend a penny' will ask for the 'loo'. In the United States it will be the 'john'. John is one of the most fashionable male names in the English-speaking world. No doubt it first assumed this position because of its sacred association. From the Hebrew, meaning 'God is gracious', it owed its early popularity to the fact that it was the name of both John the Apostle and John the Baptist, two men closely linked with Jesus. More than twenty popes were called John. No wonder, then, that for many generations it was such a favoured male name. Therefore, to refer to the men's room as the 'john' seemed an obvious choice.

Though now a typical American designation, the john has also been said to pay due respect to an Englishman, to Sir John Harrington. A godson and a courtier of Queen Elizabeth I, he proved himself far in advance of his time by being deeply concerned with hygiene and cleanliness. In this pursuit he invented, in 1596, the first of the modern flushing toilets – the valve water-closet. To acknowledge his contribution to civilisation, a place so private merited to be called after his first name. Paradoxically, it was left to the Americans to do so.

Even a chamberpot, once traditionally placed under every bed in readiness for use, was familiarly referred to as 'cousin John'. John then became the American description for an outhouse and, as early as the 1650s, of the indoor toilet. Finally it attained academic rank, so to speak, and thereby general acceptance, through a regulation published in 1735 by the renowned Harvard College. This stated that 'no Freshman shall . . . go into the Fellow[']s cus John'. The 'cus' was an abbreviation of the earlier 'Cousin John'. Dropping the cousin, john has stayed on to be of service to people of all ranks.

JOINT

In modern slang, the word 'joint' specifically refers to a marijuana cigarette. But this is only the latest stage of the word's multiple application which, through the years, has experienced some interesting changes.

Prior to the cigarette (and still to this day) a joint disparagingly described an American drinking-saloon, an establishment of bad reputation. And for a valid reason. Originally the establishment supplied not only illicit liquor but opium as well. It also provided addicts with the pipes needed to smoke the narcotic. These pipes were made of bamboo which had many prominent joints, a term still recalled in the 'joint' of present-day parlance. This led to the naming of the place where they were used as an 'opium joint'. The expression then spoke of the 'coming together', not of people but of the various sections of the bamboo.

JUDGE'S BLACK CAP

It used to be an established practice for a judge, prior to passing a death sentence, to don a black cap.

The reason was not, as is often imagined, to express sorrow at the taking of a life. The custom in fact had a religious basis.

No member of the Church was permitted to shed the blood of another or even to be instrumental in doing so. A priest, thus, could not pronounce a death sentence. Therefore, in the days when priests still acted as judges, in order to make such a fatal decision they had first to divest themselves of their ecclesiastical status. They laid aside their priesthood – at least temporarily – by symbolically covering up their tonsure. This they did with a square of black cloth – the black cap. Even after judiciary and religion had become separate institutions, the religious root of the courts of law survived in the peculiar custom.

KANGAROO COURT

A kangaroo court is a self-appointed, unauthorised and illegal tribunal. At times, its name is also applied to a mock trial.

Though the kangaroo is indigenous to Australia, the kangaroo court, it has been generally claimed, is American-born. Contrary to this is the opinion that, like the marsupial, the expression was native Australian: the first court was formed among the early convicts to settle their arguments, away from the authorities. They chose its name not only to give it a local flavour but, most of all, to distinguish it from the courts back in England – those very courts which had been responsible for their transportation.

Whichever way, its application became widespread in the United States and in Britain. American prisoners in particular used to form their own 'kangaroo courts' to settle differences among themselves, to make those not abiding by their code of rules toe the line.

The term was also adopted in trade unions to describe self-appointed groups of members who made it their task to force those disregarding policies to conform.

Upon its discovery by white man in the eighteenth century, the kangaroo astounded the world. With its pouch and its jumping, it was so out of the ordinary that anything unusual was subsequently given its name. No wonder, therefore, that even a court, different from traditional tribunals, was distinguished by the marsupial's name, to become known as a kangaroo court.

Australians, in search of wealth, joined the Californian gold rush in 1849. With the authorities far away, differences or disputes that arose between the diggers were settled on the spot. Courts were improvised and judgments executed fast. The men constituting the tribunal would then disperse, just as quickly as they had come together. It could well have reminded the Australian diggers of the mobs of kangaroos, so familiar to them from back home, which would suddenly jump out of the bush and then, equally suddenly, vanish.

A rather gruesome explanation links the kangaroo court with an unfortunate occurrence on the gold fields. It happened not infrequently that the original owner of a mining stake disappeared, most often as a consequence of having been murdered. A total stranger would then, like a skipping kangaroo, 'jump' on their claim to take (illegal) possession of it. Vigilante committees were formed to investigate such 'claim jumpers'. If these could not provide satisfactory evidence of having legitimately acquired the digging, the 'court' lost no time in 'jumping' to conclusions and, finding the party guilty, carried out its judgment.

Many of these instances are now a matter of the past, and kangaroo courts with their harsh penalties (which, at times, even led to lynchings) are merely grim memories of days gone by. However, the kangaroo court has been retained in the English vocabulary, to be used – often derogatorily – to describe tribunals not generally authorised and accepted.

KAPUT

Something *kaput* is 'done for', broken up, beyond repair. An international term now, it comes from the German *kaput* which, in turn, has its root in French gambling in the game of Piquet. A player is *capot* if he has not made a single trick. Thus excluded from the game, he is treated as if he were not present. Literally, and in the original and now obsolete sense of the word, he is hoodwinked – since *capot*, to start with, spoke of a 'hooded' cloak, something blackened out.

During the Thirty Years War, the Germans acquired the expression from the French. German soldiers then used the phrase 'to make capot' as a gruesome euphemism for killing an enemy. It is first documented as such in a report of 1643.

KEEP A STRAIGHT FACE

Everyone recognises 'blarney' as typically Irish. Few would guess, however, that – allegedly – the phrase that speaks of 'keeping a straight face' was grown in the same soil.

Among country folk, the face in this expression did not refer to a human countenance but to the front of their spade. To dig up the peat from the bog most effectively and economically, the Irish learnt to keep the face of their spades at a right angle to the ground: in other words, perfectly straight. They controlled their implements just as they would their facial expressions when teasing a person. Pulling someone's leg, they kept a straight face – a true Irishism. No smile would give away that they were not serious.

KEEP YOUR PECKER UP

Humans have learnt much from the creatures of the earth and have made use of them in many ways. They have even done so – and done so very abundantly – in the choice of their words and phrases.

An alert bird, it was observed, would keep its beak (or 'pecker') shut when it was not eating or asserting its position in the 'pecking order' of its species. Dropping its beak was tantamount to giving up the battle. A bird, exhausted in combat and no longer able to continue the fight, would naturally drop its beak. In a cockfight, when a rooster was forced to lower its beak it lost the contest – and, in many a case, its life.

Those losing courage in the battle of life were thus reminded to keep their pecker up.

KELLY'S EYE

In the game of Bingo, or Housey Housey as it is also known, each number selected at random is, when called out, given a special designation. Apart from making the game all the more entertaining, the main reason for this practice is to avoid any misunderstanding as to the number picked. Traditionally, number '1' is 'Kelly's eye', a name that has puzzled many.

Several theories have been proffered for its choice. 'Kelly's eye' has been traced to British army slang and as such is included in army dictionaries. There, however, the trail ends, for the definitions give no indication as to Kelly's identity.

Another suggestion sees Cockney rhyming slang as its source. Among its many telling phrases was 'Kelly's eye – belly's eye'. This, of course, pointed to the navel, or belly button, of which of course there was only *one* on a person's body! What better eponym could be given to the number as, like the navel to which the umbilical cord was attached, if luck so willed it the '1' could nourish a full 'House'.

KICK UPSTAIRS

An employer who is anxious to get rid of an employee without actually discharging him or her might encourage the person to look for another, 'better' job. To help the person in obtaining it, they would even furnish glowing references.

Many, indeed, have been the methods by which people have tried to dispose of someone unwanted. Their range extends from simple dismissal to assassination.

It was left to the British to achieve the paradoxical aim of deposing by promotion! A practice in their parliamentary system was the origin of the striking and otherwise puzzling phrase that speaks of 'kicking someone upstairs'. It referred to a nominal advance in position which, in actuality, resulted in the person's reduction of influence and of power.

A member of the House of Commons, also referred to as 'the Lower House', could lose his seat only at the next election. However, there was one way to remove him prior to elections, and that was by having a peerage conferred on him. His new rank made him automatically – and for the rest of his life – a member of the House of Lords. Metaphorically, he was raised to the 'Upper House'. But the honour bestowed on him was of a dubious nature. As a Lord now, he could no longer exert his influence in the Commons and prove himself a thorn in the side of those who resented his presence there.

Such a procedure of 'kicking upstairs' has moved beyond the political sphere and been applied to other areas of public and commercial life.

KILL WITH KINDNESS

To kill with kindness seems an absurd and far-fetched saying, yet it is based on an historic event dating back 2500 years.

In spite of the harsh laws Draco introduced in Athens in the seventh century BC, this statesman enjoyed great popularity. Thus when, in 590 BC, he visited the theatre at Aegina to watch a play, the large audience was overjoyed by his presence. In their enthusiasm they exuberantly tossed at him their coats and caps, which were so numerous that Draco was buried under their weight. Unable to extricate himself, he suffocated. It could truly be said that he was killed with kindness.

An alternate version of the event claims that it happened not at a show but at a gathering specially convened in Draco's honour. It got out of hand, with fatal results.

Shakespeare's *The Taming of the Shrew* is the literary source of the phrase itself. In the play, Katharina, the Shrew, a most stubborn and petulant female, is pursued by Petruchio for her wealth. The comedy describes his numerous and devious attempts to lead her to the altar and achieve his aim. Ultimately cowed and subdued, Kate becomes an obedient wife. Petruchio, indeed, is well justified in observing that 'this is the way to kill a wife with kindness. And thus I curb her mad and headstrong humour.'

Now completely taken out of context, Petruchio's words constitute yet another Shakespearian contribution to the wealth of present-day idioms.

KINKY

Nowadays, the term 'kinky' is associated with out-of-the-ordinary conduct, mostly of a sexual nature.

This has not always been the case. For more than a millennium, a 'kink' (of a Nordic root) was very harmless and meant nothing more than a twist or a bend. It was used in this sense when referring to the kink in the tail of a Siamese cat or, very early, to the kink in a rope. It was also applied when speaking of bending one's knee or bending over.

The English, on adopting the word, created from it all that was 'kinky' – which, to start with, still had an innocuous meaning. Americans, on the other hand, came to describe the curly hair of blacks as kinky, doing so first around the 1840s.

Meanwhile, however, the use of the word expanded (alas in a downward direction) to be applied to people who were mentally abnormal, who had twisted minds. It was only in much more recent days that kinky took its place in the vocabulary of sex, there to assume its freakish connotation.

KIPPERS

It might be surprising to learn that an ordinary kipper has a most interesting past: with ingenuity, something regarded as almost tasteless became a most desirable food.

The name of the kipper, some authorities say, reflects on its colour which, not unlike that of 'copper', became its linguistic root. According to another opinion, kipper refers to the fish's spawning. In fact, kipper was the Old English name for the male salmon in its spawning season. Sold untreated it was of poor quality. However, it was soon discovered that when dried and smoked its taste greatly improved.

Fourteenth-century John Woodger, a curer of fish in the small fishing village of Seahouses on the Northumbrian coast of England, is credited with having created what is now the kipper. He did so by applying to herrings the process used for preserving salmon – 'kippering' them. After having first cleaned the fish and split it, he immersed it in brine and then smoked it. In no time, people took a liking to the new product, which they much preferred to the merely dried red herrings, as they were extremely salty. Such was the birth of the kipper, which for a long time was (and remains) part of the traditional English breakfast.

KISSING THE BLARNEY STONE

Widespread is the tradition that anyone who kisses the Blarney Stone will be endowed with the gift of the gab, an irresistible power of persuasion. However, to achieve this feat is not easy.

The stone is built into the main tower of Blarney Castle, near Cork, Ireland. To kiss it, people have to climb up a steep winding staircase to the very top of the tower and then, whilst lying flat on their back, lower their head backwards over the edge to reach it. In order not to fall down the precipice they must hold on tightly with their hands to two iron bars, whilst someone else firmly grasps their feet.

An exceedingly difficult undertaking, it is considered well worthwhile because of its (imagined) effect. A popular verse light-heartedly tells us:

> There is a stone there
> That whoever kisses,
> Oh, he never misses
> To grow eloquent.
> 'Tis he may clamber
> To a lady's chamber
> Or become a member
> Of Parliament.

An Irish myth relates how this triangular block of limestone in the castle's parapet gained its miraculous power. As the gift of a witch, she had presented it to a former lord of the castle in gratitude for a special service he had rendered her. Incorporating it in his stronghold, he positioned it so that only the bravest and most daring would attempt to reach it.

It was a wise precaution, lest all Irishmen – and, more so, thousands of people coming from abroad – would acquire a persuasive and eloquent tongue which would stay with them for the rest of their lives – something greatly to be avoided.

KITSCH

Art objects of inferior quality are described as *kitsch* or *kitschy*. The derogatory term has been adopted from the German, surprisingly without changing even a single letter!

In German, *Kitsch* is 'rubbish' or 'trash'. Art critics in Munich were the first to apply the word (around 1870) to pictures of that very genre. From there, the description spread worldwide.

Paradoxically, fifty years later a German authority, Ferdinand Avenarius, claimed that the term was actually of English origin and was derived from the 'sketch'. Art lovers, not prepared to spend a lot of money for a painting they wanted to purchase, would ask for a sketch of it which, of course, would be of a much inferior quality – mere *Kitsch*. Avenarius's was an extraordinary and totally unacceptable assertion. It implied a disfiguration of the English 'sketch' which would even surpass the most outrageous object of the kitsch type.

Much more convincing is the suggestion that the German *Kitsch* was derived from the verb *kitschen*, used for 'scraping up the mud from the street with a coat-hanger'. The creation of an inferior artist looked just like the resulting *Kitsch*, the muck gathered and flattened out.

KNOCK INTO A COCKED HAT

To knock into a cocked hat spells defeat. A blow has been struck so effectively that whoever or whatever was its target has been flattened.

The phrase has been traced to the reign of King Louis XV of France, whose courtiers, to indicate their nobility, donned large wigs. This made any additional headgear superfluous, even as protection against the wintry cold. However, foppishly, if not actually wearing a hat, they continued to carry one. Made of soft cloth, they were able to fold it up and stick it under an arm. In the terminology of the time, a hat so doubled up was called a 'cocked hat'.

The choice of name had yet another explanation. To make their hat truly distinctive, they decorated it with a badge. This was known as a *cockade*, from the French *coq* for a 'rooster'. A well-chosen symbol, it was most appropriate for the men, whose general demeanour reflected their arrogance and self-perceived superiority. Did they not strut about just like the fowl? As if to debase their memory, 'to knock into a cocked hat' became the description of a thorough defeat.

A second, totally different hypothesis links the phrase with a style of pin bowling popular in the seventeenth and eighteenth centuries. According to its rules, players had to set up the nine skittles in the form of a triangle. Whoever succeeded in knocking down all but the three outer pins won the game. As the description of these three remaining pins reminded bowlers of the shape of a cocked hat, they spoke of the game as having been 'knocked into a cocked hat' – that is, of being of no further use.

LABORATORY

The laboratory, playing such a significant part in the advance of modern technology and medicine, is literally a place of 'labour' or a workshop. With all kinds of ideas 'worked out' in it – in short, '*elabor*ated', the name is well merited.

LAME DUCK

If ducks are known to waddle along, a lame duck is even more restricted in movement, getting almost nowhere! A fowl so stricken suffers from a real handicap. As a most suitable figure of speech, 'lame duck' has been applied to people who suffer great disadvantages. Crippled by misfortune or by loss of money, they become ineffectual – truly 'lame ducks'.

It is generally believed that the saying was first given currency in the nineteenth century by the London stock exchange. Defaulters were described as lame ducks, a name that soon spread.

People's body language is said to have further contributed to the popularisation of the expression. Unable to meet their obligations, some became so depressed that, like a lame duck, they waddled away.

In the twentieth century, United States politics gave the phrase a new lease of life. It was the practice that whilst a new president and his administration were elected early in November (on the first Tuesday after the first Monday of the month), they assumed their office only in March. Those defeated were expected to carry on their duties until that late date, though anything they did or decided during that long period could be annulled and therefore was of no real consequence. They were mere seat warmers – 'lame ducks'. The description soon captured the people's imaginations. It was given even wider publicity by the twentieth Amendment to the Constitution, proclaimed in 1933, specifically designed to address this situation. Halving the period of the ineffectual holding of office, it brought the date of assumption of duties by the newly elected administration forward to 20 January (ever since celebrated as Inauguration Day). Not inappropriately, the American people soon nicknamed the legislation the 'Lame Duck Amendment', further popularising – and perpetuating – the saying.

LARDER

The larder nowadays is understood to be the small room or cupboard, mostly located off (or in) the kitchen, in which food is kept. However, its original function was much more restricted and, in fact, explains the very choice of the name.

In the beginning, the larder was reserved for the storing of bacon. The French word for bacon is *lard* which, in English, became the description of rendered-down pig fat. Logically, therefore, the place in which the bacon was kept was called (in Old French) *lardier*.

Subsequently the English adopted the name in the form of 'larder'. Always practical, they expanded its use, allowing it to serve for the storing of all kinds of provisions.

'LATE' MR OR MS X

To be 'late' can have several meanings. It may merely refer to the delay of one's arrival, due either to circumstances beyond one's control or unpunctuality.

'Late', however, also serves as a euphemism for someone who has passed away. It is used thoughtfully as a mark of respect for the departed and out of consideration for the bereaved. Not wanting to call the deceased 'dead' showed deep understanding. After all, the departed lived on in the hearts and minds of those left behind.

Altogether, death was too harsh and emotive a word. It might reopen wounds and intensify the anguish of loss. This was yet another reason why people began to replace the gloomy 'dead' and 'deceased' with the much more gentle and deferential reference to the person who had died as the 'late lamented' Mr or Ms X. Eventually the 'lamented' was dropped altogether, only to keep the 'late', though by itself it made little sense.

At one time, the deceased was also spoken of as 'lately' Mr or Ms X, using the adverb in the sense of 'of recent'. However, such a description lacked dignity and intimacy; it treated the individual like an object whose absence meant little to the person speaking of them. Changing the 'lately' to 'late' was much more appropriate. Considerately, it spoke of someone who, though no longer present in person, was still vividly remembered.

All these interpretations might be seen to reveal great sensitivity of feeling. Nevertheless, even this custom, like so many others, was based on superstition. This imagined that the mention of death by name (or anything associated with or derived from the word) might have ominous effects. Death might regard it as a summons and return to collect some new victim.

LAUGH ON THE OTHER SIDE OF ONE'S FACE

To laugh on the other side of one's face indicates a sudden reversal of mood, from cheerfulness to depression, from satisfaction to deep regret.

A colloquialism based on experience, it contains some wise counsel. Those who (perversely) take pleasure in the misfortunes of others may regret having done so, as they, too – perhaps sooner rather than later – may be struck by the same fate. Then, figuratively, they will have to 'laugh on the other side of their face'.

An alternate version replaces the face by the mouth, equally relating to the dramatic change from mirth to dejection. It is so easy for those of an evil character to laugh at others' pain, not realising that they might become the victims of the identical fate.

LAUGHING ALL THE WAY TO THE BANK

Liberace has been a modern idol, adored for his music, his personal image and his performance style. In spite of his worshippers' adoration, many critics tore him apart. They castigated him for his gaudy and showy outfits, his stage trappings and his sugary melodies.

After an especially savage write-up he was asked how, in view of the critics' laughing at him, he could still carry on. His answer was short and to the point: 'I, too, am laughing – all the way to the bank.' What did it matter if so-called experts made fun of him, so long as his music brought him a fortune?

Anything Liberace used to say or do was taken note of, both by his admirers and detractors. It was no wonder, therefore, that his retort to his critics was soon picked up. In fact, surviving him, it has become a general observation by people who, successful in making money, disregard criticism of the way in which they have 'earned' it.

LAUNDERING MONEY

Just as 'Watergate' has entered the modern vocabulary from the political scandal that rocked America and the presidency of Richard Nixon in the 1970s, so have some of the phrases used during the subsequent investigation. The 'laundering of money' is one of them. It referred to the cleaning up – the 'laundering' – of ill-gotten funds to remove any traces of their source.

Such funds were passed back and forth between various bank accounts and even countries before eventually being returned – cleaned up, as it were, or laundered – as if legitimately acquired.

LEADING ARTICLE

Some terms appear so obvious that, paradoxically, they are misunderstood and are therefore truly misleading. This applies to what has been called the 'leading article' (or 'leader') of a newspaper. Misinterpreting its description, people assumed that it was so named because it was the most important feature of the paper.

Newspapers are meant to fulfil several functions. Primarily, and at their best, they supply objective and up-to-date accounts of world and local news. Significantly, too, they try to mould their readers' attitudes to current affairs by expressing views which support the policy represented by the paper, its editor or, at its very worst, its owner.

Not to confuse (and misguide) the readers, the two functions are strictly kept separate. Opinions are restricted to the 'leader page'.

Just as a leading question aims at influencing (if not predetermining) an answer, so a leading article tries to *lead* the reader to judge the subject the way its writer intends him to.

A totally different explanation links the description not with the content of the feature discussed but with its typographical presentation. To make this section of the paper particularly eye-catching, the articles it contains are given extra space. This is achieved not only by employing larger type but, even more effectively, by spacing its lines further apart than in news items. Using early methods of printing, this was attained by inserting strips of *lead* in between the lines. The metal used for this purpose suggested the name of the *lead*ing article!

Technological progress later rendered this practice obsolete. Its meaning totally forgotten, the lead-enriched feature no longer made any sense. Giving it a new and yet most appropriate meaning, the lead article was changed into the leading article, still preserving in its spelling and name the now discarded metal strips.

LEAVE IN THE LURCH

Those who are left in the lurch are in a helpless and hopeless position. They are like the gamblers at dice to whom they owe the description of their cheerless situation.

The saying originated from a sixteenth century French board game not unlike backgammon or cribbage (which possibly developed from it). Known as *lourche* or *l'ourche*, Anglicised this became 'lurch'.

A player who was 'left in the lurch' could not win, as his opponent was too far in front. The word 'lurch' itself literally related to his being 'abandoned' and 'defeated'. Going back further to a German root, *luerzen*, it spoke of being 'deceived' or 'cheated', as those who, deserted by others when in trouble, might well have regarded themselves.

It has been suggested that card players appropriated the saying from an earlier phrase used in connection with poachers and highwaymen. At the time, 'lurching' and 'lurking' were synonymous. On occasion it happened that poachers 'lurking' about to set their traps were caught in the act. He who failed to make their escape was said to be 'left in the lurch'.

The same applied to a gang of robbers. On being discovered 'lurking' – lying in wait for a victim – they quickly dispersed. In doing so, however, they had to abandon one of their partners in crime. He was 'left in the lurch'.

LEFT HOLDING THE BAG

Unfortunate indeed are those who are 'left holding the bag'. Deserted by others, they are left all on their own to clean up a mess, sort out a problem or, at its worst, to be made the scapegoat for something they played no part in or were only partly responsible for.

Bags may hold a great variety of objects – or they may contain nothing at all. The latter was implied in a phrase, current in the sixteenth century, out of which its modern rendering developed. 'To give the bag' then referred to dishonest servants who left their place of work not only without having given due notice but who carried away with them the contents of their employer's purse or bag, which was thus left empty!

The earliest mention of the saying in literature can be traced to 1787, to the first comedy ever written in America. Its Boston-born author, Royall Tyler, was an eminent lawyer. In the play, one of the characters remarks that the General had 'sneaked off and given us the bag to hold'.

LEGEND

The legend, like the stories it has handed down through the ages, has taken a meandering path to reach its current meaning. The term itself originated in the realm of religion. To start with, it was applied not to ancient myths but to factual biographical data. The word was first used in this sense in a work by Jacob of Voragine, a thirteenth-century Italian Dominican writer and Archbishop of Genoa. Among his books was a collection of stories about the saints. He entitled the work *Legenda Sanctorium*, 'Things to be Read of the Saints'. *Legenda* therefore simply meant 'to be read'.

The attractive tales Jacob had written to foster piety could be read only by those conversant in Latin. This prompted William Caxton to publish them in an English translation. He gave his edition the new title of *The Golden Legend*. The book was to become his most popular production – in fact, the first printed best seller in the world.

Jacob never attempted to embroider his saintly stories. All he wanted to do was relate factual data on the lives of the saints, and do so with authority and authenticity. However, with the passing of time, people romanticised many of the stories, adding features from myths, folklore and mere imagination so that, eventually, the term legend changed its meaning to take on a new (and its present-day) connotation. Still something 'to be read', a legend does not present a source of historic facts but an enchanting product of human fancy or, at the very least, traditions of the past greatly embroidered.

LEMON

Colloquially, a failure or anything disappointing is referred to as 'a lemon'. Similarly, whoever rejects a request or disapproves a suggestion or plan derisively does so with the words that 'the answer is a lemon'.

To many it might be a source of wonder how this vitamin C-rich fruit came to adopt such negative connotations. Its very taste may account for it. As lemons are sour, their acidity may have led people to adopt them in their speech as a pungent rebuttal.

On the other hand, this vocal lemon may owe its existence to modern gambling. It may have been plucked from the fruit machine, otherwise known in Australia as the 'pokie'. When, after players deposited coins in the slot, a row of lemons came up, it indicated to the players that they had won – nothing!

LIGHTHOUSE AND MINARET

Lighthouses were initially beacons, lit to guide ships safely into harbour. They were preceded by fires kindled on hill tops to help sailors out at sea to find their way at night. Only subsequently did the lighthouse assume the additional role of warning of hidden rocks and hazards.

One of the most famous lighthouses of ancient times was the Pharos at Alexandria, Egypt, so called after the island on which it was situated. Built of white marble in the third century BC, it was regarded as one of the seven wonders of the ancient world. The historian Josephus (AD 37 – c. 105) relates that the fire on its top could be seen from a distance of more than 50 kilometres.

According to legend, its name was the result of a misunderstanding. Returning home from Troy, Helen and her husband Menelaus lost their way. Stranded on an island, they did not know where they were. Coming across an old man, they asked him what island it was. He replied that it was Pharaoh's. Menelaus misheard, and understood him to say Pharos, a mistake perpetuated ever since.

When the Moslems conquered Egypt in 640 AD, they transformed one of the top chambers of the lighthouse into a place of worship. It seemed so apt a choice as, with their prayers ascending to God, it was nearest to heaven.

Surprisingly, this lighthouse serving two separate functions was responsible for the naming of the minaret. Now a slender tower (part of every mosque) from which the faithful are called to prayer, literally it referred to the lamp (*manarat* in Arabic, from *nar* for 'fire') of the original lighthouse that guided the ships.

The Pharos no longer exists. According to a manuscript kept in the monastery of Montpellier, it was destroyed by an earthquake on 8 August 1303.

LINEN PRESS

In the beginning, the name of the linen press described exactly the function it fulfilled. To smooth out laundered clothing or sheets, these were placed, still damp, between two large wooden boards which – by means of wooden screws – were pressed together.

The linen press of this sort has become obsolete. However, as a relic of the past, it has survived to be applied as the name for the cupboard in which linen is kept.

LITTLE KNOWLEDGE IS A DANGEROUS THING

The observation that 'a little knowledge is a dangerous thing' is not a proverb, as is sometimes assumed, but a misquotation from the works of Alexander Pope, the great English poet. In his didactic poem *Essay on Criticism* (published anonymously at the early age of twenty-one, in 1711) he discusses the laws by which critics should be guided. Giving examples, Pope shows how they often misjudged works of art, no doubt to the detriment of the writers.

What Pope really said was that 'a little *learning* is a dangerous thing'. The misquotation is a telling example of the frequent phenomenon of people merely repeating something another has said, without checking its accuracy, and thereby often perpetuating a mistake.

LOBBYING

Lobbying has become an accepted – though at times abused – political institution. It aims to influence parliamentarians and governments on behalf of or in favour of certain groups and interests. The practice derives its description from the lobby (the vestibule, corridor or special room) in which delegates met the legislators. It was in 1640 that the anteroom to the British House of Commons was first so called.

Far removed from politics, however, the lobby originated in monasteries. Many people used to call on the monks' help, and did so for the most diverse reasons. They sought not only spiritual guidance but medical advice and, themselves illiterate, clerical assistance in writing letters on their behalf or reading out to them correspondence they had received.

Without making a prior appointment, they frequently arrived at the same time and, being so great in number, had to wait their turn. They did so in the passageway that led into the monastery which, to protect them from inclement weather, was covered with foliage. Called after its 'leafy' roof, it became known as the 'lobby'. Derived from *lobum*, a medieval Latin root for 'leaf', the word is also recalled in the German *Laube*.

When society became secularised, citizens turned to the government for help. The special waiting rooms provided for them took over the original ecclesiastical name of the lobby.

LOOK BEFORE YOU LEAP

Aesop, that one-time Greek slave of the sixth century BC, has given to the world a rich legacy in the form of his *Fables*. Each of his tales, whether authentically his or merely attributed to him, illustrates some wisdom which, though of such ancient origin, has never dated or become obsolete.

That you should 'look before you leap' (from his fable of 'The Fox and the Goat') is such a piece of advice. It reminds people not to act rashly but to first give due thought to what they are about to do or to say.

According to the story, a fox had fallen into a well. In spite of all his efforts, he was unable to extricate himself. In the cunning way of foxes, he contrived to persuade a goat which was passing by to join him. Temptingly he told her that she should not miss tasting the refreshing water at the bottom of the well. Not hesitating or giving it any further thought, the goat leaped down to drink of it. The moment she touched the ground the fox sprang on to her back and jumped out, leaving the poor goat behind, helpless down at the bottom of the well.

LOOSE END

To be 'at a loose end' portrays people who are left with nothing to do. There is no fixed aim in their minds, no purpose or objective to drive them on. They have been compared to a horse which, untethered after a day's work, is let loose in the fields. There it roams hither and thither, aimlessly. The very picture of a horse with a loose end of rope hanging from its neck might well have suggested the idiom.

LOSE FACE

The face is one of the most impressive and expressive parts of the human body. People are remembered by their faces, and by their mien reveal – often unknowingly – what they think or feel. To 'lose face' has thus generally been interpreted as to be humiliated in front of others. To 'save one's face', accordingly, means to save one's reputation.

Such an explanation, however, ignores the meaning given to 'face' in Chinese culture, in which it has no connection with one's actual countenance. In Chinese tradition it describes a person's status within the community. To the Chinese, to 'have face' therefore means to be admired and respected. Accordingly, to 'lose face' (*Tiou Lien*) is the worst fate that could befall a person in the significant sphere of human relationships.

Western culture, ignorant of this special connotation of 'face', mistakenly took the word literally. Adopting the phrase, but not knowing of its different application, it has often been a source of puzzlement.

LOSE ONE'S MARBLES

Anyone losing their marbles is going insane. The marbles referred to might well be the (slightly mispronounced) French *meubles*, a word at one time also used in Britain, and still retained in the German *Möbel*, for furniture and other movable ('mobile') personal property. It could happen that, in extreme cases, those who unluckily lose their possessions become distraught and mentally unhinged. Telescoping the cause and the effect makes the loss of the furniture and the loss of one's mind synonymous.

Another bizarre explanation of the phrase links it with an alleged incident in the life of a boy who was especially fond of playing marbles. One day a monkey, suddenly appearing out of nowhere, snatched all his marbles. The loss of these playthings was so traumatic to the young child that his mind became unbalanced!

'LOT' OF LAND

To call a piece of land a 'lot' recalls a seventeenth-century American custom relating to commonly owned sections of land (referred to as 'crown land' in Anglo-Saxon countries). To impartially apportion it to individual people, 'lots' were drawn. Literally, they were a-*lot*-ted their part.

LOTUS AND LOTUS-EATERS

Called 'the fairest of flowers', the lotus has played a significant role in almost all Eastern cultures for well nigh 5000 years. The name of a great variety of plants, though mostly of a type of water lily, the lotus has been the subject of numerous myths and has served as a powerful symbol both in religion and art. It has done so in Egypt and Greece, in Indian and Chinese faiths as well as in Islam.

The Greeks believed that to eat of its fruit gave humans the gift of forgetfulness, a yearning for idleness and the happiest of dreams. Odysseus is said to have met in North Africa such a lotus-eater. Drugged by the legendary fruit, he felt free from all cares and responsibilities and had only the one desire – to lie in the sun and eat lotus forever.

Dominant is the place occupied by the lotus in the Buddhist faith. It portrays Buddha seated on the plant, which is one of the 'Eight Buddhist Emblems of Happy Augury'.

Manifold thus is its message, addressed to all people. Though often growing in murky waters, the flower itself is pure and unsullied. It inspires all that is exquisite with its beautiful scent. Closing up at the coming of darkness, at dawn it opens again, expressive of life's unceasing renewal. Not least, the lotus speaks of the flowering and unfolding of the spirit and of all existence. According to Moslem tradition, a lotus tree grew in the seventh heaven, next to God's throne.

LUKEWARM

To repeat a word usually intensifies its meaning. However, this is not the case when speaking of something that is tepid as being 'lukewarm'. Derived from the Old English, 'luke' is merely another word for 'warm'. Hence, lukewarm is a tautology, saying the same thing twice over: warm-warm.

LYING IN STATE

'Lying in state' is a solemn mourning custom intended to give people a chance to honour a leader or notable person who has passed away.

For a deceased monarch or national hero to lie in state has become a traditional way to give all citizens an opportunity to pay their last respects. Reverently they line up, at times in their thousands, to silently file past the deceased.

In contrast to this modern objective of the practice, lying in state was begun for a totally different reason. It was introduced in a period of history when regicide was not uncommon. Its purpose was to assure loyal subjects that their monarch had died a natural death. Showing no wounds or other signs of violence, they could see for themselves that he or she had not been the victim of foul play.

m

MAH-JONGG

The 800-year-old Chinese game of mah-jongg is called after the sparrows which were among the figures depicted on its tiles. Replacing cards, these tiles were introduced in Ningpo, the city of ivory carvers. These earliest pieces were made of ivory or bone, glued to bamboo.

MAKE MONEY HAND OVER FIST

Whoever makes money 'hand over fist' does so quickly and without difficulty. The figure of speech comes from the sea. It recalls a sailor's or fisherman's pulling in of a rope to fasten his boat, or the hoisting of a sail or hauling in of a net with a catch of fish. In a simple operation, an individual performed the task by putting one hand over the fist of the other.

MALAPROP

Trying to show off, uneducated people not infrequently make use of words they do not understand and therefore misapply them. At times they do so with hilarious results. Suited so badly for the purpose, their words referred to what indeed they were – 'out of place' or 'little to the point' (in the original French, *mal a propos*). Contracted into one word, this created the malaprop.

However, it was only through Richard Sheridan's comedy *The Rivals*, which he wrote in 1775, that the term caught on and became part of the English language. He chose Malaprop as the name of one of his characters, a lady who distinguished herself again and again by such malapropisms. Typical examples were her speaking of being 'as headstrong as an allegory on the banks of the Nile' and saying that 'if I reprehend anything in this world, it is the use of my oracular tongue, and a nice derangement of epitaphs'.

MAN OF MY KIDNEY

Old fallacies, once adopted in the idioms of everyday speech, have a tendency to stay on permanently. People rarely ever question their relevancy.

'A man of one's own kidney' is a telling example. Rarely used nowadays, it survives as a description of the close rapport between two people, of their similarity in temperament and attitude. Combining two different organs, it could be said that 'a man of my own kidney' is 'a man after my own heart'.

In biblical times, with medical knowledge still very restricted and, in parts, faulty, the kidney was regarded as the seat of affection, passion and temperament. Well-known now is the true function of this organ and its importance to life. That modern medicine has given the phrase a new and vital meaning may make people wonder whether it was the result of mere coincidence or an eerie kind of foresight on the part of the ancients. For, with kidney transplants having become part of daily medical practice, the typing of kidneys for their compatibility is an essential procedure. Thus the old phrase has acquired a new significance in searching for, and hopefully finding, 'a man of my own (type of) kidney'.

MAN OF STRAW

Attempts at tax evasion and dishonest business deals in general have created peculiar expressions and figures of speech. And it's not just from the modern age that they have arisen. 'Man of straw' was an expression used as early as the sixteenth century to refer to a man who, in all kinds of dubious transactions, acted as a mere front. He belonged to that unscrupulous class of people who made their living by giving wrong testimony. Hanging about outside law courts, he was prepared – for an appropriate 'fee' – to swear to anything.

To be easily identified by any would-be 'customer', the man would have a wisp of straw stuck into his shoes, hence his designation as a 'man of straw'. The expression is still retained for individuals of his type.

MANHOLE COVERS ARE ALWAYS ROUND

A manhole cover, as a description, no longer exists: the 'man' in the hole is sexist. To call it a 'person' hole just does not seem right and might be subject to misinterpretation. Hence in its modern terminology it has been referred to – rather ponderously – as an 'underground service access cover'.

Hardly ever noticed or commented on is its shape, which invariably is circular. There is a reason for everything. A round cover can never fall into the round hole.

MANX CAT AND WHY IT HAS NO TAIL

The tailless Manx cat is peculiar to the Isle of Man, that island situated in the Irish Sea between England and Ireland. It is claimed that the Manx was first bred there more than three centuries ago and, according to legend, was a cross between a cat and a hare! No evidence supports this bizarre genealogy. In fact, tailless cats have been found as far away (and apart) as Malaysia and Japan.

'Manx', of course, records the cat's habitat. The name has no relationship at all with any (hu)man. Of a Celtic root, it referred to the 'rock' of the island.

Regulations strictly define the requirement for a feline to be classed as a Manx. Its taillessness must be absolute. Even the vestige of a tail disqualifies it, making it a 'stumpy' but not a Manx. Stories abound as to how the cat lost its tail.

Oldest of all is the legend that asserts that it occurred in Noah's time. All the animals had assembled in the Ark except for the cat, who was still searching for a mouse she was determined to bring on board with her. The rains had started to pour down and time was getting desperately short. Noah could no longer wait for the missing animal. To prevent the waters from entering the vessel, he had to slam its door. Just as he did so, the cat was squeezing through, and the shutting door severed its tail.

Another story credits the Spanish Armada with having given the Manx cat to the island. In the fleet's abortive attempt (in 1588) to invade Britain, one of its vessels was shipwrecked on a reef near the Isle of Man, with all hands lost. The ship's cat, a tailless tom, was the only survivor, and he succeeded in swimming ashore. It did not take him long to find a mate and, by his genes, to give the island a new source of wealth!

According to a local tradition, a superstition robbed the cat of its so expressive extremity. Manx people believed that whoever accidentally trod on a cat's tail would suffer a fatal snakebite. Happily, thus, one family welcomed the birth of a tailless cat. Making use of its malformation, they saw in it the promise of good fortune – in more sense than one. In no time they bred a new strain of tailless cats.

It was man's cruel warfare, so yet another story relates, that was the real cause of the Manx losing its tail, which was once so beautiful, bushy and distinctive. When the Irish were occupying the island, they admired the cats' tails. But they also envied their foes' headgear, which was ornamented with birds' feathers. Trying to outdo them, they killed cats and cut off their tails to decorate their helmets with them. A pregnant mother cat, watching the horrendous sight, was much concerned for her offsprings' fate. She retreated to the highest mountain to give birth there to a large litter. To ensure her kittens' survival she bit off their tails. To protect future generations, her secret was handed on to all other mother cats. Soon nature asserted itself and 'de-tailing' became an inherited trait. Ever since, Manx cats have been born tailless.

MAPS PLACING NORTH ON TOP

At times, people take things so much for granted that they never think of questioning them. This applies to the traditional map of the world. Who has ever wondered why it has north at the top, with Australia consequently being 'down under'?

In classical Greek and Roman days, map makers actually used to place the east uppermost. There was a valiant reason: nothing surpassed the east in importance, for it was the direction from which the sun rose. As the sun bestowed light and warmth to the world, they worshipped it as the supreme deity.

Medieval Christian cartographers continued the pagan tradition of putting east at the summit. They did so for their own, equally significant, motives. According to the Bible, Paradise was located in the east. Therefore, to their minds and faith, east crowned the universe.

The eventual practice of letting north head the map goes back to second-century Ptolemy of Alexandria. The most celebrated geographer and astronomer not only of his time but of generations to follow, his teachings were accepted like religious dogmas. Because he had drawn his maps with the north at the top (though no one knew why), his orientation had to be right, authentic and in accordance with fact. His example has been followed ever since!

MARSEILLAISE

The Marseillaise, which was to become the French national anthem, was originally written in 1792 as a war song for the French army on the Rhine.

At the time, Joseph de Lisle, its composer, served as a young army engineer and was stationed at Strasbourg. The story goes that chance so willed it that he overheard the mayor of the city express his regret that the soldiers lacked a truly patriotic song. A man of many talents – a violinist, singer and poet – de Lisle immediately set to work and, on that same night (24 April), wrote and set to music a song. He felt that it would be the answer to the mayor's quest.

The very next day, it is said, the mayor had it sung. In no time it was adopted by the local military band, and within two months it was sung at a patriotic banquet in far off Marseille.

Soldiers about to march to Paris were given copies of the song. Records recall that singing it roused the men so much that they were able to cover a daily distance of 26 kilometres. It was an unprecedented feat, particularly as it was the height of summer and they were pulling heavy guns.

To the sounds of the then still unnamed song they entered Paris. Instantly, it captured the imagination of the people. The mere (and solely accidental) fact that the soldiers had come from Marseille made Parisians refer to it as 'the song (*chanson*) of Marseille', a name soon to be shortened to and perpetuated as the *Marseillaise*. Thomas Carlyle, the renowned Scottish essayist and historian, observed at the time that its sound 'will make the blood tingle in men's veins; and whole armies and assemblages will sing it with eyes weeping and burning, with heart defiant of Death, Despot, and Devil.'

Ironically, de Lisle was a staunch royalist who, when asked to swear allegiance to the new republic, refused to do so. He was then imprisoned, and barely escaped the guillotine. On his release he rejoined the army. Wounded, he was pensioned off. At the age of seventy-six, de Lisle – the man who had written the words and composed the music for a song whose effect on history has never been equalled by any other – died a poor man. At the time, his pension had been so small that kind friends had had to supplement it.

Intriguing is the claim that the national song was actually the result of a dream de Lisle had after having fallen asleep over his harpsichord. On awakening, he vividly remembered it and, in great exaltation, noted it down – the words and the music of the Marseillaise!

MARU

Japanese merchant vessels have the word *Maru* appended to their individual names. Now an internationally recognised symbol of the Japanese mercantile fleet, its use goes back well nigh 500 years. It has been given a variety of explanations.

One legend links it with the mystical past and a messenger, called Maru, sent from heaven. Maru had taught a nobleman the art of building ships, who, in turn, had revealed it to his people. To permanently acknowledge the divine source, the Japanese decided to add his name to their ships.

Another tradition tells that Maru was an ancient sea god. To obtain and keep his good will, the Japanese suffixed his name to all their merchant vessels.

In the Japanese tongue, *Maru* means a 'ring' or a 'circle'. The most perfect figure, it symbolised anything that was supreme, complete and faultless. A ship equipped with everything to serve its needs, therefore, merited to be called '*Maru*'.

Symbolically, *Maru* also expressed hope, and in early days was thought to even ensure protection. A circle displayed on a ship's flag and added to its name would make sure that it would have a safe voyage. Braving all the hazards of the sea – in other words, completing a circle – it would return home without mishap.

In the early days, Japanese castles were circular in shape, as – accordingly – were their enclosures and the bastions defending them. This tradition led the Japanese to give them the name of a circle – *Maru*. And was not a ship like a floating castle? *Maru*, thus yet another explanation claims, was a most appropriate suffix for its name, providing both prestige and – magically – invulnerability.

During the Kamakura period (1192–1333), wholesale merchants used to add to their individual trade name the word *Maru*. It was almost a foregone conclusion, therefore, that when, for the transport of their goods, they launched their own ships, they conspicuously displayed the word on them too. Even after the firms had closed down, *Maru* was retained and applied to every ship of the merchant fleet.

In ancient times, Japanese people made it a custom to add the word *Maru* (and prior to it, *Maro*) to anything or anyone they particularly cherished. Similar to the modern 'darling', it expressed intimacy and affection in personal relationships and, applied to possessions, deep sentimental attachment. Parents suffixed it to their children's names. Owners applied it to their highly prized properties. They used *Maru* as a term of endearment for their favourite musical instruments, their pet hawk, their dog. Samurais bestowed it on their most precious sword or the finest of their blades. In like manner, the addition of *Maru* to the name of a ship denoted how greatly it was treasured.

Different from the English tradition which refers to a ship as a 'she', the Japanese regarded their vessels as male. Therefore *Maru*, once a boy's name, was considered appropriate for its designation.

MAVERICK

Maverick is one of the many contributions Americans have made to the English tongue. Applied to an unbranded calf or, more generally, any stray animal, it is also used to describe a person of independent mind who refuses to be dictated by anyone as to what to think or say. Such a person is often in politics.

The term perpetuates the name of Samuel Augustus Maverick (1803–70). A rancher and native of Massachusetts, he settled in Texas on a large property of almost 400,000 acres (160,000 hectares). The owner of a large herd of cattle, he did not brand any of his animals but let them roam about freely and unidentified over his vast property. Why he did so has been explained in several ways.

First of all it was said that he refused to adopt the practice of branding because he regarded it as cruel. A second suggestion has it that Sam believed in people's honesty and therefore did not think it necessary to brand his stock. Unscrupulous neighbours took advantage of his trusting nature and, getting hold of his unmarked cattle – soon dubbed by Sam's name as 'Mavericks' – put their brand on them.

Contrary to these suggestions, many have said that the real reason for his failure to brand cattle was great cunning on his part, for he could claim that all unmarked cattle were his property!

Whichever way, the name of the naive (or exceedingly shrewd) rancher was soon applied to all unbranded animals. Once the term caught on, it spread far and wide, eventually to be applied in the 1880s not just to animals but to non-conformist politicians who refused to toe any party line.

MAYFAIR

Mayfair, the name of one of London's most fashionable districts, recalls an event of the seventeenth and eighteenth centuries. This was a fair held on the site in aid of a leper hospital which then stood where the present-day St James' Palace is located. Initiated by royal order (of which king it is uncertain), the fair was to take place annually every May and extend over a period of six days.

The fair experienced its ups and downs. Starting small, it grew to vast dimensions and attracted such unruly crowds that by 1701 it was regarded a nuisance. Stopped for some time, it was revived again, finally to cease altogether in 1760.

The hospital no longer exists and gone with it is the need to raise funds. And yet, the fair survives: at least it does so nominally, joining both the month and the fair to create the district now known as Mayfair.

MEALY-MOUTHED

Those who are mealy-mouthed do not speak up. Some might even regard them as insincere hypocrites. Oddly, though, the term by which they are known speaks kindly of them as 'sweet'. Literally, mealy-mouthed is derived from the Greek *meli-muthos* for 'honey(ed) speech'. Honey-tongued, as it were, their sweetness is that of saccharin – too sugary!

An alternate etymology does not link the saying with honey at all but discovers in it a German expression. 'Mealy', it claims, is the Anglicised version of the German *Mehl* or *Mahl* for 'flour' or 'meal'. Those whose mouths are full of food will not speak up, lest, in the process, their mouth might spill much of its nourishing contents.

METRE AND THE METRIC SYSTEM

Metre merely means 'measure'. Its adoption as a unit of measurement was the result of the French Revolution's attempt to update systems and replace obsolete ideas and cumbersome practices.

At the time, no uniform system of measurement existed. Mainly to rectify the confusion this created, the 1789 revolutionaries appointed a committee of scientists whose deliberations led to the acceptance of the metre as the new unit. They did not determine its length haphazardly or arbitrarily but based it on the (erroneous) notion that it was to constitute one ten-millionth part of the distance on the earth's surface from the pole to the equator, which was one forty millionth part of the earth's circumference. Though in 1791 the National Assembly generally adopted the suggestion, it took another seven years before the entire metric system was completed.

To permanently preserve the exact length of a metre, a bar of platinum alloyed with iridium was deposited in Paris. On it were two marks which indicated its extent.

Different classical languages were used to differentiate between the fractions and multiples of the new metre. A Greek prefix indicated a fraction and a Latin one a multiple. As 'hundred' was *centum* in Latin, the *cent*imetre designated a distance of a one-hundredth part of a metre. With *mille* being the Latin for 'thousand', a *mill*imetre was a one-thousandth part. On the other hand, *khilioi*, the Greek for thousand, created the *kilo*metre, indicating a distance that extended over a length of 1000 times a meter.

MEWS

In searching for the origins of place names, among the great variety of London thoroughfares one of the most intriguing is the mews. Small and often narrow, they were the original sites of cages or enclosures specifically built to house falcons and hawks during their moulting season.

This description was derived from the Old French *muer* for 'to change' which, in turn, from the Latin *mutare*, was responsible for all modern 'mutations'. In their case it was applied to the 'changing' of the birds' feathers, their 'moulting'.

Later, with hawks and falcons no longer in residence, the mews came to be used as stables. Then, with the coming of the motor car, they became garages. Recently they have been transformed into most attractive, fashionable and not inexpensive apartments, but still known by the original name of 'the mews'.

MEXICAN JUMPING BEAN

The Mexican jumping bean has puzzled many and has been regarded as a mere myth by those who have never seen the bean jump. However, it does exist, and a moth is responsible for the wondrous occurrence.

This bean moth lays her eggs on the flower of the plant. When this turns into fruit, it encloses the eggs. Once these have developed into moths, their movement, intended to pierce the walls of the bean, makes it jump. It is a 'natural' explanation of a mystifying phenomenon.

MIDAS TOUCH

Some people have all the luck. No matter what they attempt to do, they are always successful. Nothing ever goes wrong and all their enterprises gain them profit. Theirs is what is called the 'Midas touch'.

Midas was the legendary ruler of Phrygia, a kingdom once situated in Asia Minor, now part of modern Turkey. Midas had done a special favour to Dionysus, the god of fertility and wine. In appreciation, Dionysus promised to grant him any wish he liked. The king lost no time in voicing it: everything he touched should turn into gold!

Not having considered the implications of such a wish, Midas was soon to regret his rashness and greed. Any object the king touched turned into gold. This happened not only to the flowers, the furniture, the crockery and the cutlery in his palace but, to his horror, also to anything he was about to eat or drink. Threatened with starvation, Midas had to beg the god to take pity on him and reverse the spell . . .

The Midas touch thus preserves a legend but, at the same time, gives a warning to those who are too ambitious and are never satisfied with what they already have. Like Midas, they might deeply regret their covetousness.

MIGRAINE

The excruciating headache which usually affects only one side of the head and is often accompanied by nausea and visual disturbances has become known as migraine. Like so many other medical terms, its name comes from the Greek and refers to the ache felt across 'half' (*hemi*) 'the skull' (*kranion*). Medieval Latin combined the two Greek words and stream-lined them into *migraena*. Subsequently, the French took over the word, rendering it in their tongue as *migraine*, a description adopted worldwide.

A debilitating condition, only those who have experienced migraine can truly appreciate the agony it causes. Being so widespread, the ailment has become the subject of numerous misconceptions and unsubstantiated claims. Among them is the fallacious belief that intelligent people in particular suffer from migraines. Nevertheless, it has been observed that often perfectionists are its victims. No doubt in some cases it is the result of an allergy.

MILKY WAY

Astronomy owes the Milky Way to Greek myth and, according to one of many legends concerning it, to adultery among the gods.

As the result of having spent a night with the god Zeus, Alcmene of Thebes gave birth to Heracles. To escape from the wrath of Hera, Zeus' wife, she took the child outside the city, abandoning him there to die.

Pallas Athena, the goddess of wisdom and good counsel, aware of what had happened, was determined to save the baby. Cleverly she devised a scheme not only to keep him alive but to ensure his immortality. In pursuit of the plan she invited Hera to accompany her on a stroll, on which, as if by mere chance, she guided her to the very site where Heracles had been left. Pallas Athena had no difficulty in arousing Hera's pity and persuading her to nurse the hungry child. Ravenous, Heracles sucked her breasts with such force that Hera's immortal milk spurted out across the heavens. There it has stayed permanently as 'the Milky Way'.

Other races and cultures, equally fascinated by the wondrous phenomenon in the sky, gave their own interpretations. Some believed that it was the path along which the angels trod. The Chinese called it the heavenly river and the Basutus regarded it as the way of the gods. To American Indians it was the road that ghosts took to the spirit land.

The Greeks actually believed that this luminous girdle of stars encircling the night sky was a belt of milk. For this reason they called it, in their language, a 'galaxy'. Derived from the Greek word *gala* for 'milk', the term has been retained in modern astronomy.

The galaxy of ancient Greek myth also survives in the modern world as a figure of speech. Totally ignoring its milky substance, the word is applied to a gathering of brilliant people – luminaries in their own field, here on earth.

MOGGY – THE CAT

Moggy is now an endearing name for a cat. Originally a pet name for a calf or a cow, London cockneys adopted it for their feline companions, maybe because city life left no room for befriending bovine creatures.

To start with, Moggy was a nickname for Margaret. However, it was a name reserved for only a certain class of girls. Paradoxically, this definition widely differed geographically. In the south of England, and not least in London, to call a girl Moggy was almost an accolade, a nickname used in admiration of her good nature and kind-heartedness. In the Midlands, on the other hand, the name was applied to a slatternly woman. This diversity of heritage is now embodied in Moggy, the pussycat. Whether as a nice girl or a slut, the former Margaret changed from being a real cow to end up as a cherished cat.

MORE HONOUR'D IN THE BREACH THAN THE OBSERVANCE

Generally, to speak of a custom as being 'more honoured in the breach than the observance' is taken to express the view that it is more frequently broken than followed. However reasonable an assumption, it totally misinterprets the original sense of the saying, which is a quotation from Shakespeare's *Hamlet* (Act 1, Scene 4).

Hearing the firing of a gun and the flourish of trumpets, Horatio asked the prince what they signified. It was a traditional custom, Hamlet explained, to thus accompany the king's drinking of a toast. However in his opinion it was an unworthy tradition which would be better abandoned. Indeed, it would be 'more honour'd in the breach than the observance'!

The modern application of Hamlet's words therefore completely misunderstands what originally they were intended to convey, namely how in certain circumstances it is more honourable to break a custom than to follow it.

MORON

To call someone a moron is to insultingly suggest that the person so described is dull witted. In the original sense of the Greek word from which it is derived, *moros*, the person was truly 'foolish'.

Molière chose it for the name of a clown, a character in one of his comedies. At the time, this seventeenth-century French dramatist would never have guessed that almost three centuries later an American psychologist, Professor Henry H. Goddard, would make use of it. Borrowing 'the moron' from Molière, he suggested the term as a scientific designation for feeble-minded people whose mental development was not greater than that of an eight to twelve-year-old. In 1910 he put his proposition to a meeting of the American Association for the Study of the Feeble-minded. They voted and agreed on its adoption. 'Moron' was thus added to 'idiot' and 'imbecile', terms already in existence for other degrees of mental retardation.

If a redeeming point needs to be found for the moron, at least it can be said that he has the special distinction of being one of the few people to have entered the international vocabulary by the vote of scientists.

MOUNTING A HORSE FROM THE LEFT

The custom of mounting a horse from the left goes back to the days when men, to defend themselves, carried long swords. As most people are right-handed, the sword was strapped to their left hip, enabling them, in an emergency, to draw it quickly. To prevent the sword from getting in the way, it became necessary to mount the horse from the left.

MS

For at least 300 years, addressing men by the title of 'Mr' did not reveal their marital status. A woman, on the other hand, by her designation 'Miss' or 'Mrs', was immediately able to be categorised as single or married. Did this not present what in modern parlance might be described as a strident case of discrimination by prefix? The situation was paralleled by the custom, at one time particularly followed in some Anglo-Saxon lands, for only women to wear a wedding ring.

It was merely a matter of time and education, helped along by the Feminist Movement, before women demanded to be given equal rights with regard to keeping private their 'attachment', or lack of it. (Such sentiments expressed, almost echoed, the attempt made during the French Revolution to wipe out altogether any distinction between the sexes by referring to them simply by the common title of 'Citizen', 'Comrade' or 'Person'.)

Other efforts to remedy the situation were made from time to time, not least so in the United States. Representative Jonathan Bingham of New York, for instance, had urged the elimination of any sexual identification on all official Federal forms, except when necessity so demanded. One of the US departments paved the way by officially making it optional to use a title which lacked marital designation.

The abbreviation 'Ms' as a non-marital title ended all loathsome differentiation. It combined both the 'Miss' and 'Mrs' by taking the first and last letters of each title. Claims differ as to who had been the first to suggest it. It is on record that in 1952 the National Office Management Association of Philadelphia had advised the use of the abbreviation to solve 'an age-old problem'. The Women's Liberation Movement, another claimant, recommended it as the most suitable title, though did so only in the late 1960s. Roy F. Bailey, a Kansas journalist, asserted to have preceded all others by almost ten years.

The 'Ms' has now been generally accepted. However, many people still wonder how to pronounce this two-letter word. Left to the individual, it is being variously rendered as Mees, Meez or Miz, though the latter has been adopted most widely.

MUDSLINGING

Mudslinging, now a figure of speech used to describe political smear campaigns in particular, goes back to an actual practice. In the democratic system of the ancient Romans, candidates for office used to walk about in white togas [see CANDIDATE]. Those not sharing their views and policies showed their contempt by pelting them with mud. This badly stained their togas and made the public question the veracity of their claim. Unscrupulous opponents of the candidate, trying thus to undermine them and prevent them from being elected, were convinced that the more dirt they threw at a person the more chance there was of at least some of it sticking.

Though the physical practice has long been abandoned, its metaphorical survival is recalled in modern political life when politicians, trying to score points, defame their opponents. In effect, they continue to throw mud at them. Unfortunately, this has altogether besmeared the name of all politicians and, in the eyes of many, made politics a dirty business.

MURPHY'S LAW

'If anything can go wrong, it will' is the briefest rendition of what has become known as Murphy's law. No one knows for certain the identity of the Murphy thus remembered. Most of the claims are apocryphal, though all agree that the saying is of recent coinage, possibly dating from some time in the 1940s.

According to one theory, Murphy's law gained currency through a cartoon character of that name, who was featured in an educational publication of the United States' Navy. It depicted Murphy as someone who could never get anything right.

Another suggestion credits George Nichols to have been responsible for the popularisation of the expression. The project manager of a Californian aviation company, he worked at an American air force base at a time when tests relating to the crashing of aircraft were carried out. When yet another experiment failed as a result of a vital mistake made by a certain technician, Captain Murphy, under whom the technician worked, was overheard by Nichols to remark: 'If there is any way to do things wrong, he will!' His observation was thereafter perpetuated by speaking of 'Murphy's law'.

MUSCLES

Muscular men pride themselves upon their prominent biceps. Would they ever believe that the etymological root of 'muscle' is 'a little mouse'?

There are two explanations for the peculiar choice of name: Greek and Roman, scientific and popular. According to the first explanation, to the early Greek anatomists the dissected muscle looked very much like a small rodent and it was this that prompted them to call it by the mouse's very name. To ancient imaginative Romans, on the other hand, the sight of sinew rippling under the skin made it appear as if a little rodent was scurrying beneath. It was the reason why they called it, in their Latin tongue, *musculus* – 'a little mouse'. This term then intruded into almost every European language in the form of the muscle. It shows how a mouse can get under one's skin and stay there for a lifetime.

MUSTARD

Mustard, though a mere condiment now, has played a multiple role in history. Apart from its use at the table, it has found a place in biblical parable, proverbial lore and even folk medicine.

There is a great variety of mustards, differing in taste and constituents – French, English, German and American mustards, and even mustard sauce.

Mustard was already known 2000 years ago to the Romans, who loved its taste. They introduced the condiment into Britain, where it became popular not least because it was so much cheaper than the hot spices imported from afar.

The parable of the mustard seed, told in Matthew (13: 31–35), relates it to the kingdom of heaven. The least of all the seeds, when it is grown the grain becomes the greatest among the plants.

Mustard has served too as the source of some memorable sayings and at least one peculiar custom. Americans came to speak of those able to accomplish almost impossible tasks as 'cutting the mustard'. The proverb 'After meat, mustard' referred to one's coming too late to be of any help. Mustard's hot flavour and tartness gave rise to speaking of people who were zealous as being 'as keen as mustard'. And mustard plasters were once applied to cure colds in the chest!

There are several claims as to the origin of the plant's name. Mustard no doubt preserves the 'new wine', called *must*, once mixed with the crushed seeds of some plants of the cabbage family, making a seasoning ready to be served at the table. The

French assert, on the other hand, that mustard owes its description to them. By a circuitous route it perpetuated the city of Dijon, famous for its mustard. Philip, the Duke of Burgundy, who resided in the town, in 1382 bestowed upon the city a coat of arms in recognition of its product. Its motto, using the traditional Latin, read *multum ardeo* – 'I ardently desire'. Rendered into the then current French, it was changed into *moult-tarde*. Very appropriate to the substance, this meant to 'burn much'. People soon (mis)read the word as *moutarde* which, in no time, became the word for 'mustard'.

NAIL ONE'S COLOURS TO THE MAST

NARK

NEW YEAR'S RESOLUTIONS

NICE

NINCOMPOOP

NINE OF DIAMONDS — THE CURSE OF SCOTLAND

NITTY-GRITTY

NO FLIES ON SOMEONE

NOMINAL CHARGE

NOT BY A LONG CHALK

NOT FIT TO HOLD A CANDLE

NOT AN IOTA OF DIFFERENCE

NOT TURNING A HAIR

NTH DEGREE

NAIL ONE'S COLOURS TO THE MAST

Nailing one's colours to the mast publicly proclaims that one intends to make a firm stand. Regardless of the cost, one will never give in.

The phrase has been adopted from the sea. In naval warfare, a ship proudly would display the national flag – her 'colours'. She would only lower it if, in the unfortunate case of being outgunned and subsequently defeated in battle, she had to communicate her willingness to surrender. The practice held more than symbolic meaning. Flying at half-mast enabled the victor to proclaim his superiority by mounting his flag above hers.

However, if a flag was nailed to the mast it could never be lowered. Under no circumstances would the ship submit to the enemy; the crew would fight on to the last man.

NARK

With no home of their own, gypsies have travelled through many countries, never settling down permanently in one place. Speaking their own language, known as Romany, they have left their traces in many a local tongue, not least so in English. Best-known of such contributions is the 'nark', used to denote a spy and, particularly, a police informer. Derived from *nak*, the Rom word for a 'nose', it was well chosen. After all, spies and informers are persons who poke their noses into other people's affairs.

In a more generalised way, the word nark was also applied to a spoil-sport, and used to describe someone who was spiteful and liked to nag.

NEW YEAR'S RESOLUTIONS

New Year's resolutions have become a common feature of celebrations on the eve of the new year, though in most cases such resolutions are soon forgotten. However, in early pagan days they were taken very seriously. Based on crucial considerations and beliefs, they did not concern one's own way of life but were intended to ensure the gods' blessings. The resolutions took the form of a promise of a gift to them. This would gain the gods' good will and protection during the ensuing twelve months.

This initial type of resolution was then superseded by another kind, still steeped in pagan religious thought. In the ancient world, New Year was seen not merely as a change of date in the calendar but as a new beginning, the turning over of a new leaf. By making the right kind of resolution one was magically given the chance to change one's course of life! A solemn moment and decision, it was reinforced by the superstition that to break any of the resolutions made would bring bad luck.

NICE

'Apples and rice' is cockney slang for 'nice', and so is 'sugar and spice'. So pleasant a word nowadays, it comes as a surprise to learn that 'nice' has a dismal past, an ancestry of which it cannot be proud. Its history offers a telling example of an expression which, through the ages, has changed its meaning several times. Happily for 'nice', it has done so by becoming ever more user-friendly.

Derived from the Latin *nescius* for 'not knowing', in the beginning anyone so called was regarded as an ignoramus or a simpleton. Shakespeare used nice in this sense.

With the passing of time, however, people came to apply the word not to those who lacked knowledge or wisdom but to insignificant and unnecessary things. To be referred to as 'nice' continued to be really not so nice, in the modern sense of the word.

Yet this presented only a second stage in the evolution of the term. By the next stage it was to be reserved for the fastidious person, the pedant. Finally, the word lost all its pejorative connotations to be used for the friendly, the delightful and the kind.

NINCOMPOOP

The variety of languages involved in tracing the roots of the nincompoop shows that to take people as fools is not reserved to any one nation or group. A universal phenomenon, the naming of the nincompoop may have many sources.

In his famous *Dictionary of the English Language*, Dr Johnson derives nincompoop from the Latin phrase *non compos (mentis)*, the description of a person of 'unsound mind'.

Others have discovered in the nincompoop a curious combination of the most varied words, all linked with stupidity. Some have claimed it to be a disfigured rendering of Nicodemus, for Nicholas, by which name the French, in the form of *nicodeme*, used to call a half-wit. The added 'poop', it is said, was taken from the Dutch *poep* for a 'fool'.

A popular nickname of Nicholas was Nick(um) or Noddy. Dickens used the latter name in *Our Mutual Friend*. Lengthened again, this was expanded to Noddy-peak and thence became nincompoop. Not improbably, the custom of calling a dull-witted person a 'ninny' further reinforced all that the nincompoop stood for.

Enlisted army personnel did not always take kindly to their superiors. At times they expressed their dislike, if not contempt, for the non-commissioned officer by the (linguistic) mutilation of his rank, cutting it short to 'non-com'. Using it as a term of derision, they then stretched it into the nincompoop, a name now applied to any fool.

NINE OF DIAMONDS – THE CURSE OF SCOTLAND

Not superstition or cartomancy but a gruesome historic incident is said to have made the nine of diamonds 'the curse of Scotland', an unlucky card.

It was on the back of this card that the Duke of Cumberland, after the battle of Culloden (16 April 1746), wrote the order for the massacre of all of Prince Charles Edward Stuart's remaining men.

The choice of the nine of diamonds was the result of an ominous chain of events. Before the Duke occupied Culloden House, Prince Charles had stayed there. To pass the time and, possibly, to steady his nerves, Charles had played a game of cards with some of his officers. During the game, the nine of diamonds got lost.

It so happened that it was in this very room that, after the battle of Culloden, the victorious Duke was informed of the Jacobite soldiers who had managed to escape from the carnage. Determined to destroy even this remnant of fighting men, he issued the command to pursue and totally annihilate them, sparing not a single life. The officer so directed refused to carry out the cruel order unless it was given to him in writing. In search of paper, the Duke tripped and, catching his foot in the carpet, discovered beneath it the missing nine of diamonds. He used its back for the ignominious instruction. Ever since, the nine of diamonds has been held to be unlucky.

There are a number of other explanations for the 'curse'. One traces it to the coat of arms belonging to the Earl of Stair, Sir John Dalrymple, the then Under-secretary of the State of Scotland. The Scots bitterly hated him, and for several reasons. In 1692 he had been responsible for the notorious massacre of the Macdonalds at Glencoe, the 'Glen of Weaping', and in 1707 he had played a significant part in bringing about the Union of Scotland and England. His coat of arms displayed nine lozenges, calling to mind the nine of diamonds playing card. And according to this story it was he who had written an order to massacre the Macdonalds on this very card, which therefore became known as 'the curse of Scotland'.

Yet a further tradition tells that, during the reign of Mary, Queen of Scots, a thief had tried to steal the monarch's crown. Though he failed in his attempt, he nevertheless succeeded in removing nine of its diamonds. To replace them, a heavy tax was imposed on the people who, appropriately, dubbed the 'nine [of] diamonds' the curse of Scotland.

In the game known as Pope Joan, the nine of diamonds was called 'the Pope' who, in the eyes of the fervent Protestant

Scottish believers, was the anti-Christ – a curse indeed. In the game of Comette, on the other hand, this denomination was the winning card, causing much loss of money to many Scotch gamblers. No doubt it proved a curse to them.

Finally, to offer yet another explanation for the origin of the phrase, there is the unsubstantiated and unhistorical claim that every ninth monarch of Scotland maltreated his subjects.

NITTY-GRITTY

Getting down to the nitty-gritty of things involves dealing with the basic facts, the essentials of a situation.

One tradition tells that American blacks of the Deep South were responsible for the expression. Living in dire poverty, without running water or bathing facilities, it was difficult for the blacks to keep clean. The nitty-gritty combined two of their most troublesome personal afflictions: the nits in their hair and the specs of dried up excrement which stuck around their anus. To get rid of the deeply encrusted 'dirt' – the nitty-gritty – they had to get down to the very roots of the hair, scratching it with their fingernails. It was an experience that could well have suggested the figure of speech which portrays the concentration involved in the matter as getting down to the nitty-gritty.

NO FLIES ON SOMEONE

Long before it was known that flies were carriers of disease, people did everything within their power to chase them away or to catch and swat them. This they learnt to do by being constantly agile and alert, characteristics admired in any situation. Ready at all times to take action, some learnt to prevent even a single fly from settling on them.

Thus, to say of anyone that there are no flies on them is a genuine compliment, for it is the result of their vigilance and never-resting alacrity.

NOMINAL CHARGE

The 'nominal charge' advertised for goods, services or admission to functions is a misleading term. Now understood to convey that the price or fee to be paid is minimal, the words do not actually say so. 'Nominally' means 'in name only'. Whenever anything is given or done at a nominal charge, it should be for a token payment only, which nowadays is never the case.

NOT BY A LONG CHALK

That something far from completed is described as 'not by a long chalk' goes back to the former use of chalk to note down (on the ground or on a blackboard) the scores made in a game or the number of drinks consumed at inns.

If, in a game, the points gained were very few, it could truly be said of the player that 'not by a long chalk' could he be declared the winner.

The phrase also goes back to a custom in public houses of old. The landlord extended to trustworthy patrons a certain amount of credit. Each time he served them a drink he would chalk it up on a board. Encouraging his guests not to worry as to the number of pints and quarts they had already imbibed, he would say to them that 'not by a long chalk' had they reached their limit.

Quite possibly, the idiom might simply be an abbreviated version of the more expressive 'not by a long line of chalk marks'.

NOT FIT TO HOLD A CANDLE

The specific conditions of each period in history create their own occupations. Then, with changed circumstances and the advance of technology, some of these become redundant. Nonetheless they often survive in idioms, sayings and similes, expressions which constitute an integral part of everyday speech. Though they made good sense when first introduced, to latter-day ears they become puzzling.

A typical example is the link boy. Even his name will confound present-day readers. But for more than 300 years, ever since the sixteenth century, he played a significant role in London's night life. The streets of the metropolis were still unlit then, and those who could not afford their own carriage or were unable to use coaches had great difficulty in moving about in the pitch dark.

Young lads answered the need. For a fee (or a tip) they would light up the way with a flaming torch. This was known by the now archaic 'link', derived from the Greek word *luchnos* for 'lamp'. It was made of tow and pitch. Belonging to the down–and–outs and, unskilled in any other task, they were fit only for this menial service – 'to hold the candle'.

Many of them, greatly tempted by the opportunities offered by their employment, developed into petty thieves. This explains a feature and warning which appeared in a London newspaper of 23 September 1818. Entitled 'Caution Against Link Boys', it read:

As a gentleman who had been to Covent Garden Theatre on Monday evening was stepping into a coach fronting the box door, he felt something tugging at the handkerchief in his pocket; and on looking round he perceived the link-boy, who had been very officiously holding a light, running off under the coaches with a handkerchief. The coachman pretended to point which way the link provider was going by exclaiming, 'There he goes, sir, under the coaches and amongst the horses!' Thus these link-boys are something worse than a nuisance; and now that the exterior of the theatre is so admirably illuminated with gas, we wonder that the proprietors do not secure the public against such offensive and useless interruptions.

As London was large, with streets going in all directions, it demanded of these link boys a knowledge and alertness which many of them did not possess. They were 'not [even] fit to hold the candle'.

Lamps now light up the streets and the link boy's function is outdated, but we continue to speak contemptuously of someone we regard as inferior to another as being 'not fit to hold a candle'.

NOT AN IOTA OF DIFFERENCE

The Greek letter *iota* developed from the *yod*, a Phoenician, Hebrew and Aramaic character. The smallest of letters in these alphabets, originally it depicted a hand. The letter served not only in the spelling of words but, because of its minuteness, became a figure of speech for anything puny, negligible in size or insignificant in importance.

It is used in such well-known expressions as people 'not caring (or giving) a jot' or something making 'not an iota of difference'. It also explains the Gospel passage (Matthew 5:18) in which Jesus declares that 'Till heaven and earth pass away, one jot or one tittle shall in no wise pass away from the Law, till all be fulfilled'. The words proclaimed that his message did not intend to negate or abrogate his Hebrew heritage, the Mosaic law, but, on the contrary, by revealing its depth and meaning, to preserve it. The quotation has caused much controversy and commentary.

NOT TURNING A HAIR

Those who, in the most trying of situations, remain unruffled, showing no fear, anger or distress, are said to 'not turn a hair'. A strange phrase, it owes its existence to a phenomenon observed among horses.

A hard-worked horse breaks out in a sweat which roughens even the best-groomed coat. In the equestrian terminology of the early 1800s, its hair 'turns'.

NTH DEGREE

Some philosophers have tried to explain the world in mathematical terms and to make it fit into computable formulae. Mathematics itself has contributed its own figures of speech to the vocabulary of life, ranging from zero to infinity.

In mathematics the letter 'n' denotes an indefinite number, particularly the final and greatest in the scale of values. Applied generally, the symbol created the expression 'to the nth degree', meaning the utmost and most extreme stage of anything – the very last, the be-all and end-all.

O

OFF ONE'S OWN BAT

Sport has been a fruitful source of striking expressions. These have been applied to the most diverse situations in the game of life. To do anything 'off one's own bat' – that is, to achieve an aim or to reach a goal without relying on anyone else – comes from cricket. It is taken from a batsman's success in being able to reach the end of an innings without being dismissed, with all the runs scored 'off his own bat'. Expanded, the expression is also applied to people who embark on a task without asking for anyone's help or permission.

OLD DART

How, in Australian slang, England became known as 'the Old Dart' is uncertain. Some say that the nickname for the old country goes back to the early convict days, though opinions still differ in which way it arose.

According to one view, a number of the convicts arriving in Australia had been previously held in the (infamous) *Dart*moor Gaol. It was their practice to shorten words, a custom which has become common with Australians. No wonder, therefore, that soon they came to refer to their former domicile as the 'Dart', eventually extending the term to embrace the very country in which it was situated.

There is also the claim that not a prison but an old English symbol created the term. To be easily identified and not to be misappropriated, British government property used to be marked with a broad arrow – a dart. The clothing supplied to the convicts thus carried a large dart on its back. It was not surprising, therefore, that as a memento of the early days the dart got stuck – in the language. Detached from the sordid association it had in the past, it came to assume an almost endearing quality, and so their ancestors' country of origin was referred to as 'the Old Dart'.

OLD HAT

Though today the custom of wearing hats has almost totally been abandoned, the hat has nevertheless been retained in a number of telling sayings. Requiring people to keep a confidence entrusted to them, they are asked to keep it under their hat. Likewise, anything that is out of date and no longer in fashion is termed 'old hat'. No one 'with it' would ever wear it.

However reasonable and feasible this explanation might sound, there is a much more likely, though exceedingly obscene, explanation. It goes back to at least 1754. This claims that 'old hat' – in the form of a pun – was used by the common people to describe the female sexual organ. It was so called, according to Captain Francis Grose's *A Classical Dictionary of the Vulgar Tongue* (1796), because it was 'frequently felt'!

OLYMPIC RINGS AND THEIR COLOUR

The choice of five intertwined rings as the symbol of the Olympic Games has a significant origin.

Early in the history of the Games, such rings were carved in the altar of the stadium at Delphi. Their number then did not stand, as is wrongly surmised, for the five continents, since these were not known at the time. They represented the five-year cycle of the Games.

That the rings now are coloured black, red, blue, yellow and white has also a reason. At least one of these colours appears on the flag of each of the many nations participating in the Games. Thus the rings are symbolic of the union of all nations and the major purpose of the Games which, as Baron de Coubertin emphasised at their reintroduction in 1896, is to make people meet from far and wide and to create among all nations a spirit of goodwill and peace.

ONE MAN'S MEAT IS ANOTHER MAN'S POISON

Every period creates its own vocabulary, and the meaning of some words, like fashion, changes. Opinions and advice very appropriate in one generation might no longer be taken literally by a later one. A typical example is the well-known observation that 'what is one man's meat is another man's poison'.

It never reflected a vegetarian's attitude, as might be imagined, but dates back to the time when 'meat' covered any type of food. This former application is still recalled in the description of sweetmeats, used for sugary confections of various kinds, at one time cakes and pastries.

ONE OVER THE EIGHT

There are several ways to describe those who are drunk. These can range from calling them a little tipsy to describing them as being 'under the influence'. Until the advent of breath testing, drunkenness was rarely expressed in definite measures. There was only one exception: those who were said to have drunk 'one over the eight'. The figure was not haphazardly chosen but went back to the assumption that to have a ninth drink would make a person drunk.

In those countries in which beer was served in pints, eight pints added up to one gallon, a volume of liquor which was regarded as the most a person could consume and remain sober.

Though the expression is still used, it can no longer be taken literally or seriously, as it fails in various aspects. It does not give any thought to the capacity of the drinker to handle alcohol, which differs from person to person. Nor does it recognise the fact that nowadays beer varies in its alcoholic content. There is no reference either to yet another significant consideration: the period of time over which the eight pints are consumed.

PAL

Close friends have been called by many names, all of them giving voice to a feeling of familiarity. However, no name equals that of the pal in terms of longevity. So short a word, it might be imagined to be a mere abbreviation, or an acronym of a much longer term. But it is not.

Pal is a real word which has the distinction of having travelled much further than any of the other expressions of a friendly relationship, such as buddy, mate and chum. Pal is derived from *pral*, the gypsy word for a (clan) 'brother'. It is yet another example of how gypsies have found a home in the English tongue.

PALM OFF

People who are cheats and are underhand will get rid of things they do not want, or which are of little use and no value, by palming them off onto others who would not suspect the deception.

The expression 'palm off' goes back to card sharpers of the 1600s. When dealing their cards to gullible people they would cunningly manage to look at their own cards. If they found that one of them showed little promise for them to win the game, they would cleverly 'palm' it. This meant that they would conceal it in their palm, subsequently to deal it to one of the other players.

Their trickery has long been outdated. Nevertheless, it survives in the term now applied much more widely in the realm of dishonest tradesmanship.

PASSENGER

Originally, passengers were travellers who passed along the way to their destination. They used any kind of transport, or proceeded on foot. When using transport, it made no difference whether they were driven or drove themselves.

The term became popularised during the Crusades, when thousands of men from various parts of the western world made their way to the Holy Land. As they were seen *pass*ing through many places, their description as 'passengers' became common. This term was never discarded; however, its meaning was changed and greatly restricted. Long after the end of the holy wars, the name passenger came to be applied exclusively to anyone who used (public) transport.

PATSY

A 'patsy' is a dupe who is given or takes the blame for things that he or she has not done. Italian migrants who came to the United States possibly introduced the expression there. It has been explained as the garbled form of the Italian *pazzo* for a 'fool'. Folk etymology, in turn, has supplied two versions as to how this word acquired its meaning.

According to one tradition it recalls the Pazzi family, who lived in Florence in the fifteenth century. The Pazzis had dared to oppose the Medicis who then dominated the city. Their attempt was so hopeless that to all other citizens it was tantamount to plain stupidity. Yet the Pazzis took no notice of the people's view and judgment. Stubbornly, they continued to display their unwillingness to bow to the will of the Medicis, with the inevitable result that they were murdered.

The patsy has also been linked with the Italians' celebration of Easter. In Italian, the Easter feast is known as *Pasqua*, a word closely related (in sound) to *pazzo*. The main course served at the festive meal is roasted lamb, in commemoration of the Paschal lamb once sacrificed by the Hebrews. The name of *Pasqua* reminded the people of the *pasqualino*, the nickname given to a fall-guy. Unable to defend himself, he was easily victimised and led to the slaughter – like the Paschal lamb.

PENSIONS AND PENSIONERS

Modern western society has become deeply concerned to ensure that those who have retired from work have a life free from financial worry. The introduction of a pension scheme has become part of many countries. It is nothing novel. The payment of a pension, at least in individual cases, has been a long-established practice, both in the business world and in the public service. Almost inevitably, those receiving a pension came to be called 'pensioners'.

The term pension is derived from a Latin root and simply says what it is – a 'payment'. Used in this sense, it was once applied generally to any type of periodic payment, including for board and lodgings. Young scholars in particular had to be boarded out for 'payment' – for a 'pension'. Eventually the name was transferred to the very place providing this service.

In this sense 'pension' has been retained in Europe as the description of dwellings offering an inexpensive stay for people on holiday. A story tells of an American on a visit to Paris who was struck by the great number of houses identified outside as 'Pensions'. Not knowing the Continental application of the term, his immediate observation was that he had not realised how many Frenchmen had retired!

PHARMACIES AND BOTTLES OF COLOURED WATER

In the modern commercial world, shop windows serve as an enticement to would-be customers to purchase the goods displayed or, at least, to make them come inside the store and have a close look at the wares for sale. Quite differently, it was an old established custom of pharmacists, or apothecaries as they were then called, to identify their dispensaries by putting bottles filled with coloured water into their windows. These fulfilled the same purpose for the pharmacists as did the three golden balls for the pawnbroker, the red and white striped pole for the barber and the large clock face for the watchmaker. Some modern chemists and drugstores retain this tradition, though merely for historic and decorative reasons.

The suggestion has been made that the coloured bottles placed thus in the windows played not merely the role of a trademark but served a very practical purpose. In order to mature, certain mixtures had to be kept standing for some period of time, a process further accelerated by heat. And what better place was there for it than the show window, exposed to the rays of the sun?

Prior to the days of ready-made medications, pharmacists used to prepare their own draughts, potions and tonics. To make them look attractive (metaphorically speaking, to sugar the pill) they dyed them in a variety of colours. Hence the differently coloured liquids in the bottles displayed.

PIG-IRON

The name of pig-iron has mystified many people. They have wondered what association there could be between the swine and the metal.

In actual fact, pig-iron has little to do with the pig itself. Its description may be due either to an imagined resemblance to the animal of one of the final stages in a now obsolete process of its production or, completely differently, to a system of weights discarded long ago.

On leaving the blast furnace, molten iron used to be conducted through a channel into moulds placed at right angles to it. There it would be left to cool down and harden. When filled, in their fanciful configuration they reminded imaginative onlookers of piglets sucking a sow. This made the workmen speak of the channel as 'the sow' and the ingots as 'the piglets'. No wonder, therefore, that when the solidified iron was removed from the moulds and broken up into pieces, it became known as 'pig-iron'. The name has been kept on long after the old method had been replaced by streamlined modern machinery.

The alternate explanation of how the pig got into the iron sees in it not the animal but an ancient measure, common in England from the time of the Norman Conquest up to the fifteenth century. At that time, 'pig' was used as a standard measure of weight, equal to 70 pounds (31.5 kilograms). It owes the choice of its name to the fact that the average domesticated pig was about that heavy. As each lump of the broken-up pieces of metal also approximated that weight, pig-metal was called after the measurement.

PILL

Though its name has come to be applied to tablets of any form, even if these are far from round, a pill is really a small 'ball', its earliest shape.

Etymologically and historically, the pill can be traced back to the ancient Romans and their games. The balls they used at that time were made of felt which, in turn, was produced from hair, responsible for the Latin name *pila*, derived from the Greek *pilos* for 'hair'.

This spherical body has rolled a long distance to reach its modern and best-known destination. 'The Pill', the popular name for the oral contraceptive, was first developed in the 1950s by Dr Gregory Pincus, an American.

PIN MONEY

Pins, such simple objects, were at one time not cheap. In fact, they were so precious that women needing them for their clothes were given a special allowance from their husbands. This was appropriately called 'pin money'. Once pins became mass produced and obtainable at little cost, the gift was no longer necessary. Nevertheless, the term was retained but given the more general sense of an allowance a husband gave to his wife for the purchase of any minor personal items she fancied.

PLAIN AS A PIKESTAFF

The phrase 'as plain as a pikestaff', now used to emphasise the ease with which a matter can be understood, should itself be very plain in explanation. And yet, its origins have been disputed, with several possibilities propounded as to how it came about.

Some say that it recalls a medieval weapon – a staff with a metal spearhead with which to stab the enemy. To keep a safe distance from the foe, this staff was especially long, which made it clearly visible.

Others believe that its origin is far from bellicose, going back to pilgrims and itinerants of various kinds. On their arduous journeys, these travellers learnt to support themselves on a short stout staff, a forerunner of the modern walking stick. It was totally plain and unadorned.

A third derivation recognises in the pikestaff a (mispronounced) packstaff. Wanderers used it, and so too did peddlers. Slung over a shoulder, it helped them to carry their pack. To ease their burden, the staff they chose was straight and smooth. By constant use it became worn and almost polished. No one could miss it.

There is yet a final possibility. By its conspicuous simplicity, the staff of those itinerants was easily distinguished from the staffs of office, which were traditionally richly ornamented. It justified people to speak of something being 'as plain as a pikestaff'.

PLEASED AS PUNCH

A puppet show presented at English fairs, first in the seventeenth century, popularised the figure of Punch. Traditionally a hunchback, he had a hooked nose and a protruding belly.

Judy, his wife, was also part of the entertainment. She was a domineering, difficult and shrewish person. Nevertheless, in all 'Punch and Judy' shows, invariably Punch proved himself the master, able to prevail in the most trying of situations. Whatever happened in between, he always finished up having the upper hand, and gloatingly would he show his delight. It made people speak, ever since, of being 'as pleased as Punch' when utterly satisfied.

Not indigenously British, the 'Punch and Judy' show was adopted by the English from Italy. It is alleged to have been created (around 1600) in Naples, by Silvio Fiorello, a member of a well-known local family of comedians and actors. In his production, the boastful stock character was known as Pulcinella. The Neapolitan word for a 'young turkey cock', its choice was prompted by the fact that the nose on the mask of the original Pulcinella greatly resembled the bird's hooked bill.

After having Anglicised Pulcinella into Punchinello, the English further shortened the name into 'Punch'.

Punch's name was adopted as the title of Britain's best-known illustrated humorous periodical. First published in 1841, it conspicuously displayed on its cover the figure of Punch.

PLUMBER

In days gone by, people obtained their water from wells, lit up their homes with oil lamps or candles, and cooked their food on open fires. To relieve themselves, they used chamber pots, outhouses or merely a hole in the ground. Civilisation then brought the blessings of running water, gas fires and the flush toilet. To supply these amenities it became necessary to provide houses with pipes. To protect the pipes from becoming corroded, they had to be made of the best material available for the purpose. At the time, this was lead. It ensured durability and rust resistance.

'Lead', in Latin, was *plumbum*, and adopting the classical tongue, all piping in a home was called 'plumbing'. Almost inevitably, the craftsman installing or repairing the pipes came to be known as a 'plumber'. Even when lead was no longer used for the pipes, the name was retained in the plumber.

POP MUSIC AND POP CULTURE

Pop music, as part of pop culture, first made itself known in the early 1960s. The product of the younger generation, it was their (noisy) protest against the old order, a result of and a criticism against the prevailing gross materialism. Living for the moment, the young wanted to be up-to-date and *pop*ular. It was the latter aim and achievement which gave the culture and its music its name.

Initially a local colloquialism, the term 'pop' gained renown in 1970 when the first performance ever of a pop group was staged at the famous Proms held at the Royal Albert Hall in London.

Pop music attracted young people worldwide and in such numbers that, on one occasion in 1973, a rock concert held at Watkins Glen and attended by 600,000 pop fans caused one of the worst traffic jams ever experienced in the State of New York.

POSTMAN AND THE MAIL

Before the advent of the modern fax and internet it was the postman who kept people in touch with each other all over the world. Being such an everyday figure, little thought was given as to why he was so called.

Early on, communications between distant places were kept up by dispatch riders. They made their way across the often vast expanses of land on fast horses. Covering long distances 'post haste', the mounts would get tired, so in order not to slow down the delivery of mail the rider regularly changed his horses. He did so at previously arranged stopping places, where a fresh horse, tethered to a *post*, would be waiting for him. It could therefore be said that the animal was 'posted' – ready for the next section of the route.

In further developments, numerous such post-roads were created, criss-crossing great parts of Europe. Initially they were reserved for official purposes only, and for royalty. With the growth of commerce, however, it did not take long to see the advantage of expanding the service and, for a charge, opening it up to private citizens, particularly those engaged in trade.

The posts to which the horses were hitched have vanished long ago. However, the crucial part they once played in the history of communication is recollected every time the *post*-man calls, and society continues to speak of the post office, though it lacks the posts for horses which were responsible for its name.

In the United States the Anglo-Saxon postman changed into the mailman. This not only updated his name, in keeping with the disappearance of the early wooden tethering posts, but was a most fitting designation. After all, he carried the mail.

The mail presents a story in itself. Literally, it does not refer to the letters sent and delivered but to the bag in which documents used to be carried from post to post. ('Mail' is derived from the Old French *malle* for 'a bag'.) And yet, irrespective of how the letters are now conveyed, people still 'mail' them.

POT

'Pot', now used as a word for marijuana, is said to have been first grown on the loom of American slanguage. Early on, in the south of the United States, it was linked with the making of illicit whisky. Produced in private backyards in a 'pot', this crucible's name was then bestowed on the substance itself. Already applied to something done illegally, the word was to be transferred from a drink to a smoke.

Some etymologists differ. They claim that the root of the word is the Mexican Indian *potiguaya*, of which the 'pot' was all that was left after it had crossed the border into the United States.

PRETTY PICKLE

Whoever is in a pickle is in an awful mess or an awkward situation.

A very descriptive phrase, the victim could be said to be immersed in a briny solution which makes them feel exceedingly uncomfortable and from which it is hard to escape.

The liquids used for pickling are as varied as the objects they are meant to conserve. Brine, salt, oil and vinegar all serve as preservatives.

The worst kind of pickling – in a morbid and (literally) final sense – applied to the preservation of a corpse. If someone died whilst away and their family or community wished their body to be interred at home, it would take some time for the corpse to be returned. To prevent its deterioration it was placed in a pickling solution. To be in a pickle in this sense thus pointed to a most dismal state of affairs – one which was really deadly.

Most likely, however, the phrase has been adopted from the Dutch. Its English equivalent would be 'to be in hot water'.

PUNCH LINE

Basically, a punch refers to a thrusting blow which knocks down an opponent. Adopted figuratively in 'the punch line', it is the last sentence or phrase which forms the climax of a humorous story or joke. Without it, these would remain meaningless. They knock one down – laughing! Fred Allen, the comedian, has been quoted as having said that the punch line is the gag that got you right in the belly.

PUT ON ONE'S THINKING CAP

Caps have played a significant part in everyday life. In the majority of cases, of course, they were worn to provide greater comfort, to protect the head from both cold weather and the sun. However, apart from serving as an item of clothing, the cap came to fulfil yet another significant role.

In some periods, the kind of hat worn indicated one's social status. Dull pupils at school were at one time made to don the dunce cap, a conical paper hat. Its purpose was to humiliate the child and, in an almost sadistic way, to encourage it to do better. On the other hand, in a variety of respected positions the individual's cap became a symbol of wisdom, a sign that the person wearing it was highly qualified in their sphere of work, or steeped in deep thought.

Clerics studying religious lore wore a skull cap. Judges donned their special cap for the thoughtful consideration of the sentence they were about to pronounce. Academics wore a cap with conspicuous tassels to symbolise their learning and scholarship.

It was no wonder, therefore, that anyone pondering over a problem or promising to give serious consideration to a subject was said, metaphorically, to put on their 'thinking cap'. They thus were assumed to become like those learned people identified by a cap which not only indicated their superior intelligence but, perhaps, in mysterious ways, even further fostered it.

PUT ON THE SCREW

However civilised humanity has become, it still preserves traces of former sadistic practices – in, if nothing else, its speech. A telling example is the expression 'to put on the screw', used to describe the act of applying pressure to obtain an objective or a payment.

The saying recalls one of the instruments of torture common in medieval times, and part of man's dismal story of so-called judicial procedures.

To extract a confession or to exact money, a suspect or victim was subjected to all kinds of physical torture. Among the various forms devised by man's cruel mind was the thumbscrew. A clamp or a vice was attached to one or both thumbs of the victim and gradually tightened by turning a screw. Eventually it would exert such unbearable pressure that the person so afflicted could not help but submit – to pay up or to confess to whatever it was they were meant to say, irrespective of what was the truth.

Though the mechanical screw has long been abandoned, its figurative application survives. To verbally put on the screw can inflict immeasurable psychological pain and damage. No longer dislocating a person's thumbs, it can do so to their minds, often permanently.

That prison guards became known as screws might have been a further linguistic application of the medieval instrument. The harsh treatment gaolers meted out to the prisoners led these to compare them to the screws of former days. It might also be possible that the guards were so called because of the 'screws' – the slang word for 'keys' – with which they locked up the prisoners.

PUT A SOCK IN IT

'Oh, go and put a sock in it!' is a colloquial request for someone to stop talking (too much).

The saying dates back to the days of the earliest wind-up gramophone, which used a horn for amplification. Lacking all electronic volume control, it was soon found that, if necessary, the best way to muffle the sound was to put a piece of cloth into the horn. What better object could serve this purpose than a woollen sock!

PUT A SPOKE IN THE WHEEL

Those who, by their interference, try to stop a scheme from progressing are said to 'put a spoke in the wheel'. The expression, like so many others, was time-conditioned and is now antiquated. Nevertheless, it has got stuck on the loom of language and people, without knowing its original meaningful sense, continue to use it as a metaphor.

The invention of the wheel is recognised as the most revolutionary step in the history of transportation. For the first time it enabled people to carry and move loads with comfort and speed. One of the greatest discoveries ever made, the wheel proved the beginning and very basis of modern mechanised civilisation.

Never known to primitive races, no one is certain what first prompted the idea of the wheel. It might have been suggested by the rolling along of loads on tree trunks. This, most likely, was the method by which the ancient Egyptians moved the huge blocks of stone needed for the building of their pyramids.

Archaeologists' finds have suggested that the wheel was first devised in Mesopotamia, the present-day Iraq, as long ago as 4500 BC. The earliest wheels were made of wood and consisted of solid disks. Modified, they were provided with a hub and, subsequently, with hollowed out spaces around the centre. Further expanded, these ultimately led to the creation of the first spokes. The spoked wheel is known to have existed in Asia Minor from around 2000 BC.

Other problems to be solved were how to stop or slow down the wheels once the vehicle was in motion, or to 'scotch' them when stationary. These problems were resolved by a simple method. Carters learnt to carry with them a spare spoke or stout stick. Whenever the need arose, they would thrust it between the spokes of a wheel. Acting as a brake, this practice originated the expression to 'put a spoke in the wheel'.

QUAKERS
QUEER STREET

QUAKERS

The name of the Quakers has an inspiring story, going back to seventeenth-century Britain and a sect whose members called themselves 'the Children of Light' or 'the Children of Truth'.

Claiming direct communication with the divine, they abolished all forms and creeds. They refused to attend the services of the Established Church, to pay tithes, to take oaths and to fight in war. Consequently, in 1650, George Fox, who was the founder of the group, was accused of blasphemy. Appearing on this charge at court in Derby, Justice Bennett found him guilty and sentenced him to a prison term.

Accounts differ as to the circumstances responsible for the first use of Quaker. According to Fox's *Journal* it was because, on the occasion of his trial, he had admonished the judge to 'quake and tremble at the word of the Lord'. Justice Bennett, taking the words as a cue, tried to ridicule Fox and his group by referring to them as Quakers.

In actual fact, Fox did not create the term; he only picked it up from another source. Shortly before Fox's trial, in 1647, 'Quaker' had been used as the nickname for the adherents of a foreign religious sect who were seen during their worship to 'swell, shiver and shake' whenever they felt that the divine spirit moved them.

Far from feeling humiliated or ridiculed, 'the Children of Light' almost at once adopted the name. In the course of the years they changed a name intended to make them an object of fun into one which was highly honoured and respected. Though officially the former 'Children of Light' became 'The Religious Society of Friends', commonly they are still known as Quakers.

Theirs was not the first case in which a designation, given to make fun of or humiliate people, was turned by them into a name of honour. Examples range from the teetotaller to the modern Afro-Americans who, derogatorily called blacks on account of their colour, changed the name into one of pride because, as they said, 'black is beautiful'.

QUEER STREET

The word 'queer' has had many connotations and has spelled out a variety of situations. However, for anyone to be said to be 'in Queer Street' clearly indicated that they were in financial trouble. Why those unfortunate people were so described has been explained differently.

Queer Street has been thought to have its origin in a simple question mark, a 'query'. Put in a ledger against the names of potentially bad debtors, it denoted that it was questionable whether it was safe to extend any further credit to them. That is how, in the way of a pun, those who were 'in Queer Street' could no longer be trusted – money-wise.

An alternate suggestion links the phrase with a former treatment of debtors. According to an old English Common Law, abolished only in 1869, debtors could be sent to prison to be kept there till they had settled their accounts. It was not only a cruel but a stupid method. How, after all, could they find the money if they were thus incarcerated? The courts of Chancery were situated in and around what became appropriately known as Chancery Lane. Among them, in a side lane called Carey Street, was the Bankruptcy Court. It did not take long for those having to appear there to disfigure (or rather, corrupt) the name of its location, changing Carey Street into Queer Street.

Maybe the expression might also have been created by the mere fact that those finding themselves financially embarrassed were in queer circumstances. Not least, in slang Queer Street also stood for something that was 'contrary to one's wish'.

RABBIT, RABBIT, RABBIT

The superstition to say 'rabbit' at the beginning of a new month for good luck goes back to antiquity and to a strange combination of assumptions and beliefs.

The moon has dominated life in many ways. For those who followed the lunar calendar, the beginning of each month was determined by the appearance of the new moon. Aware of the effect of the phases of the moon on the tides, it seemed only reasonable to assume that the whole of life, its ups and its downs, was equally influenced by this heavenly body.

Of all the creatures, the rabbit was regarded as most closely associated with the moon. In ancient Sanskrit literature it symbolised this luminary and was portrayed as its ambassador on earth. Seeing a rabbit gambolling about the countryside whenever there was a full moon confirmed people in their conviction of the special link that existed between the animal and the lunar body.

Several curious features about the rabbit led people to believe that it had occult powers. Born with its eyes open, they imagined that it made the rabbit invincible to the evil eye and gave it magical faculties to annul malevolent influences. Prolific in its reproductive capacity, it was associated with every type of growth: with fertility, prosperity and success.

All these factors combined to make people call on the animal for its aid, particularly when a new month was about to start. The rabbit would not only help to keep the month free from misfortune but, with the increasing moon, bring good fortune and an increase of luck.

To make sure that the call would be heard, it was repeated three times, if possible in quick succession, as the rabbit could not ignore this magic and most potent figure.

RAMSHACKLE

Anything ramshackle is derelict and very shaky. The word itself is a legacy from the Old Norse language, probably originating on the Vikings' tongue. This spoke of the 'search' (*saka*) of a 'house' (*rann*) for the purpose of plundering it, as still retained in anything 'ransacked'. And does not a ransacked house look ramshackle?

READ THE RIOT ACT

Nowadays, when speaking of 'reading the riot act' to someone, the expression is not meant literally. What it refers to is a severe reprimand and warning. However, such an 'Act' really existed. Passed by the British Parliament in 1715, it was prompted by the Jacobite rioting and the unpopularity of the Hanovarian king.

A magistrate or other representative of the law had to read the Act to any gathering of more than twelve persons believed to be about to cause trouble. It informed those assembled that if they did not disperse within an hour of having the Act read to them they would be charged with committing a felony, a crime punishable by death. In later years the sentence was mitigated to imprisonment, in extreme cases for life. The Act was repealed only in 1973.

RECKONING WITHOUT ONE'S HOST

To be 'reckoning without one's host' means to anticipate the result of one's efforts and to come to conclusions without taking into consideration anything the other party may do or think.

The original wording of the phrase, which spoke of 'reckoning *before* one's host', clarifies its sense by putting it back into the context of the circumstances which created it. Guests staying or having a meal at an inn frequently worked out ('reckoned') the cost before their host presented them with the bill. The sum at which they arrived rarely tallied with the amount charged, as this almost always included many an additional item for services rendered.

REMOVE GLOVES BEFORE SHAKING HANDS

Few people still wear gloves, and certainly not in hot climates. At one time, however, it was the custom to do so, and not only in winter. Prior to shaking hands with someone, courtesy demanded that a person remove his or her gloves, a custom still followed in some parts of the world.

Such apparently innocuous item of etiquette in fact covered up a world of distrust, crime and insecurity. The removal of the glove was not symbolic but was the result of a combination of significant factors.

First of all, the bared hand assured the other person that no weapon was concealed in one's palm and, therefore, removed the need of worry on their part of being attacked. It also showed that one was not wearing a poisonous ring, once a very effective way (and not so unusual a practice) of getting rid of a foe. In fact, royal law once decreed that no one who was wearing gloves was permitted to come into the king's presence. Like the modern metal detector, it was a wise precaution.

Going back even further, according to early English law those convicted of a crime were perpetually branded – literally so, by having a mark burnt into their right hand. On meeting people they would be only too anxious to keep it covered up for fear of being shunned by them. Thus for the lawful to display one's innocent past was yet another reason for removing the glove. Courts of law actually demanded anyone about to take an oath to do so.

RIGMAROLE

Rigmarole is a long and complicated procedure. Equally confusing are the claims made as to its origin and even the date of its first appearance which, in different traditions, varies by almost one hundred years.

Most likely, the correct and initial term was not rigmarole but (the) 'Ragman's Roll'. Exceeding 12 metres in length, this medieval document combined numerous oaths of allegiance made by Scottish barons and other noblemen to King Edward I during his progress through Scotland in 1296. Reading them out must have become a most monotonous practice which, no doubt, led to the name of the roll being associated with tedium. In addition, with so many seals attached to it it must have presented a ragged sight. Jointly, these were sufficient reasons to give the Ragman's Roll its new connotation. With its original meaning and purpose forgotten, its name was streamlined (or corrupted) into rigmarole.

Another theory traces the term to much less serious circumstances, to those of a medieval game of French origin. The various people taking part in it drew scrolls of parchment containing descriptive verses and clues. The players had then to guess their meaning. As the chief character represented in the game was *Ragemon le Bon*, 'Ragman the Good', the entire set of small scrolls was called after him, to become the Ragman's Roll. Playing the game must have been quite confusing – truly a rigmarole.

With its true origin uncertain, the name of the scroll(s) in time acquired the present-day meaning. As confusing as ever, rigmarole metaphorically preserves the original 'scroll', no matter what the items were which rendered it so ponderous, long-winded and incoherent.

ROB PETER TO PAY PAUL

Those who pay one debt by incurring another, or take something from one person to give it to someone else, are said to 'rob Peter to pay Paul'.

The practice portrayed by this metaphor was condemned as early as 1380 by John Wycliff, the great English reformer. He called it an act of robbery of which God most certainly would not approve.

The phrase has also – and most commonly – been traced to a transaction within the Church that took place in 1550. At the time, St Paul's Cathedral in London was in dire need of repairs but had no funds to pay for them. To have the work done in spite of it, the ecclesiastical authorities used money which legally belonged to St Peter's Abbey at Westminster. Hence it could rightly be said that they robbed (St) Peter to pay (for St) Paul.

It has been pointed out, however, that the transaction was not a case of misappropriation of funds but was in fact completely legal, based on a transfer of property. A Royal Letter Patent of 17 December 1540 had raised the Abbey Church of St Peter to the status of a cathedral, giving it total independence. When, ten years later, St Peter reverted to its former, lower, position, the order was revoked. Once again reunited with St Paul's Cathedral, it became part of the diocese of London with its own property (and finances) becoming part of the vast estate of St Paul's. Quite properly thus, it was said, its revenue could be used to help where it was needed most – which, at the time, was for the repair of the grand cathedral, St Paul's. Rightly or wrongly, the fact remains that what had belonged to St Peter was used to pay for St Paul.

ROMAN NUMERALS

The earliest and most obvious way to count was by using one's fingers. As the right hand was needed to tick them off, the left served as a kind of abacus.

Noting down the numbers one to four they merely copied the outstretched fingers, creating in what is now known as the Roman numerals the I, II, III and, originally using four vertical strokes, also the IIII. The figure V was provided by the entire hand, with its four fingers pointing upward and the thumb stretched out away from them at an angle.

To go beyond that number, both hands were needed. Adding the fingers of the right hand enabled people to continue counting – up to ten. It was a simple process of addition, in every sense of the word. To find a symbol for ten presented no problem either. After all, ten was twice five, and the character could be formed by combining both hands – not laterally, placing one V next to the other, but by reversing one and placing it on top of the other. Thus they created the X.

All that followed in completing the system of Roman numerals was merely a matter of modification and refinement. 'C', the Roman symbol for one hundred, used the initial of *centum*, the Latin designation of that figure. 'M', standing for 1000, was the first letter of the Latin *mille*.

It is interesting to learn that, though totally unconnected with the Roman tradition, the Arab figures from 0 to 9 are referred to as 'digits', a term derived from the Latin *digitus* for 'finger'.

RUM ONE

To call an odd and eccentric fellow 'a rum one' is English slang. Commonly accepted is the theory that gypsies introduced it into Britain.

Rom was part of their *Rom*any language and was the very name by which they called themselves. In their vocabulary, *rom* was a 'man' or a 'husband'. For rom to become rum was merely a matter of accent.

As gypsies, coming from far off lands, looked so different and seemed to practise what, to Englishmen, appeared such strange and peculiar customs, they – and with it their name 'Rom' – were soon identified with anything that was odd. Long after the gypsies had moved on to other regions, *rom*, pronounced 'rum', stayed on, with its roots forgotten.

There is also a suggestion, still linking the word with the gypsies, that 'rom' is derived from 'Rome'. Gypsies were not Egyptians, as their name might suggest. They were only so called because, prior to arriving on the Continent, their last stopping place had been Egypt. Coming from the east, the gypsies had passed through many cities and countries without ever becoming part of the local community. Nonetheless, it has been said that, whilst in Rome, the grandeur of the city had so fascinated them that they adopted its very name (slightly altered on their tongue to 'rum') as their description of anything that was remarkable and 'grand'. Eventually, they used it for any male gypsy, as well as for their entire people.

When others came to look down on the gypsies, they transferred their dislike for them to their name, their language and the things they admired. What was great to the gypsies had therefore to be small, queer and odd, disreputable and eccentric.

Further to complicate matters, rum has also been traced to a Teutonic root. Signifying 'famous', it still survives in the German *Ruhm*, as in the names Roger and Roderic. (Both names are compounds, one part of which is derived from the old German for 'fame'.)

Rum, indeed, presents a veritable mystery, just as does the gypsies' existence. Both have been a source of puzzlement for many centuries.

S

SACRED COW

SAFARI

SAILORS' BLUE UNIFORM

SALAD DAYS

SAY 'BOO' TO A GOOSE

SCHLEMIEL

SCOTCH A RUMOUR

SCREW

SELL DOWN THE RIVER

SELL ONE A PUP

SEMINAR AND SEMINARY

SHANTY

SHEMOZZLE

SHERBET

SHILLYSHALLY

SHIP'S BRIDGE

SHIPS IN BOTTLES

SHODDY

SHOPPING TROLLEYS
IN SUPERMARKETS

SHOW A LEG

SHYSTER

SILK PURSE OUT OF
A SOW'S EAR

SIXTY – AS A NUMERAL

SIXTY-FOUR DOLLAR
QUESTION

SKELETON

SLEDGEHAMMER

SLEEP ON A CLOTHESLINE

SMART ALEC

SMORGASBORD

SNACK

SNAFU

SOMETHING IS BUGGING ME

SOUR GRAPES

SPA

SPINACH FOR STRENGTH

SPOUSES

SPRING CHICKEN

SPUDS

SQUARE HANDKERCHIEF

STATIONER

STEAL THE MARCH

STICK ONE'S NECK OUT

STOOL PIGEON

STREET LAMPS

STRUDEL

STUFFED SHIRT

STUNNED MULLET

SURE AS EGGS IS EGGS

SWAP or SWOP

SWEET FANNY ADAMS

SACRED COW

A sacred cow is something untouchable: a custom, an institution or even a person so highly respected that in no circumstances can they be changed or criticised.

Hindu tradition has generally been quoted as the source of the term, based on its worship of the cow. In India, all cows are sacred. No one dares to harm them or even try to move them should they obstruct the way. The worship of the cow in this subcontinent has been traced to the far-distant past and was possibly already practised in pre-historic days.

Popular is a legend linked with Prithu, a mythical hero who was deeply concerned to provide his subjects with edible plants. The earth resisted, however, and assuming the shape of a cow tried to escape into celestial heights. She did not succeed. Prithu took hold of her and made her promise forthwith to bring fertility to the ground and nourish the people with her milk. Prithu himself was said to have been the first to have milked the cow which, ever since, has been sacred as a symbol of the sustenance of life.

Another version of this legend tells that Prithu changed himself into a cow to encourage his people, like him in this shape, to become vegetarian. Traditions are obscure and confused. However, already the Rig-Veda, that vast compilation of Hindu poems dating back to at least 2000 BC, reflects the belief in a sacred link between the earth and the cow.

Belief in the transmigration of souls not only reinforced but perpetuated the sacred status of the cow as an animal that was not to be killed or to be molested in any way. The gift of cows became one of the noblest of deeds, duly to be rewarded. Anything that came from the cow, from its milk to its dung, was held so sacred that it became an essential ingredient in some rituals of purification.

The British presence in India no doubt imported the sacred cow, as a figure of speech, to England, whence it spread worldwide.

Nevertheless, the sanctity of the animal itself was not confined to India. It played an equally significant role in ancient Egypt and in Greco-Roman mythology. In Egypt, Hathor, a universal goddess, was worshipped as the ruler of many things, both in the heavens and on earth. Among the numerous forms she could assume, most conspicuous was that of a cow, which thus became sacred to many in that part of the world. No wonder that princesses of distinction were frequently buried in cow-shaped sarcophagi.

Just as in ancient Egypt, so in classical Greece and Rome did cows become the subject of sacred myths. One of them tells how Io, the beautiful daughter of a river god, was transformed into a cow. Whilst walking along a river she caught the attention of Zeus, immediately rousing his desire. Pursuing her, he ravished her. When his wife Hera became suspicious, she descended from her seat in Olympus to get hold of Io. Zeus, to prevent his wife from discovering his love affair with Io, transformed her into a beautiful white heifer.

SAFARI

Safari, a Swahili word (possibly influenced by Arabic), simply means a 'journey' or an 'expedition'. When whites first used the expression, they did so in this very sense. Its association with the hunting and killing of game and the acquisition of trophies only came later.

William J. Burchell, an English naturalist, was the first to go 'on safari' and to introduce the term into modern European language. For almost five years – from 1810 to 1815 – he travelled through central Africa in search of new botanic specimens. The region he covered was then mostly occupied by the Hottentot people. To befriend them, he carried with him in his huge wagon all kinds of goods, including tobacco, coloured beads and handkerchiefs. That he had also loaded into his cart a few muskets and some gunpowder was not for the purpose of killing animals but for his own protection should hostile tribes or ferocious beasts attack him.

His successful venture inspired others to follow his example. Unfortunately, however, they did not set out in search of exotic flowers and plants but of adventure, to hunt game and bring home their quarry in the form of trophies.

Over the years this type of safari gained ever greater popularity, with the result that the ecology and, specifically, the animal world, suffered a great deal of damage.

The wheel has come full circle at last, for going on safari has regained its original meaning of a 'trip'. If any shooting takes place, it is done with a camera, to carry home as booty not animal trophies but memorable photographs.

SAILORS' BLUE UNIFORM

The reason why sailors all over the world wear blue uniforms has been attributed to naval warfare dating back at least two millennia. As the sea was blue, it was realised almost from the beginning that this colour would serve sailors as their best camouflage. The identical consideration prompted the Romans to issue an order soon after their invasion of Britain in 55 BC decreeing that the sails of the long boats of their fleet should be dyed blue as well. The colour would avoid easy detection of their approach or whereabouts by enemy forces.

SALAD DAYS

That the years of immaturity are called 'salad days' is easily explained. At that early stage of life, one is still green and fresh, just like the vegetables used in the making of a salad. The phrase, like so many others, was coined by Shakespeare. In *Anthony and Cleopatra* (Act 1, scene 5), Cleopatra speaks of 'My salad days, when I was green in judgment.'

SAY 'BOO' TO A GOOSE

As a word or exclamation, 'boo' (or 'bo') is used in a variety of circumstances and tones of voice. Loudly and protractedly, people 'boo' a bad performer on the stage or a speaker whose views they strongly disagree with. On the other hand, uttering the word suddenly and briefly has the effect of surprising or startling, particularly so a child in a game.

As the goose has always been regarded as a harmless but somewhat stupid creature, anyone afraid 'to say [even] "boo" to a goose' must be of the most timid nature. The phrase became a proverbial saying and was recorded as such as early as 1588.

The goose is also known as a bird that is easily frightened, and taking flight or starting to hiss when there is hardly any reason for it. Therefore not much courage is needed to say 'boo' to a goose. Not to do so indicates, to mix metaphors, chicken-heartedness.

SCHLEMIEL

The *Schlemiel* is a clumsy and unlucky sort of person. He always seems to miss his chance, and whatever he touches goes wrong. Bad luck dogs him all the way.

A Yiddish word, numerous proverbs describe the figure of the Schlemiel and his fate. He has been described as someone who, when landing on his back, bruises his nose, and when winding up a clock, makes it stop. Obscure in origin, the name has been given a variety of explanations.

One claim traces the Schlemiel back to biblical ancestry. It was a corruption of Shlumiel, a name quoted four times in the Book of Numbers in the Pentateuch. Appointed as the head of the tribe of Simon, a tradition asserts, he proved a most inefficient leader and experienced an unhappy end. Etymologically, Schlemiel has been interpreted as the contraction of a Hebrew phrase which spoke of him as having been 'sent away from God' or 'who is useless'.

Yet another derivation attributes the character's modern meaning to a folk tale, popular in medieval times. A man by the name of Shlumiel, so it relates, went on an extended trip. On his return home more than a year later he found that his wife had just given birth to a son. Not prepared to believe that, during his absence, his wife had been unfaithful, he consulted the local authorities. Taking pity on the slow-witted husband, by devious arguments they tried to prove to him that, contrary to the laws of nature, the child was his. Ignoring all logic and the reports of his neighbours, Shlumiel became convinced of his paternity. And this, it was suggested, was the real origin of the modern Schlemiel.

Adalbert von Chamisso, a German writer and poet, used the name for the main character of his *Wondrous Tale of Peter Schlemihl*, a work he published in 1814 and which made his reputation. His Schlemiel who, in return for earthly goods, sold his shadow to the devil, soon caught the imagination of the people. They adopted the figure as a prototype of those suffering undeserved adversity and chronic bad luck.

From Germany the Schlemiel made his way out into the world at large and can still be met with everywhere.

SCOTCH A RUMOUR

Quite apart from Scotch whisky, numerous are Scotland's contributions to civilisation. Yet the scotching of a rumour is not one of them. The phrase is derived from *escocher*, the Old French word for to 'cut', 'slash' or 'scratch'. To 'scotch a rumour' literally says to cut it off or, as in the case of a race-horse, to scratch it.

SCREW

Copulation is an act which has been described in many ways. To 'screw' is one of its more vulgar versions.

The term combines a variety of sources, two of them going back to ancient Rome. First of all, the screw can be traced back to the sow, *scrofa* in Latin. However, the word does not relate to the animal itself but to its curly tail, which to the Romans was somehow reminiscent of sexual relationship. Also in Roman times, common people compared the vulva to a 'ditch', which was *scrobis* in Latin.

In Middle English, on the other hand, *scrue* meant to 'dig'. This meaning was responsible for the naming of the joinery screw, which digs into wood ever more deeply, just as the penis does during intercourse into the vagina. All three words – *scrofa*, *scrobis* and *scrue* – by a process of assimilation were then joined to create in English the 'screw' and become part of the vocabulary of once strictly tabooed sexual terms.

SELL DOWN THE RIVER

Anyone being 'sold down the river' is being taken advantage of, badly treated or betrayed. Without knowing the circumstances of its earliest use, it is difficult to understand how this indigenous American phrase assumed its present-day meaning.

To 'sell down the river' goes back to one of the darkest periods of American history, to the time when blacks were the slaves of the whites. In various degrees of severity, black servitude lasted for well nigh 250 years, from 1619 till just after Abraham Lincoln's Declaration of Emancipation in 1863.

One of the punishments meted out to unruly slaves in the 1800s was to sell them to plantations situated 'down the [Mississippi] river'. Renowned for their harsh conditions and total lack of amenities, it was impossible to escape from these plantations.

The days of slavery are long past, but as a relic of that dismal time the practice survives – linguistically – in the now common saying.

SELL ONE A PUP

Whoever is talked into a worthless purchase or has bought goods at a price that far exceeds their value has been 'sold a pup'. They have been being swindled. It is like buying an as yet unborn puppy which turns out to be of a much inferior quality than promised.

Another malpractice once common at some English country fairs may equally be responsible for the saying. People who had bought a pig were handed it, for easier transportation, wrapped in a sack. When, on arrival home, they opened it, they often discovered that they had been cheated. The bag did not contain the pig but a worthless puppy. Indeed, they had been 'sold a pup'! Identical circumstances created the well-known similes of 'buying a pig in a poke' and 'letting the cat out of the bag'.

SEMINAR AND SEMINARY

A seminar, arranged to exchange ideas and gain up-to-date information, perpetuates in its name some 'seeds' sown long ago. Its very name embodies *semen*, for 'seed', the linguistic root of the seminary from which the seminar is an offshoot.

The first seminaries were established in early medieval days. Their name was wisely chosen, as they were to serve as 'seed beds' to implant religious lore. They thus were nurseries for faith. This explains why theological training colleges are frequently still referred to as seminaries.

For an institution of learning to be known as a seminary favourably compares with the etymologically selective 'college', which means 'chosen together'.

SHANTY

There are two kinds of shanties. Each has a totally different meaning and, though both might share French as their mother tongue, their roots are far removed from one another.

One kind of shanty, going back to the days of sail boats, owes its name to the French *chanter* for 'to sing'. Shanties were the songs sung at sea when the men were attending to their many duties. In fact, they could be described as their working songs and often fitted a specific task, such as the pulling of the ropes or the pushing of the capstan. The special rhythms of the songs seemed to ease the labour and even to hasten it. It was the general custom for one of the sailors, standing by, to chant them, with the rest of the men periodically joining in a refrain.

When steam replaced the sail, the shanty lost its purpose. If heard at all today, it is no longer on board ship but on the concert platform.

The second type of shanty lacks all beauty. A ramshackle sort of dwelling, it survives in present-day shantytowns, those sections of cities inhabited by very poor people. Even its name, though only slightly, is out of shape. From *chantier*, the French description of a workshop or a building site, French-speaking Canadian lumbermen applied it to their forest headquarters. Crudely built timber huts, they were mere shacks.

A totally different derivation traces this type of shanty to the Irishmen who formed the majority of the gangs employed in building the American railroads. Not inappropriately, they compared the temporary huts in which they were quartered to an 'old house'. In their Gaelic tongue this was *sean tig*, which Anglicised became the shanty.

SHEMOZZLE

Shemozzle, also spelled *shimozzel* or even *schlemozzel*, is used nowadays in the sense of a 'mess' or 'muddle'. Literally, it means 'bad luck', a fate the term itself experienced on the tongues of people. A hybrid, the word was derived from two languages. In their combination, each word became disfigured almost beyond recognition.

Shemozzle joins *schlimm*, the German-Yiddish word for 'bad', with the Hebrew *mazal* for 'luck'. Anglicised, the German-Yiddish-Hebrew phrase then became the *shlemozzel* which people, uncertain of its proper pronunciation and linguistic roots, came to render in so many different and confusing ways.

To complicate, if not aggravate, the 'bad luck' even more, it must be realised that the original meaning of *mazal* was not 'luck' at all. *Mazal* was the Hebrew astronomical term for a 'constellation of the stars'. Properly understood, therefore, speaking of a shemozzle reflects a belief in astrology. It implies that those experiencing 'bad luck' do so because of a bad constellation of the stars.

SHERBET

As a water ice flavoured with fruit, sherbet is mostly served as a dessert or, in between main courses, to clear the palate so as to better enjoy the taste of what is to follow. Its name is derived from *sharbarh*, the Arab word for a 'drink'. Initially, indeed, it was a favourite drink of the Turks who, in their tongue, rendered the Arab term as *serbet*.

Sorbet is merely an alternate, originally French version of the identical word and sweet, which is primarily known in the United States but is now served in other countries too.

SHILLYSHALLY

To speak of those who are unable to make up their minds in even insignificant matters as 'shillyshallying' is to use an expression of fascinating origin. Vacillating between a 'yes' and a 'no', they ask themselves 'Shall I? Shall I (not)?'. This, in former days, also took the form 'Shill I? Shall I?' Joining the two and assimilating the vowels yielded the ultimate description of their irresolute and hesitant state of mind as 'shillyshallying'. Another euphonious expression of a similar kind is 'dilly-dally'.

SHIP'S BRIDGE

People have rightly wondered what has led to the peculiar naming of the bridge, that raised (and now enclosed) platform from which the captain and the officer in charge direct the course of a ship.

The name goes back to the days of sail and to an early safety measure introduced to avoid collisions at sea in the darkness of the night. So that vessels in the vicinity of each other could be made aware of each other's presence and the course each took, ships were equipped with coloured lights: a red one indicating the port side and a green one the starboard. To be visible from afar, these were fixed high up on masts. At that early period, of course, oil lamps were used. These needed constant attention. They had to be refuelled regularly and their wicks trimmed. This necessitated, twice daily, the climbing up and down of the lofty masts – a dangerous procedure, especially in stormy weather. To make the task easier and safer and to reduce the number of climbs to one, an ingenious sailor came up with the idea of linking the lights by a plank or platform of some kind – a bridge.

With the coming of electricity, the red and green lights were retained as a permanent safety feature. However, no longer using oil, there was no need for their constant maintenance. This made the bridge obsolete. Nevertheless, it was not dismantled. Kept on, it was given its new, useful function of the present day. Its former name was never updated.

SHIPS IN BOTTLES

Bottles containing the model of a fully-rigged sailing ship have made many people wonder how anyone got the vessel through the narrow neck. An intricate art, it was especially popular during the nineteenth century, when it was taken up by sailors to pass the time on their long and often tedious crossings of the oceans.

Not put into the bottle in one piece, the individual parts were packed flat before being pushed into it, there to be assembled and secured. They were raised by pulling a thread attached to them, and stuck into place by means of a wire dipped into glue.

The original purpose of enclosing a ship in a bottle was not merely ornamental. Much more significantly, there was a practical and even an occult reason. Safely enclosed and corked, nothing could damage the precious little ship. It was genuinely believed that, by sympathetic magic, the real ship represented by the model was now protected from any harm, no matter where it was. Its miniature replica, so safely guarded in the bottle, would make it withstand storms, wild seas and any other mishap it may encounter. Indeed, the ship in a bottle, by supernatural power, would ensure the sailors' safe return from their voyage.

SHODDY

Shoddy things are thrown together from material of inferior quality. In the Yorkshire dialect, 'shoddy' was applied both to yarn which had been produced by tearing refuse rags into shreds and to the cloth woven out of it. It was also used as a name for quarried stones which proved of little value, and coal so poor that it hardly burnt. In the United States, rubber workers referred to reclaimed rubber as 'shoddy'.

The word gained widest currency during the American Civil War, when it was used to describe the cheaply made uniforms which greedy merchants supplied to the Union army.

Torn off, as it were, from all those previous usages, 'shoddy' came to assume its modern, much wider meaning. Etymologically, the origin of the word has been classed as obscure. Unsubstantiated suggestions claim that it grew out of a word that was used for something 'split', fragmented and no longer whole. This would be very applicable to things, no matter what, that were so badly made that they would soon fall to pieces.

SHOPPING TROLLEYS IN SUPERMARKETS

The shopping trolley (or shopping cart, as it is called in the United States) presented a major development in the history of merchandising. It was first introduced in the 1930s by Sylvan Goldman, the owner of a supermarket in Oklahoma City. His initial motive was not merely to help shoppers carry their purchases but to increase the volume of goods sold. Watching his customers carry the baskets into which they put their shopping, he noticed that they stopped buying the moment these were full or too heavy. It greatly limited the amount of items sold. Somehow he had to overcome this problem.

His imaginative mind set to work and, ingeniously, made use of an existing object to create a totally new contraption, one which would change the entire process of shopping.

Travelling salesmen at the time carried with them, for their own convenience, folding chairs. Why not make use of these, Goldman thought. He mounted the legs on wheels and raised the seats, placing on them one or two baskets. This would make it possible for shoppers to wheel away goods which, in volume and hence in value, would far exceed anything ever sold before.

Goldman did not let the grass grow under his feet. In no time he had fifty chairs converted into this novel cart. Having done so, he placed advertisements in the local paper, promising would-be shoppers 'a new sensational way in food buying'.

To his disappointment, however, his endeavour seemed to prove a failure. Business did not increase. Shoppers were reluctant to make use of the trolley, fearing that it might get out of control and hence be dangerous.

Goldman did not give up. Well aware of how easily people could be influenced, he employed a ruse. He re-advertised the innovation and, surprisingly, this time, it appeared to be most successful. Crowds of shoppers were wheeling carts, fully laden, outside his store. Would-be customers, seeing them, were convinced that the carts would not after all present any hazards. No longer hesitant, they went inside to be offered – by a woman specially positioned at the door for the purpose – one of the vehicles . . .

They did not realise that they had become the victims of a stunt. Goldman had hired people, some of them actors, to impersonate those customers happily pushing the loaded carts out the front! It took no time for the trolley to prove its value and, using the words of the title of Terry Wilson's biography of Goldman, to become *The Cart that Changed the World*.

Having patented his idea, Goldman founded, in 1936, the Folding Carrier Corporation to manufacture his trolley and to take up the building of supermarkets and shopping centres. He died in 1984 at the age of eighty-six, two years after having retired as the head of Goldman Enterprises. Leaving a fortune estimated to amount to US$200,000,000, even more significant was the legacy he left to the world – his shopping trolley.

SHOW A LEG

'Show a leg' was a one-time waking call used in British warships. In those days, men were not conscripted for a period of time as those joining the navy nowadays are, but had to serve for the duration of the ship's commission, however long that might be. Fearing that they would not return for duty when the ship was at dock, sailors were not allowed to leave the ship. Instead, to make it possible for their wives (or friends) to join them, these visitors were permitted to come on board and stay on whilst the ship was in port. Women could spend the night with their man in his hammock.

When, after the call for duty early next morning, a hammock was found still to be occupied, the occupant would be asked to 'show a leg'. If this was hairless it was taken to be that of a visiting wife, who then was left undisturbed. However, if hairy, it was assumed to be that of a man who had shirked to report for duty. He was made to get up and to do so in a hurry – to 'shake a leg'.

In 1840, the practice of allowing 'ladies' on board overnight was discontinued. Nevertheless, the waking call survived. It became part of civilian life and is still a colloquial way of waking someone up in the morning, especially a child.

SHYSTER

Shyster is the original American vernacular for a crook, particularly a disreputable lawyer known to pursue his calling to the discredit of his profession.

The term portrayed the obnoxious element of his pursuit. He was like human excrement, vulgarly referred to in German-Yiddish as *Scheisse* (pronounced shy-say). He did a dirty job, and to touch him was besmirching.

There is also the suggestion that his was the (Anglicised) name of an actual person, a Mr Scheuster who, in the 1840s, had followed his unscrupulous career in New York City. Specialising in criminal cases, his name became synonymous with corruption, in more senses than one.

The change into shyster might have come about because of the similarity of the word in sound with both the figure of Shakespeare's Shylock and the German-Yiddish vulgarism for a person who defecated, which was *Scheisser* (pronounced shicer). After all, did not the shyster's lack of integrity soil his profession?

Shicer (spelled Schicer or Shiser) was also used for a 'swindler', especially so for someone who welshed on the racecourse. In an English dialect, shice was known as and applied to something that was 'worthless' and 'no good'.

Less disreputable – though least likely – are derivations that discover in the shyster either a distorted gypsy word or the (mispronounced) Gaelic *Siostair* for a 'troublesome litigant'.

SILK PURSE OUT OF A SOW'S EAR

The observation that 'you cannot make a silk purse out of a sow's ear' is a striking way of stating a common experience. The words are those of a proverb, current as long ago as the sixteenth century. With rural life then predominating, pig sties were part of many a home. A silk purse, on the other hand, was a highly treasured possession.

The ear of a sow was nothing special. Of little use or value, it would never serve as the raw material for such a precious item as a silk purse. Likewise, a person lacking the qualities and background essential for a position or a task would never be able to hold or achieve it. Applied to everyday things, the message of the saying was this: to make something of value, inferior material would never do.

There are variations of the saying. Some do not use the simile of a sow's ear but that of a goat's fleece. Others replace the silk with satin. Whichever way, they all convey the same meaning. The choice of a sow's ear might well have been suggested by an imaginative mind discovering a rough resemblance between the ear and a purse.

SIXTY – AS A NUMERAL

The accepted method of measuring time and geometric figures owes its existence to ancient Babylonian culture. The Babylonians were the first to divide the hour into 60 minutes, the minute into 60 seconds and the circle into 360 degrees. Even more surprisingly, the scoring in the game of tennis owes its 60 points for a game to that identical source: the sexagesimal system invented by the highly developed civilisation of the Babylonians.

These people regarded the figure 60 as being of cosmic and universal significance. They discovered how it could fulfil a most useful role in everyday life and calculations. It possessed qualities hardly equalled by any other number, and lent itself to a multitude of numerical operations. Sixty could be divided by 2, 3, 4, 5, 6, 10, 12, 15, 20 and 30. Awed by such a multiplicity of possibilities, it was no wonder that the Babylonians gave this figure the status it has never lost. Universally accepted, the number 60 has influenced daily life throughout the ages, right up to the present day.

SIXTY-FOUR DOLLAR QUESTION

Easily accounted for is the origin of people's reference to a problem which is exceedingly difficult to solve as a 'sixty-four dollar question'.

In the beginning, the saying was not used metaphorically. The words meant what they said and the sum of money mentioned was real. It was all part of a popular quiz show, broadcast first on radio and then on television. Introduced in 1941 under the title of 'Take it or Leave it', the saying has never lost its appeal. Contestants who gave the correct answer to a question were rewarded with a prize of money. This sum increased progressively, with ever more difficult questions asked. In the early days of the show, the amounts paid ranged from the paltry sum of $2 dollars (for the easiest question) to the top award of $64, at the time a considerable sum.

Inflation and the promise of much higher prizes (reaching, on the show, the fabulous height of $64,000) made the early sum totally unrealistic. In spite of it, the saying survived. Independent of the show, and with the sum of money now meaningless, it continues to be applied to a query which truly stumps the person questioned.

SKELETON

Through the years, the skeleton has found many a place in the world of idioms and symbolism. 'A skeleton in the cupboard' may destroy a reputation. A skeleton displayed at a feast, as the ancient Egyptians first did at their banquets, was a reminder of death and the impermanence of the pleasures of earthly life.

In the early days, people did not realise the significant role the skeleton played in holding up the body. Paradoxically, the 'skeleton' is derived from a Greek root, *skello*, which means 'I dry up' or 'I wither'. The Greeks first applied the term to a withered corpse, a mummy. It was as late as the sixteenth century that the skeleton was to assume its modern meaning, describing the bony structure of an animal's body.

SLEDGEHAMMER

A sledgehammer, to begin with, was the largest hammer a blacksmith used. As it was so heavy a tool he needed both his hands to hold it. This explains why the expressions 'sledge-hammer blow' and 'sledgehammer argument' came about. They were so called because, ruthlessly, they knocked down all opposition.

The name 'sledgehammer' is a tautology, saying the same thing twice. The word combines *sleggja*, the hammer's Old Norse description, with the Old English *hamor*, of identical meaning. People might easily imagine that the reason for this doubling up was the wish (in speech) to emphasise the powerful blow this large and heavy implement could inflict. In reality, there is a very simple explanation, going back to the time when Norsemen invaded Britain. Not understanding the English 'hammer', they translated its name into their own tongue but, for the sake of the English, retained the other word as well. Like a blacksmith, they forged the two words into one to create the sledgehammer.

SLEEP ON A CLOTHESLINE

Insomniacs envy people who can sleep anywhere and at any time, even if 'pegged out' on a clothesline. The phrase is not simply a figure of speech but goes back to nineteenth-century England and concerns a real rope.

Destitution and poverty then abounded in the country. It was estimated that in London alone there were 100,000 homeless people. Workhouses were overcrowded. The rent charged by so-called lodging houses was exorbitant, far beyond the means of those ordinary men and women still able to earn a pittance. Down-and-outs regarded themselves lucky if able to bed down on the bare floor of a stable, or in a sewer.

More 'fortunate' were those who were permitted by a landlord to spend the night sitting on a hard bench in one of his rooms. Invariably they had to share this with many others. A rope, stretched tightly in front of them, served as a makeshift support on which they could lean. But even for this convenience they had to pay – two pennies (2 cents) per person. At daybreak their host removed the line and they were jolted back into reality.

It is a sad paradox that the tragic need of those who had to literally 'sleep on a clothesline' is recalled by a phrase which has acquired a totally new meaning. It is now the happy gift of those who are able to nod off anywhere – even, metaphorically speaking, stretched out on a clothesline.

SMART ALEC

It is uncertain whether 'a smart Alec', that conceited extrovert who thinks himself all-wise, is called after an actual person or is a mere figure of fiction.

Alex, the popular abbreviation of Alexander, was once a common name, eventually to become Alec. Many people were so called, which makes it difficult to identify the 'original' smart Alec, if ever there was one. Even to mention some of the individuals suggested would be scurrilous, as there is no historic foundation for any of them. If a smart Alec did exist, his very astuteness would have prompted him to make quite sure that future generations would be unable to trace him.

SMORGASBORD

The smorgasbord – as an institution and as a word – is indigenously Swedish. Literally, it means a 'sandwich table', from the Swedish *smorgas* for 'sandwich' and *bord* for 'table'.

This sandwich board goes back to the specific Swedish custom of never eating plain bread with their food. It had either to be buttered or topped with a slice of cheese, ham, a piece of herring or some other delicacy. These (open) sandwiches were attractively displayed on a table, the 'board', ready for the diners to make their choice. Initially, the sandwiches served merely as an hors d'oeuvre. With the passing of time, however, the smorgasbord began to fulfil many other functions, offering a hasty lunch or a snack in between meals.

The tradition of the smorgasbord has been abandoned in private homes. It has become a feature instead of restaurants, which have vastly extended the range of food offered.

Swedes carried their custom to wherever they migrated. They did so, first of all, to the United States during the middle of the nineteenth century, where it soon became a popular fare. It was then adopted, in diverse versions, in many other countries of the western world.

SNACK

The modern snack goes back to the fifteenth century, at which time it did not refer to light refreshments, usually taken in between meals and mostly in a hurry, but to a dog's bite.

The word tried to imitate the sound made by the animal's snapping jaws, which were not so much intent on hurting as in snatching some food! When first applied to humans, the earliest snack was a drop of liquor, no doubt meant to fortify oneself when one's spirits flagged.

Snack bars were first established in America, in 1895.

SNAFU

Modern life has become so complicated that, at times, chaotic conditions seem the normal state of affairs. This applies not least to those most regimented.

British Tommies, renowned for their humour but on occasions also victims of official muddle, created – in the early 1940s during World War II – their own description of such chronic chaos. They referred to it by way of an acronym. This combined words which, if fully voiced, at the time would have shocked many people.

First coined by an unknown member of His Majesty's Forces, SNAFU soon caught on. When the United States entered the war, GIs too found the word very applicable and adopted it. Like a snappy military report, SNAFU stood for *S*ITUATION *N*ORMAL: *A*LL *F*UCKED *U*P. To sound less offensive to the ears of genteel people, it was explained as being descriptive of things that were merely 'fouled up'.

The wartime coinage survived hostilities to be applied ever since to non-military situations of like kind.

SOMETHING IS BUGGING ME

Insects, annoying a person by their bites, may well have been responsible for the colloquial complaint that 'something is bugging me'.

A bug, however, originally did not refer just to an insect but to a ghost. As such it survives in various forms, such as in the bogey, the bugbear, and the bugaboo of the Welsh. It might well explain why people who are bothered say that something is 'bugging' them. Their state of mind and irritation are not the result of the sting of a bug as we know it now, but the effect of malevolent forces.

Of the various editions and translations of Holy Scripture, one, published in 1535, is known as the *Bug Bible*. Its odd name is due to one single word in its text. In its version of the 91st Psalm, the faithful are exhorted not to be afraid of 'any *bug* by night', a passage traditionally rendered as 'any terror by night'. As in the present-day saying, the specific reference to the bug here is not concerned with the small creatures infesting homes or hovering around in the air, but with evil spirits and demons flying about in the dark.

SOUR GRAPES

When people pretend to dislike things they are unable to obtain, their attitude is described as 'sour grapes'.

'Sour grapes' is a rationalisation of feelings of frustration. It helps people to overcome disappointments and to explain away a missed opportunity, a lost chance. This mental mechanism tries to prove that not attaining a certain aim was in reality not a loss, as achieving it would have proved of no value anyway and not worth the effort.

The term is yet another example of the influence of Aesop's fables on everyday speech. The 'sour grapes' come from his story about a fox who, anxious to eat of a vine's luscious grapes, sneaked into a vineyard. To his great disappointment, however, the grapes grew at a height beyond his reach. He consoled himself with the deceptive thought that it really did not matter, he did not miss anything. For all he cared, anyone could have those grapes, as they were sure to be sour.

SPA

The modern spa, as a designation of a mineral spring or resort where such a spring can be found, goes back to the Belgian township of Spa. It is believed that the health-giving properties of its waters were discovered as early as the fourteenth century.

The town of Spa developed into one of the most famous watering places, attracting a vast number of visitors who came to drink its curative waters for the improvement of their health. World-famous, Spa was patronised by the illustrious and the powerful. Among them was Peter the Great of Russia. In 1717, further to develop its amenities, he had a pump room built for its main spring.

The fame of Spa has never vanished. In fact, it has been perpetuated in the international vocabulary. Spelled with a small 's', spa has become a generic word for a spring the waters of which are of medicinal value. Other cities, like Leamington Spa in England, were clever enough to adopt its name.

SPINACH FOR STRENGTH

Not infrequently, eating habits have been influenced by fads and misconceptions. One of them has been the idea that, because of its high iron content, spinach gives special strength to those eating it. This fallacy was particularly popularised through the 'Popeye the Sailor' cartoons. Created around 1930 by the famous American cartoonist Elzie C. Segar, the series became his most successful production. At the climax of each of its strips, Popeye, facing a gigantic opponent, gained superhuman strength by gulping down the contents of a tin of spinach.

It was an example of how a simple cartoon can mislead people. The belief that spinach was rich in iron, an ingredient that greatly contributed to one's strength, was (and is) totally erroneous. The quantity of iron found in spinach is insignificant, and even if there were plenty of it, it could have no influence on people's vigour, as the body cannot easily assimilate the small amount of iron contained in the vegetable. More so, though the iron might help those who suffer from anaemia, it has no influence on bodily strength.

SPOUSES

The history of the spouse is colourful, at least linguistically so. Now applied to one's partner in marriage, to start with the term merely referred to one's fiancé(e), the one betrothed. Derived from the Latin *spondere*, it spoke of a solemn 'pledge' or a 'promise'. The marital status was only the final stage in the development of the term.

Tracing the spouse back to its origins leads to an ancient trade practice. When, in classical Greece, two parties had agreed on a business deal, they solemnly sealed their transaction by a sacrifice which, in most cases, took the form of wine poured on the altar of a god. This act of libation was known as *spendo* which, by its association, came to assume the wider meaning of 'making an agreement', eventually to become the root of the modern spouse and also the sponsor.

SPRING CHICKEN

Raising chickens was a skill learnt by early civilisations, as attested by archaeologists' finds. However, for many centuries, the lack of heating or anything resembling modern methods of incubation made it impossible to breed poultry during the winter months.

Farmers soon realised that this restriction and apparent disadvantage could be turned into a source of enrichment. Chickens hatched in spring could be sold at top prices in summer. Dishonest traders, cashing in on the demand for chickens, tried to palm off old and tough birds, claiming that these had been reared in the spring.

Astute customers did not fall for the trick. Rejecting the offer, they would say that the bird was 'no spring chicken'.

It did not take long for the expression to be transferred from the fowl yard to a person who, past the prime of his or her life, was also 'no spring chicken'.

SPUDS

Colloquially, a potato is called a 'spud'. It is a term acquired by mere association. Originally, the spud – in the form of *spudde* – was the spade used for digging up potatoes. By their intimate contact, the *spudde*'s name was transferred from the implement to the tuber itself.

SQUARE HANDKERCHIEF

France has for a long time been recognised as the trendsetter of fashion. Yet who would guess that the world owes the simple square handkerchief to that country as well? It is the result of the logic and pragmatism of one French woman – Marie Antoinette.

In contrast to her weak and dull-witted husband, King Louis XVI, she was not only an ambitious queen but a woman full of ideas and plans to render life more pleasant and enjoyable. Her interests extended even to such trivial items as the handkerchief.

Originally, handkerchiefs were of varied shapes and sizes: triangular, rectangular, oval, round and square. Marie felt that, of all of these, the one cut square was the most useful.

Nowadays, royalty may happen to launch a fashion merely by their example. In Marie's days, prior to the Revolution, kings not only reigned but ruled. At the queen's suggestion, Louis XVI issued a law (on 2 June 1785) which instructed his subjects that henceforth 'the length of handkerchiefs must be equal to their width through my entire kingdom'.

The French monarchy fell seven years later. Both the king and the queen were executed. Whether or not the royal decree was repealed is unknown, but the square handkerchief survived to become a universal and enduring accessory of dress. Even fickle fashion has not changed it.

STATIONER

Writing material of any kind is generally referred to as stationery. This word is also attached to the store or shop which sells it and is responsible for those in the trade being called 'stationers'.

The word has nothing to do with the actual goods but recalls a significant change in the way they were sold. Itinerant hawkers initially supplied paper, envelopes, pens and ink. In time they established a permanent abode, opening a booth or a stall. To have become thus 'stationary' presented a notable stage in the growth of their trade and gave them a new respectability, so much so that their new 'position' became their very name. No longer moving about, they deserved to remain conspicuous, even in the specific spelling of their name: 'stationery' (with an 'e' instead of an 'a'). In reality, this is merely an older spelling of the same word.

STEAL THE MARCH

To steal someone else's march is a clever manoeuvre. By guessing their intention and anticipating their move, it puts one ahead of others.

Obviously of military origin, the phrase goes back to the time when the outcome of a battle very much depended on the movement of the army's foot soldiers. The route they took, the speed with which they advanced and, most of all, the time in which they reached points of strategic importance, could make all the difference between victory and defeat. It was therefore of paramount importance for a commander to accurately calculate the enemy's arrival at a given point, and then to make sure that his own forces reached it prior to them. This necessitated that his troops marched all night and at double speed, beating the foe's men to their destination. Quite literally, they stole a march and thereby gained the advantage in battle.

STICK ONE'S NECK OUT

Those who meddle in affairs which are really no concern of theirs are said to 'stick their neck out'. They ask for what is coming to them, whether it be criticism or retribution. The expression and its dire complications reflect a combination of experiences both in nature and in life.

People who, unasked, interfere in the affairs of others have to suffer the consequences of their actions, to be taught a lesson to mind their own business.

A tortoise sticking its neck out of its shell leaves its safe protective cover and exposes one of its most vulnerable parts to other animals' attacks. A boxer who does not keep his chin tucked in provides an extra target to the attack of his opponent. There is also the example of butchers who, prior to chopping off a chicken's head, stretch out the bird's neck.

STOOL PIGEON

That police informers came to be known as 'stool pigeons' goes back to the days when the catching of pigeons was a favourite and profitable pastime. Pigeon meat then belonged to the average person's diet.

Not really a sport, it was a matter of trapping the unfortunate birds, a task which was mostly done by using one of their kind as a decoy. To prevent the bird from escaping it was tied to a stool. The cord used was long enough to give the bird sufficient leeway to move about, as if free. This practice was followed not out of concern for the poor pigeon but as a clever ruse. It was intended to avoid any suspicion on the part of other pigeons who, always wanting company, would join the bird. This was exactly what the fowlers hoped for. Lying in wait for them, they would lure the birds to their deaths, trapping them in nets or shooting them.

Because the pigeon serving as the bait was tied to a stool, it came to be known as a 'stool pigeon'. The fact that it was used as a trap was responsible for the term being transferred to police informers!

There was a very practical reason for the specific choice of a stool. Frequently, those hunting the birds had to spend many hours in the field, waiting for the game to 'catch on'. The stools they carried with them to sit on while they waited therefore served as a ready 'anchor' for the often lengthy rope.

There is yet another explanation for the term, a linguistic one. In Old English the word *stale* denoted a 'live bird', a name which therefore perfectly fitted the pigeon used as a bait. More significantly, it was also an ancient term for a decoy.

The pigeon's wonderful gift for finding its way back to its loft made people employ it too as a carrier pigeon. In the 1830s, the American police force took advantage of the bird's extraordinary ability. They enlisted it, as it were, to provide them with essential information of criminal activities. This, not least, made the name of the stool pigeon synonymous with a police spy or informer.

STREET LAMPS

The illumination of public places started in Europe only in the late 1600s. After some initial abortive attempts by the king of Naples to introduce streetlights, he was able to have his plans at least partially realised – through religion! At street corners frequented by people he placed holy shrines. As was then the custom, the faithful lit lamps at those icons, which were kept burning day and night. Obviously they did so solely to honour the saints. Nevertheless, by their religious act they also guided pedestrians in the hours of darkness. Thus they pioneered street lighting. It still took some considerable time till secular street lamps were put up.

STRUDEL

Though a pastry, the *Strudel* has a watery name. It speaks (in German) of a whirlpool. This was appropriate, as the dough was rolled in the shape of a spiral, reminiscent of a powerful circular current. The name was first used for a dessert (or 'cake') in 1715.

STUFFED SHIRT

Someone who is pompous and conceited is called a 'stuffed shirt'. Their description goes back to women's fashion in the early 1900s in America. At that time, women wore 'shirtwaists'. These were dresses or blouses tailored like shirts.

As dummies were not yet in existence, stores, to display the garments in their show windows, stuffed them with tissue paper. They may have looked good from afar, but on closer inspection they proved to be flimsy, without substance.

STUNNED MULLET

To compare situations, people and things with sights or experiences provided by nature and everyday life is not uncommon. In fact, the custom has created many a striking Australianism. A typical example is the analogy used for anyone who seems totally dazed or slow to respond: they are described as being 'like a stunned mullet'.

The specific choice of this fish is due to its abundance in Australian waters, and its consequent popularity as a food fish. There are at least thirty different species, outstanding among them the sea mullet.

From the process of catching and then killing the fish, the memory of a stunned mullet must have left its lasting impression in the minds of the people. Eventually they applied it as a figure of speech to humans who showed insensibility and lack of comprehension.

SURE AS EGGS IS EGGS

To confirm a certainty by stating that something is 'as sure as eggs is eggs' is not only grammatically faulty, it also makes no sense. Paradoxically, the original observation contained not a single egg. Mathematically speaking, originally it used 'X', the symbol of algebraic propositions. To underscore the validity of something said, it was very appropriate to apply the formula that it was 'as sure as X is X'. The 'egg' is merely a corrupted 'X'. To add to the oddity of the phrase, it uses a symbol standing for an unknown quantity as an assurance of an irrefutable fact.

SWAP or SWOP

It was once the custom for people to confirm a deal by shaking hands or, in more forceful manner, to strike them. Like an echo of the sound they thus produced, their transaction, particularly if it concerned an exchange of goods, came to be known as a 'swap' or 'swop'.

SWEET FANNY ADAMS

The phrase 'sweet Fanny Adams', specifically used in naval and military circles, is English slang. It denotes 'nothing at all' and expresses worthlessness.

The saying has a gruesome origin – the cruel murder in 1867 of an eight-year-old girl at Alton, in the English county of Hampshire.

On 24 August of that year, just after one o'clock, little Fanny Adams was playing with her younger sister and a friend in a meadow near a church adjacent to the River Wey when a well-dressed young man approached. After treating the girls with some apples, he managed – for a gift of a halfpenny – to make Fanny, a pretty girl, accompany him into a hopsfield close by. When at 7 o'clock at night she had not returned home, a search party was sent out. It led to the discovery of one of the most horrendous murders. Fanny had not only been brutally killed but, sadistically, her body had been dismembered. *The Standard*, reporting the ghastly case, commented that 'no tiger of the jungle, no jackal roaming famished about a city of the dead, could so fearfully mutilate its victim'.

It did not take long to identify and apprehend the murderer, Frederick Baker. There was a history of insanity in his family. At the inquest, which was held on the day after the murder, Baker's diary was produced. In it he had recorded on the day of the crime, 'Killed a young girl – it was fine and hot.'

The trial lasted a mere two days, and after two hours of deliberation the jury returned a verdict of 'guilty' and he was sentenced to death. Baker was executed on Christmas Eve 1867 at the Winchester County Gaol, watched by 5000 people.

Strange circumstances made the Royal Navy perpetuate the name of the unfortunate murder victim, 'Sweet Fanny Adams'. By mere coincidence, it was just around that time that the navy introduced tins of mutton as a regular ration. Sailors, finding the meat far from palatable, in a kind of sick humour suggested that the tins contained the remains of Fanny Adams – 'sweet nothing'. It was a description almost as obnoxious and nauseating as the crime itself.

t

TABLOID

The modern 'tabloid' owes its description to pharmaceutics!

Once upon a time, oral medical preparations used to be provided in the form of liquids, powders and large lozenges (also known as pastilles). Two American pharmacists who had migrated to Britain, Sir Henry Wellcome and Silas Burroughs, felt that there was much room for improvement. They reasoned that the identical remedies could be supplied in much smaller form. They were, in fact, aware of such successful attempts already made in the States and even in Britain. Acquiring the rights, they improved on the methods so far employed, and succeeded in compressing all the necessary ingredients into a little pill. To start with, they called their new type of medicine a tablet. Combining the words tablet and alkaloid, Sir Henry coined as its new name the 'tabloid'.

The idea came to him at 4.30 one morning in 1884. In spite of the early hour, he immediately summoned his secretary and dictated to her a memorandum on the introduction of the tabloid as the new trade name of their products. On 14 March 1884, the name was registered.

It did not take long for the many advantages of the tabloid to be realised and for the novel tablet to swallow, as it were, all previous types of medication. The tabloid soon became so well known that its name was applied in spheres far removed from pharmaceutics, to describe things presented in condensed form. Most prominent among them was a newspaper. In 1902, the *Westminster Gazette* published a small-page edition to make the paper easier to handle and to read. Making use of the new word, it adopted 'Tabloid' as its title. Its aim was, the editor pointed out, 'to give in tabloid form all the news presented by other journals'.

The drug company took exception to the newspaper and regarded the choice of the name as misappropriation of a term which was specifically theirs. In an ensuing court action, Sir Henry won the exclusive right to use the term. He then had the further satisfaction of seeing see his word included in the *Oxford Dictionary* as of his making.

Nevertheless, in its pharmaceutical sense the tabloid eventually resumed its original 'tablet' form. It survived in journalism, however, with tabloid coming to be applied generally to newspapers which, with less words but more pictures, presented the news in a condensed form.

TAKE UMBRAGE

Umbra, the Latin for 'shade' or 'shadow', is the most likely source of the idiom that speaks of people taking umbrage. They take a dim view of things said or done to them. Themselves bereft of light, their resentment makes them throw a shadow over the people involved.

Another interpretation links the phrase with human susceptibilities. Though not everyone likes to be in the limelight, people do not want to be put into the shade either – to be overshadowed, as it were. In its Latin rendering, the idiom incorporated the offensive shadow and spoke of people 'taking umbrage'.

Totally different is yet a further explanation, which traces the term to French horsemanship and the encounter with a *cheval ombrageux*, a horse that took fright of its own shadow.

TAKING THE MICKEY OUT OF SOMEONE

To 'take the Mickey out of someone' means to pull their leg, to tease them or, even worse, to show them disrespect.

The phrase reflects Englishmen's early dislike for the Irish, whom they regarded as dull and slow-witted. As an Irishman's nickname was Mike or Mickey, to take the Mike or Mickey out of someone denoted to make fun of people by expressing (or highlighting) their stupidity. It is a sad left-over of former prejudice and antagonism.

Tabooed is another derivation which claims that the phrase is a euphemism for extracting urine from a person, by inserting into them a catheter for the simple purpose of humiliating and making a laughing stock of them. Vocally and without shame, this explanation found expression in the rhyming slang which speaks of 'Mickey Bliss [for] Piss'. Though the expression does not specifically refer to the act of urinating, more generally it is linked with 'taking the piss', in the sense of giving offence, of deriding and disparaging.

TALK TURKEY

To 'talk turkey' is to come down to brass tacks, to talk seriously. The saying started in the United States, though versions vary in which circumstances.

Some say that it recalls early encounters between the Pilgrim Fathers and the indigenous population. English migrants soon found in the Indians a welcome supplier of turkeys, a bird previously unknown to them. The newcomers purchased so many of them so frequently that the moment white people approached, Indians, anticipating the purpose of their visit, greeted them with the words, 'You come to talk turkey.'

Best known, though most likely apocryphal, is the tale which traces the origin of the saying to a hunting expedition, jointly undertaken by a white colonist and his Indian companion. At the end of the day, all they had managed to bag were four crows and four wild turkeys. On dividing the spoils, the white man, underestimating the Indian's intelligence, handed him a crow whilst putting a turkey into his own bag. He did this four times in succession. On each occasion he remarked, 'You take this crow and I take this turkey.' The Indian did not hold back in expressing his resentment. 'You talk turkey for you, but not once did you talk turkey for me', he said. 'Now I talk turkey to you!' He meant business.

Different again is yet another explanation of the phrase. It, too, goes back to the early days of white colonisation, when the immigrants first came across the turkey in the forests of their new home. They soon realised that by imitating the birds' sound – that is, by learning 'to talk turkey' – they would attract them. This was particularly effective during the mating season, when the often love-sick birds would mistake the call as that of a promising partner. Hence 'to talk turkey' was most effective and lucrative.

TEA CADDY

A container for tea is referred to as a caddy. Its name initially indicated a unit of weight, equal to approximately 1¼ pounds (0.56 kilograms), which obviously related to the amount of tea that could be stored in the receptacle.

Derived from the Malay *kati*, the caddy as a unit of weight can be traced to pre-revolutionary China, where it was commonly used in trade. According to both the region and the type of substance measured, the quantity tended to differ. Least among tea vendors in Peking, it was largest among Honan coal merchants.

Traders then 'carried' the weight with them abroad, where, first called *catty*, it eventually reached Britain at the end of the eighteenth century. There it replaced the previously used canister. At the time, tea was so precious a commodity that only the wealthier classes could afford it. They kept it in caddies which, appropriately, were made of silver and to avoid theft of their contents were provided with locks!

TEACH ONE'S GRANDMOTHER TO SUCK EGGS

There are various ways to eat an egg. One method, now obsolete, is to puncture the shell at either end and suck out its contents through one of them.

This is the background of the phrase which compares the attempt to teach someone something they already know with 'teaching their grandmother to suck eggs'. Grandmother had learnt to do it so many years ago that any attempt to instruct her in the practice would not only be totally superfluous but, most of all, presumptuous.

TELEPHONE NUMBERS

The telephone plays a significant part in calling for help in emergencies, which are frequently of a medical kind. Its function as such is now taken for granted. No one would ever imagine that sickness itself was responsible for the introduction of telephone numbers. They owe their existence to the circumspection of a concerned doctor.

In 1879 a measles epidemic had broken out in the town of Lowell in Massachusetts, USA. At the time, telephone connections were still made manually by four operators. To make a call, subscribers told one of the operators who they wanted to speak to and the connection was made at once. Those working the exchange were well acquainted with the individual subscribers.

With the epidemic spreading ever further, the local doctor became worried that it might infect the entire staff of four operators, with the result that the exchange would break down. Anyone acting as their temporary replacement would not be familiar with the individual subscribers and their voices. By replacing their names with numbers, the problem would be solved and any such debacle prevented. It was the birth of the telephone number. The sickness abated, but the numbers stayed on to prove a blessing to the world of communication.

TENTERHOOKS

Those in a state of suspense are said to be 'on tenterhooks'. Their anxiety is stretched to the limit, and that, exactly, is the literal meaning of the word. 'Tenterhook' is derived from the Latin *tendere*, for 'to stretch', a word also responsible for all that is 'tense'. Even the modern 'tent' comes from the Latin word. After all, it is little more than a 'stretched' canvas.

The tenterhook, however, is not merely a linguistic contribution to the vocabulary. Much more practically, it owes its heritage to the early process of weaving and cloth-making. To retain the shape of the finished material whilst drying, manufacturers used to stretch it on a framework known as 'tenter', fastening the cloth to its edges by appropriately named 'tenter-hooks'.

Gruesome is yet another explanation for the expression. This associates tenterhooks with one of the horrendous practices of medieval torture – putting people on the 'rack' (called a *tenter* as well) to be stretched till their joints were dislocated. This painful experience might well have left its scars in everyday speech.

THAT'S A BIT STEEP

Whoever is told a tall story, is overcharged or rejects an unreasonable demand may well voice the opinion that 'that's a bit steep'. Unknowingly, in saying so they might either quote a remark alleged to have been made by the Duke of Wellington, or refer to a huge cleft in the landscape of southern England.

One day, George IV told the Duke of Wellington that a cavalry troop under his command had charged down an extraordinarily steep ravine near Brighton. Wellington did not believe the king, but he did not dare to express his doubts. Instead, straight-faced, he merely responded, 'Very steep, Sir, very steep!'

The gorge of the king's story is known as the devil's dyke, and a legend explains its name. It tells that the cleft was not a natural feature in the Sussex Downs but the result of the devil's work. Determined to thwart the further spread of Christianity, the devil had embarked on a project of digging a deep chasm through which he hoped the waters of the English Channel would pour, flooding the entire area and exterminating its population. Before he had finished, however, a woman stopped him in his nefarious scheme. Holding a lit candle up to him, she watched as he, mistaking the light for the sun, a divine body, took fright and fled, leaving his work unfinished and his hope unrealised. Only the steep gap he had made has remained. It has been called after him ever since and, according to this version, is the real source of all 'that's a bit steep'.

THAT'S HOW THE COOKIE CRUMBLES

A note of resignation and acceptance of an unalterable situation is expressed by saying, 'that's how the cookie crumbles'. At times the words are also rendered as, 'that's the way the cookie crumbles'.

An American phrase first used in the 1950s, it gained wide currency through Billy Wilder's 1960 movie *The Apartment*. In one of its scenes, Miss Kubelik (played by Shirley MacLaine) asks C.C. Baxter (Jack Lemmon), 'Why can't I ever fall in love with somebody nice like you?' Baxter replies, 'Yeah, well, that's the way it crumbles, cookie-wise.'

Cookie, the Americans' equivalent of the English biscuit, was adopted by that nation late in the eighteenth century. It was Dutch settlers who brought the word with them from Holland, where the *koekje* was a 'small cake', a diminutive of the Dutch *koek*. Though its name might have suggested that it was cooked, it was in fact baked.

THAT'S YOUR PIGEON

The saying 'that's your pigeon' does not refer to the bird at all. What it really means is, 'that's your business'. The confusion is the result of pidgin English.

When the British began to trade with the Chinese, the latter had difficulty in pronouncing the word 'business'. Trying to do so, the sound they produced was very much like *begin*, which was (mis)understood as 'pidgin'.

When, subsequently, the British introduced into China a simplified form of English which was accommodating to the Chinese syntax and tongue, they called it after this most conspicuous mispronunciation – 'Pidgin English'. The earliest business of the British with the Chinese has thus survived and, changing the abstruse pidgin into a pigeon, has given the English idiomatic vocabulary the telling phrase, 'that's your pigeon!'

THREE Rs

Modern technology has changed many of the methods of traditional education. Most schools are now equipped with computers. Nevertheless, the fact remains that the basics of education for any school curriculum are to learn to read, to write and to do sums. It was early in the nineteenth century that this triad of faculties was first referred to as 'the three Rs'.

Obviously, the expression combined Reading, Writing and Arithmetic. It is rather ironic that the abbreviation offends the very principle it advocates, by misrepresenting (in speech, at least) two of the three subjects: it drops the 'w' and the 'a'.

The phrase is said to have been first used in a toast made by a London Lord Mayor. Explanations differ as to the reasons for his choice of 'the three Rs'. One suggests that, as an eloquent speaker, he wanted listeners to remember his message, and to achieve this aim chose to use the method of verbal alliteration. Less kindly is another suggestion which claims that the Lord Mayor himself had been an illiterate person who did not realise the mistakes he made. Whichever way, the three Rs he created were never corrected, replaced or forgotten. They became a memorable addition to our vocabulary.

THREE SHEETS TO THE WIND

People who are totally drunk and are seen to stagger along, swaying to and fro, are said to have 'three sheets to the wind'. So portrayed, they recall the early days of sailing.

Though obviously the sheets referred to are not bed linen, nor are they, as may be assumed, the sails of a vessel. A sheet, in nautical terminology, is a line, rope or chain used to control the position of the sails. Shortened or lengthened as the situation demands, sheets enable a ship to sail along steadily and at top speed. If the sheet is not kept tight, however, the sails become uncontrollable. This makes the ship unsteady – like drunkards on their feet.

The number of sheets referred to in the expression grades the intensity of the person's intoxication. Whilst one sail to the wind indicated a slight degree of inebriation, those who were 'three sheets to the wind' were completely 'out'.

THYROID

Although the first reference to a thyroid in medicine can be traced to 1693, the word, used in a different sense, was part of everyday speech thousands of years before that date. To begin with, it denoted a safeguard. From the Greek, thyroid indicated a 'large stone' which people placed in front of a door to keep it shut. Warriors then adopted the term to describe the shield that protected them. Homer used the thyroid in this sense.

To imaginative minds, the largest cartilage in the larynx somehow resembled the ancient shield. For this reason it was called a thyroid ... but only temporarily so. Ultimately the name was transferred to the gland located in front of the larynx. In a metaphorical sense it was a proper choice, as the thyroid served as a protector – specifically of one's health. This it did by secreting hormones for controlling the metabolism of the body and its growth.

TICKLED PINK

Speech has always been colourful, not least so in expressing human emotions: people can be in a black mood; angrily, they see red; jealous people are green with envy. In similar vein, those who are greatly pleased and delighted with something are said to be 'tickled pink'.

It is a phrase well chosen to portray their feeling of satisfaction. Pink is a colour that reflects well-being, if not happiness. A pink complexion denotes good health. To be 'in the pink' refers to the very best of conditions. Tickling, on the other hand, produces pleasure. It is a sensation that – inevitably – makes people laugh and, with it, causes blood to rush into their face.

The combination of both the colour pink and the result of tickling reinforce each other in portraying a mood of pleasure. A person so gratified has been 'tickled pink'.

TIGHTFISTED SCOT

Scottish people have suffered many a calumniation. Qualities deserving admiration have been misjudged and, at times, even quoted to denigrate them. Their acumen and ability to make a little go a long way have been misinterpreted as miserliness. They have been called 'tightfisted'.

The term certainly applies to them, but not in the sense it is now used and understood. If a Scotsman clenched his fist, he did so not to retain the little money he possessed but to make sure of his next meal!

In days gone past, many a Scotsman used to carry oatmeal in his sporran – and very wisely so. It enabled him to prepare a snack for himself at almost any time in any place. All that was necessary was to roll the meal into balls and then cook these in the hot ashes of a fire. To bind the oats, however, he had first to wet them. He did so by taking a handful and dipping them into a brook or river. This created a problem: the running stream tended to wash away the cereal. To prevent this from happening, the astute Scotsman made a tight fist around the oats. It was this simple but ingenious practice that gave him the reputation of being 'tightfisted'.

TIN-PAN ALLEY

A general practice all over the world has been for those pursuing the same kind of occupation or trade to congregate in a specific district. These districts eventually became identified with them. In London, for instance, Petticoat Lane in the East End became renowned for the bargains it offered, whilst Harley Street was identified as the location of eminent doctors.

Publishers of popular music in New York chose the district around Time Square as their centre. Trying out numerous tunes behind the open windows of their rooms, studios and offices, it was inevitable that this part of the city reverberated with a medley of sounds. In combination, the sounds were more noisy than tuneful. Was it any wonder, then, that some people (first in 1908) came to compare the strident notes with the cacophony produced by the clashing of tin cans? (Credit for having invented the term is usually given to Monroe H. Rosenfeld, the author of many popular songs at the time.) The comparison soon caught on, creating the Tin-Pan Alley, a name adopted in England in 1934.

There is also the suggestion that the 'Alley' took its designation from early musicians' slang for the cheap tinny pianos they had to use. Very appropriately, they dubbed them 'tin-pans'.

TIT FOR TAT

To give 'tit for tat' is an unfortunate trait of humans. The original wording spoke of a tap, in the sense of a slight blow or a slap. Those who were hit would not take it lying down. Promptly, they returned what they have received – a blow for a blow, one stroke in return for another.

As a universal phenomenon, similar sayings are part of other tongues. The English, renowned for their 'fair play', may have borrowed the phrase from one of these languages, though which is not certain. The most frequently quoted sources are the Dutch *dit vor dat* ('this for that'), the French *tant pour tant* ('so much for so much') and, going much further back in time, the Latin *quid pro quo* ('something for something').

The earliest mention of the phrase appears in a collection of English proverbs, published in 1546 by John Heywood.

TODDY

A once popular home remedy for those suffering from a bad cold was to go to bed, take a couple of aspirins and drink a hot toddy, a potent mixture of rum, lemon juice and hot water, or of slightly diluted whisky sweetened with sugar.

Both as a word and a drink, the toddy goes back a long way. In India more than 2000 years ago it was used both as a drink and as yeast for making bread. Made from the fermented sap of palm trees, particularly the palmyra, its original Hindi description referred to it as *tari*, a word then corrupted on English tongues to 'toddy'.

The British took the word and drink back home. Adding other ingredients, and heating up the inebriating beverage, they created the hot toddy. Especially welcomed in Scotland, it was served there as a warming drink on cold winter nights.

Its earliest mention can be found in Robert Burns's *Holy Fair*, which he wrote in 1786. It tells of the lads and lasses who sat around the table, enjoying their toddy.

TOE THE LINE

Anyone expected to conform to rules has to toe the line. Used figuratively now, originally the expression was meant literally. It comes from sport, where it was first applied in foot races. To make sure that none of the runners started ahead of the others, not even by the slightest of margins, each of the contestants had to place his toes against a line marked on the ground. Put briefly, he had to toe the (starting) line.

'Toeing the line' also became a practice in early boxing bouts. With very few rules and regulations, contestants were not limited in time. They went on till one of the boxers was almost completely exhausted. Nevertheless, he was given a chance to recover by being permitted a breathing spell of thirty seconds, during which he withdrew into his corner. If he was then able – within eight seconds – to 'toe the line' scratched into the centre of the boxing ring, he was permitted to continue the fight. Unable to 'come up to [the] scratch', he was declared the loser.

TROPHY

Trophies are treasured mementos of a victory, usually of a sporting kind. They may be gained individually, as in the games of golf or bowling, or nationally, like the America's Cup or the Ashes. Now a completely peaceful object of pride, the trophy originated in fierce battles and was one of the earliest war monuments put up by the victorious army.

From the Greek *trapaion*, the 'trophy' literally referred to the 'turning point' of a battle, the 'putting to flight' of the enemy. The word was chosen to designate a monument erected on the site where the enemy was forced to turn back. Initially, this monument could simply be a pile of booty, made up of some of the arms the vanquished soldiers had thrown away when they fled.

Alternately, the trophy could be the banner of the beaten foe, discarded by or captured from him. The victor hung it up on the branch of a tree, where it was worshipped as sacred.

Eventually, the trophy, of whichever type, was taken from the actual field of battle to a selected place, to be kept there as a highly valued war memorial. It was only in later years that the concept of the trophy changed and, completely divorced from the battlefield, took its place on the playing field. Henceforth the contest it recalled was no longer a clash of arms but a match between sporting rivals, and the trophy not booty but a silver cup.

TRUE BLUE

'True blue' is a mark of staunch loyalty to a cause or a person. It denotes dependability and faithfulness of many kinds. Those who are true blue do not change colour, whatever the cost and the circumstances.

Many sources have been given for the phrase. Sailors linked a blue sky with the absence of storms, promising reliable seas and, with it, a safe voyage. The choice of the colour to express constancy may have been suggested by a dyeing process, pioneered in the English manufacturing town of Coventry and even called after it – 'Coventry blue'. Blue cloth produced in that city was of superior quality, due to the fact that it was colourfast. No matter how often it was washed, it never faded. It was the 'true blue', as people came to call it.

Religious faith, too, has played its part in giving 'true blue' its special meaning. Blue, as the hue of the sky, symbolised heaven and truth. However many clouds darkened it, they could do so only temporarily; sooner or later its blue colour would reappear. Nothing could ever destroy it.

Scottish Presbyterians of the sixteenth and seventeenth centuries chose blue as the colour of their banner. Known as the 'Covenanters', they bound themselves by religious and political oaths never to yield their beliefs to any power. The colour of their banner explains why their unswerving loyalty became known as the 'true blue', perpetuated in Samuel Butler's *Hudribas* (1663) in which he spoke of 'Twas Presbyterian true blue'. It was also the reason why preachers of the faith used to cover their improvised pulpits with a blue apron.

Butchers might have played a part in at least popularising and perpetuating the expression and its application to allegiance. Their choice of blue as the colour of their apron had a very practical reason: it disguised blood stains. Responsible for the proverbial saying that 'true blue will never stain', this expression was soon applied to all life situations. People of loyal character and dependability would never change their colour.

More a relic of an age which has almost totally passed is the specifically British use of 'true blue' for members of the upper class, dyed-in-the-wool aristocrats. Maybe they regarded themselves 'blue blooded'.

TURN A BLIND EYE

Self-explanatory is the description of those who do not want to take notice of something as 'turning a blind eye'. Taken literally, though, the saying makes no sense. After all, even if bereft of one eye, a person can still see.

The saying relates to a famous episode in the life of Lord Nelson. During the Battle of Copenhagen, fought in 1801 against the Danes, the British Fleet confronted the Danish Fleet in the narrow sound between Denmark and Sweden. Under the command of Admiral Sir Hyde Parker, the British Fleet battled under a great disadvantage. The very size of the vessels (numbering twenty altogether) made it difficult for them to operate in the narrow shoal waters against the massive units of the Danish Fleet, which were further supported by shore batteries.

Unexpectedly, the encounter proved of extraordinary ferocity. At the height of the battle, Hyde Parker, realising the extreme danger to which Nelson's forces were exposed, sent him the signal to 'Discontinue [the] action!'

Nelson, however, was not prepared to retreat. Pretending not to see the signal, he turned to his captain, remarking on the blessing of having only one eye. Legend tells that he put the telescope to his blind eye, not seeing his commander's instructions . . .

Nelson's refractory decision proved right, for it resulted in a truce. Subsequently Hyde Parker was removed from his position and Nelson, in spite of his having disobeyed his superior's orders, was appointed as the new Commander-in-Chief. Ultimately, indeed, his action resulted in dashing Napoleon's hope of gaining the upper hand over the British Fleet.

Though many may be totally ignorant of the circumstances of its birth, Nelson's 'turning a blind eye' has become a telling metaphor, applied to situations in life when it pays not to see things.

TYCOON

Japan plays a significant role in the commercial life of the world, and it seems fitting therefore that the title now given to business magnates of any nation stems from that country. They are called tycoons, the description once given to Japan's shoguns who, for well over 600 years, ruled their country with absolute power.

Derived from the Chinese *ta-kiun*, the name spoke of 'the great prince' or, more literally, 'the army leader'. Americans adopted the title and, adapting it to their English tongue, created the modern tycoon. Affectionately they bestowed it on President Lincoln, possibly because of his being the 'military leader' during the Civil War. Eventually, however, the word was applied exclusively to the captains of industry, finance and trade, to those who occupied positions of extraordinary influence and wealth.

TYING A KNOT INTO A HANDKERCHIEF

The practice of people tying a knot into their handkerchief to remind them of something they wanted (or promised) to do, far from being a mere aid to memory, originated in a climate of fear. It was 'tied up' with gross superstition.

The knot they tied was intended to act as a potent antidote to evil spirits. Totally confused by its odd shape, the demons' attention would be diverted from the harm they were about to inflict.

u

UNABLE TO MAKE HEAD OR TAIL OF SOMETHING

UP TO DOLLY'S WAX

UPSET THE APPLECART

UNABLE TO MAKE HEAD OR TAIL OF SOMETHING

To be unable to make head or tail of something expresses how confusing a situation or story can be. One cannot even guess what is the beginning and what the end.

The metaphor immediately recalls the practice of tossing a coin, whether for sport or for deciding a matter on which one has been unable to make up one's mind. The determination is left to chance – or, in pagan days, to the gods! On some such occasion, the coin tossed might be placed so awkwardly on the ground that it is impossible to recognise which of its sides – 'head' or 'tails' – is uppermost. Things are thus left 'up in the air'.

This is the explanation usually given, but it does not provide the real answer, which goes back many thousands of years ago and is part of the story of coinage. The earliest coins were lumps of metal. Of gold, silver or baser metal, their value was determined by their weight. These often unshapely coins were replaced by round pieces, which were so much more easily handled. Initially they had their value marked on one side whilst the other was left blank. To ascertain the worth of a coin, one had to turn it over to its proper side. This was responsible for the later, Latin-derived name for it: the 'obverse', meaning the side turned towards one. Accordingly, the opposite side came to be known as the 'reverse', from the Latin for 'turned back'.

In a further development, the head of the ruler of the country was stamped on the coin. In recognition of his supreme status, this became the chief side, which resulted in it being referred to as the 'head'. Quite logically, then, the reverse side became the 'tail'.

Frequent usage and bad craftsmanship caused some coins to so deteriorate that people were no longer able to differentiate between the head and the tail. This lent itself as a most fitting metaphor for any occasion which was perplexing.

UP TO DOLLY'S WAX

Not a few expressions have found their way into everyday speech from the nursery. Of Australian coinage is the description of having over-indulged in food as being (full) 'up to dolly's wax'. Rather puzzling words, they only make sense if put back into their proper context.

Dolls have always been one of the most favoured of children's toys. Not mere objects to them, children treat them like human beings. Using a doll as an example, therefore, was once considered the best way to teach children a lesson.

Whilst the body of dolls used to be made of cloth or some other material, their heads were frequently of porcelain or wax. To impress on a child how inappropriate it was to be greedy, with the child's love of a doll in mind it was told that the food reached up to the dolly's wax (head).

The saying caught on, to be applied in the adult world when speaking of any glut or excess as 'up to pussy's bow and dolly's wax'.

UPSET THE APPLECART

To spoil a project or plan carefully laid out is, in a figure of speech, to 'upset the applecart'.

The saying has been seen as the result of a once not infrequent experience of sellers of fruit, or of country people bringing home their harvest. Carrying their produce on a cart, often along bumpy country roads or the cobbled streets of a city, it was not always a smooth run. On many occasions the cart got stuck and toppled over, its contents scattering and, at times, getting badly damaged. As a result, any profit hoped for was either reduced or totally wiped out.

Though the saying has been traced back to the end of the eighteenth century, its real source may be classical Rome. People who had failed in achieving some longed-for aim were known to have expressed their disappointment and near despair by using similar words. In their anguish they exclaimed, 'I'm done for – I've upset my cart.' A record of such a saying might well have suggested its modern version, which improved on it by loading the cart with apples!

A totally different explanation links the expression to an old slang term in which the human body was called an 'applecart'. Applied to contact sports, 'to upset the applecart' meant to knock down one's opponent, to throw him to the ground and thus spoil his hope of gaining the upper hand.

VAUDEVILLE

V FOR VICTORY

VAUDEVILLE

Theatrical variety shows presenting songs of a light-hearted nature, interspersed with dance and other entertaining items, are known as vaudeville. As the word is French, so is the origin of this type of performance, which goes back to fifteenth-century France.

Tradition tells that at that time, in the Normandy Valley of Vire (Vau-de-Vire), a craftsman by the name of Olivier Basselin wrote lively satirical drinking songs. They became so popular that, almost instantly, they caught on. Sung far and wide, they even reached Paris.

Acknowledging not the composer but the site of his compositions, they were soon referred to as *Chansons du Vau-de-Vire*, the 'Songs of the Valley of Vire'. Too long a description, it was contracted (and in the process slightly corrupted) into Vaudeville.

Eventually the circumstances of its origin were forgotten and the songs became the basis of music hall entertainment, no longer restricted to France but adopted in countries around the world.

Another derivation, totally divorced from the valley in Normandy, sees in vaudeville the shortened version of *Voix de Ville* – the 'Voice of the Town'.

V FOR VICTORY

During the life and death struggle against Nazi tyranny, the V-sign played a powerful role in inspiring the Allies and supporting those oppressed. There is no doubt that Winston Churchill contributed greatly to making the signal famous, not least by making the letter 'V' with two of his fingers whenever he appeared in public. However, Churchill did not create it. Several explanations have been offered as to its origin.

According to one suggestion, Belgian students were the first to have introduced it. To join the forces fighting for the liberation of their country during World War II, these students escaped to England where they enlisted in a freedom movement.

They chose *Vrijheid*, their native Flemish word for 'freedom', as their slogan. Imaginatively, they adopted its initial as their symbol. To produce it, it needed only the raising of the index and middle fingers of a hand.

Victor de Laveleye, a member of the exiled Belgian government in London, then took it up. In a broadcast made to his country on 14 January 1941, he suggested using the V-sign as a salute from one patriot to another. In fact, he further advised, it could serve as a most effective psychological weapon against the invader. Easily and quickly chalked on to walls, buildings or pavements, it would act as a potent message of defiance, unnerving the enemy.

Six months later, on 20 July, Churchill adopted the V-sign. In his forceful and eloquent way, he proclaimed that it was to serve 'as a symbol of the unconquerable will of the occupied territories and as a portent of the fate awaiting Nazi tyranny'.

Ceaselessly, the European service of the British Broadcasting Company repeated Churchill's message, uniting the people in their determination to fight the invader and never to succumb.

Strangely, it so happened that the letter 'V' was also the initial of the word for victory in the language of many European nations who were battling for their survival or liberation. *Vryheid* in Dutch and *Victoire* in French, it was *Viteztvi* in Czech. Dutch people soon joined two 'Vs' to form the letter 'W', the initial of Wilhelmina, their beloved and undaunted queen.

Going much further back in time – well over 500 years, in fact – the V-sign might be traced to the confrontation of the French and the English in the Hundred Years' War. The English, though often greatly outnumbered, nevertheless proved themselves far superior in their fighting power. They had learnt to make use of the long bow, a weapon still unknown to their enemy. Whenever the French succeeded in capturing one of the English archers, the first thing they did was to cut off his fore and middle fingers. The mutilation disarmed him for life, making it impossible for him ever again to draw the long bow.

Tradition tells that, after their decisive victories both at Crecy (in 1346) and Agincourt (in 1415), the English taunted the defeated foe by holding up their hands with their fore and middle fingers conspicuously pointing upward. Proud and defiant, their gesture indicated that, in spite of the fierceness of battle, they had remained unharmed and, if need be, were ready for further combat. Churchill, being a historian, was possibly well acquainted with the gesture and thus adopted it as the V-sign for the twentieth century struggle.

Perhaps merely odd is the coincidence that in ancient Egyptian worship the V-shape, made by two fingers of the hand, served as a gesture of petition to one of their gods, asking for his protection.

The V-sign has also been seen as the stylised representation of the crotch. As the seat of the genitals, it was symbolic of the continuation of life and of its victory over death.

W

WAKE

WALL STREET

WARPATH

WARTS AND ALL

WASHER UNDER A NUT OR IN A TAP

WEATHERCOCK

WEDDING RING SEWN ON TO A PILLOW

WELL-HEELED

WELLINGTON BOOTS

WELSH SINGING VOICE

WENT TO THE WELL ONCE TOO OFTEN

WET ONE'S WHISTLE

WHAT A PLUM!

WHEN THE BALLOON GOES UP

WHISTLE BLOWER

WHISTLE STOP

WHITE AND DARK MEAT OF A CHICKEN

WIGWAM FOR A GOOSE'S BRIDLE

WIMPS

WIN HANDS DOWN

WOG

WAKE

A wake is now traditionally linked, particularly in Ireland, with the watch kept over the body of a deceased person during the night prior to the funeral. In fact, the very word is derived from the Old English *wacian* for a 'watch'.

People stayed awake not merely because their grief did not let them rest. There were very practical reasons as well. They guarded the body and watched over it lest it be defiled by a rodent or some other (imagined) creature that could do it harm. When friends came to join the mourners, both to comfort them in their loss and to pray with them for the eternal rest of the soul of the departed, the original dreary task was livened up. All joined in making countless toasts in honour of the deceased.

A coffin table is still part of the furniture of some Irish inns, kept specially for wakes. Whilst the casket is placed at its centre, all-around drop leaves provide ample room for the guests to put down their glasses. No wonder that the solemn nightwatch often deteriorated into veritable drinking orgies which led the ecclesiastical authorities to issue special regulations to control the dignity of the occasion.

Strangely, however, to start with wakes had no association with death at all. People used to keep festive vigils the night before a feast in honour of a local patron saint, or on the anniversary of the consecration of a church. At times, the term 'wake' was applied to the entire holiday, which was not always restricted to one day but to an extended period, often linked with the holding of a fair. Preceding its funeral significance, joy, entertainment and happiness were the very essence of such wakes.

WALL STREET

'Wall Street' is now synonymous with the American centre of the money market, the New York Stock Exchange and numerous other financial institutions located in downtown Manhattan.

Its name, originally, applied to an actual street. In 1652, in the days of the early settlement by the Dutch, Peter Stuyvesant, the then governor of New Amsterdam (the future New York) had a wall built to protect the (Dutch) residents from attacks by Indians and, most of all, from the British. Fortunately, his fears never materialised. Totally neglected, the wall eventually collapsed. It was replaced by a dirt track which, recalling the original purpose of its site, became known as the 'Wall Street'. The designation, though long having become redundant, was never abandoned and is now applied to the entire district.

WARPATH

Frequent usage often contracts or even distorts expressions, making them unintelligible or subject to misinterpretation. In some cases, it gives a figurative meaning to something once taken literally. This applies to people who are said to be 'on the warpath'. They are ready, if not anxious, to engage in some kind of confrontation. The warpath, however, originally referred to the '*war*riors' *path*'. This expression was used not in a metaphorical sense but related to the actual path American Indian warriors took when about to attack.

WARTS AND ALL

To relate things and describe people as they really are, without embellishment or omission of negatives, is described as 'warts and all'. The words are a (partial) quotation of what Oliver Cromwell (1599–1658) is alleged to have requested of the artist commissioned to paint his portrait. He was not to ignore any imperfection, but show his true image. 'Mr Lely,' he remarked, 'I desire you would use all your skill to paint my picture truly like me, and not flatter me at all; but remark all these roughnesses, pimples, warts, and everything as you see me, otherwise I will never pay a farthing for it.'

WASHER UNDER A NUT OR IN A TAP

Intriguing is the question why the flat ring of metal or rubber, placed under a nut or inside a tap (the American faucet) to tighten a joint or distribute pressure, is called a washer. Plausible and least involved is the suggestion that it was so named because early washers were made of *wash*-leather, a soft kind of leather, mostly of sheepskin, so named because of the 'washing' involved in the process of manufacture.

Its description, however, may have no connection at all with water. It may go back to an old Anglo-Saxon word for straw, stubble or grass – *ways* (pronounced 'waize') – and be explained by a practice of fishmongers at the famous Billingsgate (fish) market in London. To ease the pressure of the heavy baskets of fish they had to carry on their heads, they cushioned it by means of a ring of straw. It acted as a buffer between head and basket.

This wreath or wisp of straw, the *wayzer*, did not take long to deteriorate in speech to become a 'washer'. And as the ring in the water tap looked like a mini replica of that improvised buffer, it was called after it. To begin with, in fact, the washer under a nut actually consisted of straw wound around the screw. Its name was therefore very much to the point.

The washer thus found its way from on top of a head to inside a tap. No matter where it was found, however, its purpose was the same: to ease a load or to prevent friction.

WEATHERCOCK

Long before the use of present-day windsocks in aviation, to determine the way in which the wind was blowing was the preoccupation of many people, particularly farmers. Early indicators of the wind's direction were of a very simple kind. They consisted of a strip of cloth attached to a pole and were appropriately referred to as wind flags. As the Old English word for 'flag' was *fana*, they became known as weather vanes.

The piece of cloth was then abandoned for a more sophisticated kind of device, such as a thin plate of metal or wood, which pivoted on a vertical spiral. Still, that was not the end of the weather vane's evolution. Eventually the vane was given the shape of a rooster. Because of this, its alternate description became the weathercock. Though the name was very much to the point, at one time it was deeply resented by Puritans, who immediately linked it with the slang expression for a penis. For that reason they never forsook the weather vane.

The choice of a cock was much more meaningful than might at first be thought. Its presence did not signify mere beautification of the vane but was due to superstitious beliefs, religious tradition and, most significantly, to a papal decree.

The cock was known to crow early in the morning, just when the first rays of the sun appeared. Confusing the sequence, this made people imagine that by its crowing it actually dispelled the darkness of night and, with it, its demons. Ultimately, the cock was believed to fulfil this task at all times, both during the day and at night. As a constant protector against evil it was thus placed on steeples, towers and even private homes, simultaneously serving as a vane.

Its role as a guardian and a religious symbol was reinforced by Christian tradition. The Gospels tell how Peter, on the arrest of Jesus by the Romans, had strongly denied ever to have been his friend or disciple. It was exactly what his master had foreseen. When Peter had assured Jesus that he would never forsake him or fall away, Jesus had said that this very night, even before the cock had crowed twice, he would deny him thrice (Mark 14:30). In response, Peter reassured Jesus of his unswerving loyalty, saying that he would never do so.

Events proved otherwise, exactly as Jesus had predicted. When Peter had denied for the third time ever to have belonged to his group, he suddenly became conscious of his betrayal and, deeply repentant, 'went out and wept bitterly'. This very incident led Pope Nicholas I (858–67) to issue an enactment which decreed that the figure of a cock should be set up on every church steeple. As the emblem of St Peter, it should recall his denial and his subsequent repentance, to serve as a warning to all the faithful. No matter in which direction the wind blew, people would be constantly reminded of their sins and, just as Peter had done, seek and obtain forgiveness.

Other symbolic meanings were added to the vane, just as other figures, such as fish, birds and a diversity of objects, were chosen for its shape. The vane was intended to teach people watchfulness. As it swung around in every direction, so should they keep a constant watch for possible antagonists and temptations. Like the proverbial cock, they should put to flight the powers of evil and darkness.

The weathercock has made yet another contribution to everyday life in the way of a simile. People who are fickle and always change their opinion are said to be 'like a weathercock in the wind'.

WEDDING RING SEWN ON TO A PILLOW

Still occasionally observed, though little thought about, is the custom for a pageboy to carry the ring loosely stitched to a pillow prior to it being placed on a bride's finger. Apparently it being tacked to a cushion is a very practical precaution: it prevents the ring from rolling off. Originally, however, there was a much more weighty reason for it being thus secured. For the ring to fall to the ground before the marriage was solemnised would not augur well for the union.

WELL-HEELED

Someone who is 'down and out' cannot afford to have his or her shoes repaired and hence is described as being 'down at the heels'. Accordingly, to be 'well-heeled' means to be a person of means.

Such an apparently obvious explanation may not in fact be the real one. The figure of speech may well have been derived from cockfighting. Birds selected for the cruel sport were known for their pugnaciousness and fighting power. To fortify them even further, their sponsors attached artificial razor-sharp spurs to their heels. Thus it could truly be said of them that they were 'well-heeled', words easily adopted to describe human situations.

American slang, too, has been quoted as the source of the saying. In the early frontier days, pioneers constantly had to be ready to defend themselves against attacks. For them to carry a gun was essential. In the American argot, 'to arm oneself' was to 'heel'. Those who could pride themselves on having not just one gun but a rich store of weapons could rightly be described as being 'well-heeled'.

WELLINGTON BOOTS

A variety of memorials has served to honour and remember famous people. Some are of stone and usually represent the face or figure of the specific individual. Others, of a more practical nature, are items of clothing called after them.

Wellington boots are so called to honour one of Britain's great warriors, the Iron Duke who (with the aid of the Prussian Blucher) crushed Napoleon in the Battle of Waterloo in 1815. The story is told that one day, when Queen Victoria received in audience one of her generals, she had remarked on the boots he was wearing. 'They are "Wellingtons"', he explained. The queen would not accept the answer. It was quite impossible, she said, that there could ever be a pair of them; Wellington had been unique.

Earliest records of Wellington boots go back to 1817. Doubts exist as to whether they were merely named in his honour or were actually the kind of boots the Duke wore. It is generally assumed that he had them made, not just for himself but for his soldiers, for the campaigns fought in Belgium and in Spain. Not to be impeded when traversing swampy and muddy ground, the soldiers needed to be equipped with knee-high boots made of water-resistant material. Specially manufactured on the Duke's orders, they truly merited being called after him.

Subsequently, Wellington adopted them for everyday wear, even when attending the Houses of Parliament. No wonder that they soon caught on and, for some time, became the fashion.

WELSH SINGING VOICE

The Welsh have always been known as a musical race, but less known is the possibility that their gift of singing might be the result of common sense and a healthy instinct.

Employed mostly as miners, Welshmen worked deep down in the coal pits, a pursuit that carried many occupational hazards. When, after long hours of work, they came up from the pit, they used to climb to the top of the nearest hill, not only to inhale some fresh air but to clear their lungs of coal dust (even at a time when its dangerous implications to their health were not yet realised). They did so by singing, and it was this continuous practice that gave them their beautiful, resonant voices.

WENT TO THE WELL ONCE TOO OFTEN

An interesting study is the rendering of idioms and sayings into other languages. To literally translate them often proves inadequate, as it can obscure, if not totally distort, their meanings. Taking them out of their contexts can further complicate them.

A typical example applies to the proverbial remark that someone 'went to the well once too often'. A quotation from the German, it very freely translates the saying 'the pitcher goes to the well till it breaks' (*Der Krug geht so lange zum Brunnen bis er bricht*). Without interpretation, the words make little sense.

Actually, the observation refers to a fact of life well worth remembering. To obtain an objective, one can presume upon people many times. Eventually, however, even the kindest of persons will lose his or her patience and put a stop to it. Others have interpreted the saying differently. A person can do much harm, and repeatedly so, without being found out, but sooner or later justice will catch up with the offender.

A totally different French tradition gives the proverb a symbolic, sexual meaning. A girl going to the well, apparently to fetch water, uses it as an excuse to meet there her lover – and loses her innocence: the jug breaks.

The quotation gained widest currency through a famous comedy, *The Broken Jug*, written in 1808 by Heinrich von Kleist. The saying itself does not literally appear in the play, but it was fostered by its very title and plot. Wittily, von Kleist tells the story of a country judge who is himself the culprit of an offence he is trying – the attempt to seduce a young girl. Caught in the act by her boyfriend, he is thwarted and beaten up by him. He makes a hasty escape, upsetting and breaking a valuable jug and losing his wig as he goes. The judge arrives at court badly injured and with his wig missing, noticeable facts he tries to explain by devious means. He falters and fails to do so. As his guilt becomes ever more apparent, the net closes tighter around him. All that is left for him is – for the second time – to flee. His repeated efforts to escape being discovered as the real perpetrator of the crime are finally shattered. Once again, but metaphorically now, the jug is broken.

Though a writer of inspired comedy, von Kleist was an unhappy man who ended his life by drowning himself (in 1811) in a Berlin lake.

WET ONE'S WHISTLE

As we whistle with our mouths, it is understandable that people identified the sound with its source and, colloquially, called the mouth one's whistle. With a dry mouth it is hard to speak. In such a situation, the obvious thing to do is to have a drink – to wet one's whistle.

This is one explanation for the idiom. Another intriguing one links it with an early type of mug. This was so ingeniously constructed that it started to whistle, like a kettle on the boil, the moment it was empty. To wet one's whistle therefore came to mean to have a(nother) drink!

A further suggestion traces the phrase to a practice of hardy Norsemen. During their carousals they did not want to have to wait too long between one tankard and the next. To speed things up they blew a whistle, attached to their drinking vessel, the moment the cup was (about to be) drained. On hearing it, a servant would make haste to refill it.

Completely different again is a derivation that sees in the expression the survival of a custom among harvesters. Having stopped working in the field in order to sharpen, or 'whet', their whittle (scythe), was to them a welcome break which they used to refresh themselves with a drink. Eventually, thus, to 'whet one's whittle' became synonymous with having a drink and, in the process, the words were transformed into 'wetting one's whistle'.

A once popular assertion claimed that, originally, the phrase spoke of 'whetting' one's whistle. After all, drink might sharpen one's mind, as one whets a knife on a stone. In the course of time however or, more likely, by slurring the words, people had dropped the 'h' – merely to 'wet' their whistle.

WHAT A PLUM!

Hidden away in a pudding and in a nursery rhyme is a veritable fortune – in the form of a 'plum'. In hard cash, this plum was originally worth £100,000 (well over $200,000). Historically and religiously, it recalls a turning point in British history.

When Henry VIII broke his ties with the Pope and used it as an opportunity to confiscate the holdings then owned by the Roman Catholic Church, the Abbot of Glastonbury Monastery was determined to have the vast estates under his jurisdiction excluded. To keep them, he tried to buy the king's good will. In 1535, as a special Christmas gift, he sent him the deeds of twelve properties owned by his monastery. He assigned Jack Horner, his trusted chief steward, with the mission.

Horner duly carried out the task. However, he did so with one significant omission. On the way he appropriated for himself, out of the treasure trove he was conveying, the most precious deed, a property valued at £100,000. Though his extraordinary theft did not go unnoticed, no action was taken against him. Soon, however, a satire lampooned the 'deed' in the form of a rhyme. It spoke about little Jack Horner, the man who stuck his thumb into a Christmas pie to pull out 'a plum'.

The plum has not only become part of a popular nursery rhyme but has been retained as a figure of speech to describe juicy pickings, the best of anything, whether merited or undeserved. Horner's 'plum' is now a remarkable bonus.

WHEN THE BALLOON GOES UP

'When the balloon goes up' is a sure indication of impending trouble. Initially, the phrase was not used metaphorically, as it is now, but was ominously real. It goes back to the trench warfare of World War I, when the opposing forces were facing each other from their dugouts. The moment the troops occupying the front lines saw observation balloons go up on the other side, they knew that a bombardment by the enemy was imminent.

WHISTLE BLOWER

Police used to blow a whistle to sound an alarm, and referees still do so to stop a game because of some fault or infringement of rules on the part of a player or a team. This practice made 'to blow the whistle' an apt description of concerned people's determination to stop a wrong or corruption by revealing its existence.

Whistle blowers have become part of modern industrial, political and economic life. Their revelations are fraught with danger, as they expose themselves to retaliation by those whose misdeeds they have disclosed. Unless they act out of mere spite or self-interest, whistle blowers show great courage, as they well know that what they do, though it may right things, might be to their own detriment.

WHISTLE STOP

A whistle stop, originally an Americanism, refers to a short stay at a place, especially by a politician. Such a stop leaves just enough time for him to shake hands and say a few words.

The figure of speech stems from the time of steam trains. A passenger who wanted to get off at an unscheduled stop, too insignificant for a regular halt, notified the conductor who, in turn, conveyed the request to the driver. The latter acknowledged it by blowing the whistle of his engine. Truly, the brief halt merited being called a whistle stop.

WHITE AND DARK MEAT OF A CHICKEN

To speak of the 'white' and 'dark' meat of a chicken, for its breast and legs respectively, has an intriguing background. Once upon a time people were too coy to name these parts of the fowl's anatomy by their proper designations. Identical susceptibilities were responsible for other such euphemisms which, for instance, made Victorian society refer to a man's trousers as his 'unmentionables'.

WIGWAM FOR A GOOSE'S BRIDLE

Many people have been puzzled by the saying that 'it's a wigwam for a goose's bridle'. The words do not make any sense. There is no such thing as a goose's bridle, hence to provide a wigwam (a North American Indians' dwelling place) for something which does not exist only adds to the confusion.

A jumble of words, mere verbiage and gibberish, the expression says nothing at all. And this is exactly its intention. When asked a question to which they do not know the answer, or when unwilling to supply it, people will not say so outright. Instead, either to cover up their ignorance or to avoid having to reply in the negative (whether to an adult or a child), they say something that sounds so sophisticated that, awestruck and flabbergasted, the questioner does not dare pursue the quest further. They accept the answer as final.

A slang phrase, it is said to have been used on the Australian goldfields in the 1860s. Diggers, asked what they had been doing lately, would reply, 'Making a wigwam for a goose's bridle'. Unwilling to give a straight answer, they used the phrase, and everyone knew what they meant by the meaningless words.

In the course of time, wigwam was occasionally replaced by whim-wham or wing-wong. Whichever the version, the senseless phrase achieved its aim, eventually being also applied to give a (well-merited) silly answer to an even sillier question.

WIMPS

Society has little respect for persons who are weak in character. They are decried as 'wimps' (or whimps). The description, most probably, is derived from their *whimp*ering, the continuous complaints they make about the way they are treated or how bad things are.

In a totally different sense, the word wimp was further popularised by Wimpy Bars, those outlets which, originating in Chicago in 1935, called their product after the hamburger-loving character J. Wellington Wimpy from the comic strip 'Popeye the Sailor'.

WIN HANDS DOWN

Those who win 'hands down' almost effortlessly succeed. The phrase was born on the race course. A jockey who led the race well ahead of all the others was sure of his reaching the winning post first and could therefore relax. With no need to use his whip to prod his mount or pull the reins to control it firmly, he could drop his hands – to 'win [with his] hands down'.

WOG

Once a nickname for people of oriental or European extraction, 'wog' is now shunned and proscribed as a discriminatory, pejorative, racist term. A variety of explanations exist as to its origin, though most agree that it is an acronym.

It is generally believed that the British first used the word during their control of the Suez Canal. To easily identify the native labourers they employed, they had the back of their shirts conspicuously marked with the letters W.O.G.S. These stood for 'Working On Government Service'.

An alternate suggestion claims that 'wog' was the nickname given to Indian students who, having graduated at British Universities, on their return home spoke with an Oxford accent. Whether an affectation or genuinely acquired, their way of speaking caused resentment, and they were referred to as 'Westernised Oriental Gentlemen', contracted into WOGS.

Slanderous indeed were the implications of another interpretation. This asserted that the word stood for a 'Wily Oriental Gentleman'.

Much more acceptable and pleasant, though most unlikely, is yet a further explanation. This claims that, just like the word POSH, the WOG was created by the pursers of the P & O shipping line, which once plied its ships between Britain and the orient. Not rarely, these carried Indian passengers of high status. They were conspicuous by their courtesy. For future reference, pursers, in listing their names, put next to them the letters WOG to indicate that the passenger so marked was a 'Wonderful Oriental Gentleman'.

Possibly, however, the wog is not an acronym at all, but a left-over of the golliwog. A once favourite doll, it was made of black cloth and had fuzzy or curly hair. The character was created jointly by two Americans: Bertha Upton, the writer (d. 1912), and her illustrator, Florence Upton (d. 1922). They introduced it in their series of children's books. The golliwog became a popular toy in British homes. It remained a favourite till the 1960s when, decried as racist, most doll manufacturers discontinued making it. All that was left of it, though only surviving for a limited time, was the unfortunate 'wog'. Meanwhile, Cockneys had acquired it in their slang as a nickname for boys with a mop of dishevelled hair.

X-RATED

YARBOROUGH
YEW TREES IN CHURCHYARDS AND CEMETERIES

ZIP FASTENER

X-RATED

It was not until the 1960s that the United States Motion Picture Association began rating films as a guide to film-goers. This system was soon to be followed by other countries.

The classifications were easily understood – with one exception. 'G' indicated that the movie was for *General Exhibition*, 'M' signified that it was limited to *Mature* audiences and the cipher 'R' stood for *Restricted Viewing*. But why the 'X' was selected to designate films that showed explicit sexual scenes or extreme violence was less obvious.

The 'X' in fact stood for *Extra Restricted*. It was introduced to protect those who, irrespective of age, might be offended by such scenes or even suffer psychological damage by the depiction of risque topics, horrendous actions and hard-core sex.

YARBOROUGH

A yarborough is a term used in the game of bridge. It refers to a hand of thirteen cards of which none is higher than nine, a rare occasion indeed.

The word recalls an actual person of that name, the (second) Earl of Yarborough (1809–62). Little is known of his life, except that he was an enthusiastic sportsman and card player. His name has been perpetuated by a wager he made when meeting with his companions at bridge. When about to commence the game, he laid odds of 1000 to 1 that a player would not be dealt a hand in which no card was higher than a nine. Ever since, such a hand has been called after him.

Actually, modern methods of calculation show that his estimation was wide off the mark. The real odds on being dealt a yarborough are 1827 to 1.

YEW TREES IN CHURCHYARDS AND CEMETERIES

That yew trees can be found in and around churchyards and cemeteries has been given manifold explanations, some going back to antiquity.

Yews are slow-growing, sturdy trees and are exceedingly long-lived. No wonder that they were sacred to the ancient Druids. With Christianity replacing paganism, the early churches were often built in the vicinity of those trees already regarded holy. Hence, contrary to general belief, the trees were often older than the church itself, and not the other way round.

As the dead were buried in the consecrated ground surrounding the sanctuary, appropriately known as the 'churchyard', inevitably, in the minds of people, the yew trees growing in it became closely associated with the graves. Soon their presence there was given a significant (new) meaning. The long-livedness of yew trees, combined with the fact that they were evergreens, made them symbols of immortality. So aptly sited among the dead, they stood as a promise of everlasting life.

There was a further, and this time practical, reason for growing yews in churchyards. In the thirteenth and fourteenth centuries particularly, their timber was used for the bows of archers. Because of the sanctity of the ground, their wood was protected from unlawful use.

Yew trees also proved ideal as wind breaks. This prompted King Edward I of England to issue a decree ordering that they be planted to protect churches from the elements. Being poisonous, farmers took good care to keep their cattle away from the trees, thereby adding extra protection to the church and, not least, preventing the desecration of the burial places.

ZIP FASTENER

The *zip* in the zip fastener is a shortened version of 'zipper'.

In 1921 the B.E. Goodrich Company of Akron, Ohio, marketed waterproof overshoes which used a unique type of fastener, the first of its kind. With a tab sliding along two parallel rows of metal teeth, it surpassed in effectiveness and ease of application all previous and similar inventions. In 1923 the firm advertised them as 'zipper boots'. In no time, people transferred the name from the boots to its novel fastener, and thus the 'zipper' was created as a new word and a device of multiple usage.

grim reaper, 101; 'late' Mr or Ms X, 146; lying in state, 157; preserving a corpse – *see* pretty pickle, 201; wake, 271; yew trees in churchyards and cemeteries, 286

debunk, 68

deprived of one's rights, 68

difference, not an iota of, 186

disease, 70

dishevelled, 71

doctor, 71; apple a day keeps the doctor away, 6

dogs: dog days 72; sell one a pup, 222

dogwood, 72

doily, 73

dollar: bottom dollar, 28; buck, 33; sixty-four dollar question, 29

dolly's wax, up to, 264

door knockers, 74

drag, dress in, 75

drink: champagne spraying, 45; drinking horns, 75; saloon – *see* joint, 133; tea caddy, 249; toddy, 256; wet one's whistle, 279

drinking horns, 75

drunkenness: one over the eight, 191; three sheets to the wind, 253

duck: Bombay duck, 26; lame duck, 145

E

east, graves facing, 99

eggs: curate's egg, 59; devilled eggs, 69; egg on one's face, 77; egg rolling, 77; sure as eggs is eggs, 243; teach one's grandmother to suck eggs, 249

etc, 80

evil spirits, warding off: baby rattles, 13; best foot forward, 17; door knockers, 74

eye, turn a blind, 259

F

face: cut off one's nose to spite one's face, 62; egg on one's face, 77; keep a straight face, 136; laugh on the other side of one's face, 147; lose face, 155

fate worse than death, 82

February, 82

feet: best foot forward, 17; feet of clay, 83

films: cliffhanger, 48; X-rated, 285

first-rate, 85

fish and chips, 85

flies on someone, no, 183

food: antipasto, 4; apple, 6; avocado, 9; bagel, 13; biscuit, 19; Bombay duck,

26; buttered bread, 36; caviar, 44; Caesar salad, 39; chicken, 281; coleslaw, 51; corned beef, 55; crepe Suzette, 58; curry, 61; devilled eggs, 69; fish and chips, 85; french fries, 88; garlic, 91; grapefruit, 98; ice-cream cone, 125; kippers, 140; larder, 146; mustard, 176; oatmeal – *see* tightfisted Scot, 254; overeating – *see* up to dolly's wax, 264; sherbet, 224; smorgasbord, 234; snack, 234; spinach, 237; spuds, 238; strudel, 242

forestall, 86

forlorn hope, 87

forty winks, 87

freelance, 88

Freemasons: apron, 7

French anthem: Marseillaise, 163

french fries, 88

G

gab, gift of the, 95

gambling: beginner's luck 16; Bingo, 137; bottom dollar, 28

games and sports: bowling alley, 29; boxing – *see* toe the line, 257; Bridge – *see* yarborough, 285; cards – *see* nine of diamonds, 181; cricket – *see* innings, 126; darts, 66; fowling – *see* stool pigeon, 241; gymnasts, 104; hunting – *see* hue and cry, 120; jousting – *see* horse of a different colour, 119; mah-jongg 159; Olympic rings, 190

gargle, 91

garlic, 91

gavel, 92

gazumping, 92

gerrymander, 93

get down to brass tacks, 94

Giro banking, 95

give a dressing down, 96

go by the board, 97

go off half cocked, 97

good chap, 97

good luck: beginner's luck, 16; best foot forward, 17; Midas touch, 169

goose: say 'boo' to a goose, 220; wigwam for a goose's bridle, 281

grapefruit, 98

graves facing east, 99

green: in Islam, 99; with envy, 100

greeting cards, 100

grim reaper, 101

grotty, 102

guided tours, 102

guttersnipe, 103

gymnasts, 104

H

hair: hairbrained, 106; not turning a hair, 186; unkempt – *see* dishevelled, 71

handkerchief: for show but not for blow, 86; square, 239; tying a knot in, 261

hanged, drawn and quartered, 106

hanging fire, 107

hanky-panky, 107

hard up, 107

hat: knock into a cocked hat, 142

have one in stitches, 109

haversack, 109

hawks and doves, 110

head or tail of something, unable to make, 263

health and illness: apple a day keeps the doctor away, 6; buttered bread, 36; cure, 60; disease, 70; garlic, 91; migraine, 170; pill, 197; tabloid (medication), 242

hell for leather, 111

hell-bent, 110

heyday, 111

hide one's light under a bushel, 113

hip, hip, hooray, 112

his nibs, 114

hobo, 114

hoisted by one's own petard, 115

hoity-toity, 116

hold a candle, not fit to, 184

homo sapiens, 116

honky, 117

hooligan, 118

hooray, 112

horse: equestrian statues, 79; horse of a different colour, 119; mounting a horse from the left, 173

horseracing: further back than Walla Walla, 89; win hands down, 282

host, reckoning without one's, 210

howling success, 120

hue and cry, 120

humbug, 121

humour: have one in stitches, 109; keep a straight face, 136; laugh on the other side of one's face, 147

hustler, 123

I

I, capitalised, 41

ice-cream cone, 125

illness – *see* health and illness

Indian giver, 125

innings, 126

innuendo, 126

inventions: Axminster carpets, 10; bifocals, 18; brooch, 31; cash register, 43;

Q
Quakers, 206
Queer Street, 207

R
rabbit, rabbit, rabbit, 209
raglan sleeves, 42
ramshackle, 209
rattles, 13
resolutions, New Year's, 179
rigmarole, 211
riot act, read the, 210
river, sell down the, 222
rum one, 214
rumour, scotch a, 221

S
safari, 218
salad days, 219
Schlemiel, 220
Scot, tightfisted, 254
Scotland, the curse of, 181
screw, put on the, 203
seminar, 223
sex: aphrodisiac – see
    avocado, 9; bonking, 27;
    illicit – see hanky-panky,
    107; kinky, 139; screw, 221;
    virginity – see fate worse
    than death, 82
shaking hands, gloves
    removed before, 211
shanty, 223
shemozzle, 224
sherbet, 224
shillyshally, 225
ships: bridge, 225; in bottles,
    226; Japanese merchant –
    see Maru, 164
shirt, stuffed, 242
shoddy, 226
shopping trolleys, 227
show but not for blow, for, 86
shyster, 229
silk purse out of a sow's ear,
    230
singing voice, Welsh, 277
sixty-four dollar question, 231
skeleton, 232
sledgehammer, 232
sleep: forty winks, 87; sleep
    on a clothesline, 233
smart Alec, 233
smorgasbord, 234
snack, 234
SNAFU, 235
snag, hit a, 114
sour grapes, 236
Spa, 236
speech: apology, 5; gift of the
    gab, 95; eloquent – see
    kissing the Blarney Stone,
    140; hesitant – see mealy-
    mouthed, 176; misuse of
    words – see malaprop, 159;
    quieten – see put a sock in it,

203; senseless – see Irish
    bull, 127
spoke in the wheel, put a, 204
spouses, 237
spring chicken, 238
spuds, 238
stationer, 239
statues, equestrian, 79
steep, that's a bit, 251
stick one's neck out, 240
stitches, have one in, 109
stool pigeon, 241
straight face, keep a 136
strength, spinach for 237
strudel, 242
stunned mullet, 243
superlatives: first-rate, 85;
    howling success, 120
superstitions: deathwatch
    beetle, 67; dirty work at the
    crossroads, 69; garlic, 91;
    'late' Mr or Ms X, 146;
    rabbit, rabbit, rabbit, 209;
    ships in bottles, 226;
    something is bugging me,
    235; tying a knot in a
    handkerchief, 261
suspense: cliffhanger, 48;
    tenterhooks, 250
swap, 243
Sweet Fanny Adams, 244
symbols: Ankh, 4;
    cornucopia, 56; key – see
    coming of age, 51

T
tablet: tabloid, 242; see also
    pill, 197
taking the Mickey, 247
tea caddy, 249
teach one's grandmother to
    suck eggs, 249
telephone numbers, 249
tenterhooks, 250
terms of abuse or disdain:
    country bumpkin, 56;
    guttersnipe, 103;
    hairbrained, 106; hoity-toity,
    116; honky, 117; hooligan,
    118; hustler, 123; Indian
    giver, 125; Irish bull 127;
    man of straw, 160; moron,
    172; nark, 179; nincompoop,
    181; not fit to hold a candle,
    184; patsy, 194; plain as a
    pikestaff, 197; Schlemiel,
    220; shyster, 229; smart
    Alec, 233; stool pigeon, 241;
    stuffed shirt, 242; stunned
    mullet, 243; tightfisted Scot,
    254; wimps, 282; wog, 282;
terms of approval: good chap,
    97; man of my kidney, 160;
    nice, 180
theatre: claptrap, 48;
    vaudeville, 267

thinking cap, put on one's, 202
three Rs, 252
three sheets to the wind, 253
thyroid, 253
Tin-Pan Alley, 255
tit for tat, 256
toddy, 256
travel agencies, 102
trophy, 257
true blue, 258
trumpet, blow one's own, 22
turkey, talk, 248
turning a hair, not, 186
twenty-one: coming of age, 51
tycoon, 260

U
umbrage, take, 247

V
V for victory, 267
vaudeville, 267
voice, Welsh singing, 277

W
wake, 271
Walla Walla, further back
    than, 89
warfare: battle cry – see hip,
    hip, hooray, 112; forlorn
    hope, 87; freelance, 88;
    hawks and doves, 110;
    hoisted by one's own petard,
    115; Marseillaise, 163; nail
    one's colours to the mast,
    179; warpath, 272; when the
    balloon goes up, 280
warts and all, 272
wealthy: tycoon, 260; well-
    heeled, 275
weathercock, 273
wedding ring sewn to a pillow,
    275
well-heeled, 275
Wellington boots, 276
went down to the well once
    too often, 277
wheel, put a spoke in the, 204
whistle: whistle blower, 280;
    whistle stop, 281; wet one's
    whistle, 279
wimps, 282
win hands down, 282
wog, 282

X
X-rated, 285

Y
yarborough, 285
youth: salad days, 219; spring
    chicken, 238

Z
zip fastener, 286